Rightsizing the
New Enterprise

The Proof, Not the Hype

Harris Kern and Randy Johnson

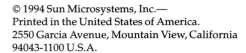

Editorial/production supervision: *Mary P. Rottino*
Cover design: *Anthony Inciong*
Buyer: *Alexis Heydt*
Acquisitions editor: *Phyllis Eve Bregman*

The publisher offers discounts on this book when ordered in bulk quantities. For more information contact: Corporate Sales Department, P T R Prentice Hall, 113 Sylvan Avenue, Englewood Cliffs, NJ 07632 . Tel.: (201) 592-2863; Fax: (201) 592-2249

10 9 8 7 6 5 4 3 2 1

ISBN 0-13-132184-6

SunSoft Press
A Prentice Hall Title

Dedication

Thanks to Scott McNealy for never blessing our decision to go with a mainframe solution, for forcing us off the mainframe as quickly as possible, and for telling us: "I want you to run Sun on Sun!"

— Harris and Randy

Table of Contents

Rightsizing the New Enterprise

Figures

≡

Tables

Foreword

Rightsizing, downsizing, side-sizing — these are the latest business buzzwords for the 90s. What does *rightsizing* mean? To some companies, these words mean reducing staff to run the business; to other companies, they mean changing business strategies to compete only in markets where a competitive advantage is seen. For the purpose of *Rightsizing the New Enterprise*, we define rightsizing as the way to more effectively implement business systems — through the Information Technology (IT) organization — that improve business processes and productivity and help the IT organization become a competitive advantage to the business it supports.

How can we write a book about this rightsizing strategy?

We have been with Sun Microsystems Inc. (Sun) for over five years and we each have more than five years of experience implementing and supporting business systems in a distributed environment that really does improve business processes. Prior to joining Sun, our careers spanned a combined 35 years of IT experience supporting the operational management processes in a mainframe environment.

How can we place the processes to support Reliability, Availability, and Serviceability (RAS) in this new environment? How can the same controls be put in place to support UNIX® distributed systems?

Our background in mainframe systems, data centers, and IT management gives us a solid understanding of the requirements to support the running of mission critical systems in a UNIX distributed environment. *Rightsizing the New Enterprise* shares our experience implementing the same mainframe disciplines to support mission critical systems running around the world, and details the new processes and methodologies we developed to support them. One of these new processes, the UNIX Production Acceptance (UPA), is the key process and was specifically developed to support and implement distributed systems using mainframe disciplines. Yes, disciplines still work and are even more important in this new distributed environment.

Five years ago the technology was not yet available to support running mission critical systems on a UNIX platform. At that time, all business systems at Sun were running on midrange computers. Sun initially hired us to implement the network and a mainframe business systems environment. Sun was approaching a $1 billion company and had begun to have real capacity problems. Our long-term strategy was to "run Sun (the corporation) on Sun (systems)." But, since the technology was not yet available, we installed a mainframe environment with MVS, VM, and an IDMS database for the interim. The capacity included 140 MIPS of processing power and 480 gigabytes of disk storage. After we put the systems into production in 1989, executive management issued a firm directive that stated any new business function we supported needed to be in a distributed environment. This directive required us to off-load processing from the mainframes to maintain performance for existing critical mainframe transaction systems that supported the business. As Sun's business grew from about $1 billion to almost $4.5 billion in 1993, the transaction volume tripled (from a peak of about 250K transactions per day to a peak of over 650K transactions per day) — *without* adding mainframe capacity or headcount. These UNIX distributed systems now meet Sun's business requirements and support improved business processes.

Our approach to rightsizing, therefore, is implementing new business systems in a client-server distributed environment and transitioning legacy systems from mainframe to client-server distributed environments — or getting the right information to the right people in order for them to run their business, using mainframe disciplines to support them. One important ingredient is to provide and implement integration tools between the mainframe and the distributed systems to allow a smooth transition based on business requirements, not capacity issues.

Most companies are not wondering whether to rightsize; rather, they are wondering *how* to rightsize. If you are a CIO, an IT manager or director, or a technical support person who is facing this challenge, this book is written for you. *Rightsizing the New Enterprise* details the processes and tools put in place to support this heterogeneous environment of midrange, mainframe, and UNIX distributed systems based on our experience at Sun. The facts contained in this book will provide you with the proof that rightsizing can be done — and that it does improve business productivity and can lower IT costs.

We have given presentations and seminars around the world; we have participated in many seminars. While we cannot predict what the future might bring in terms of business issues and the IT organizations that support them, we can share our experience and give our views for the remainder of the 90's. Keep your sizing right!

— Randy and Harris

Acknowledgments

Special thanks to Mike Graves (our boss and friend) for abiding and mentoring us and for having the insight and intelligence to design the tools that put us three years ahead of our competition. Mike has been instrumental to our success because he allowed us to do our own thing based on what we thought was good for Sun's business.

Special thanks to the following people for their significant contributions, which were key in developing the standards, procedures, processes, and tools:

Our System Programmers: Andrew Law, Becky McNulty, Wayne Chan, Ruey Chyi Wang, Fred Ting, Rich Stehn, and Jim Heredia (managed by Matthew Ricks);

Our Production Control Staff: Marcus Howery, Donald Walker, Karen Chau, and Emma Lewis;

Our Database Administration Staff: Jay Raman, Vicki Cramer, Linda Halloran, Steve Schuettinger, Pedro Lay, Debbie Santos, Cheryl Wallace, Carolyn Paulsen, and Judy Wan (managed by Linda Flores);

Our Software Developers: Teresa Beyer, Dennis Montgomery, Barbara Ferber, Frankie Lau, and Mita Vyas (managed by Randy Ott);

Richard Webster, our colleague;

Paul Lawryk, for helping to evangelize our efforts in selling our concepts for the commercial marketplace throughout Sun;

Rosemary Rossell, for her work on server room audits;

Our Software Distribution staff, supporting SunDANS;

Our Network Services Support staff (managed by Shyam "Sam" Rangole);

Our East Bay System Administration staff managed by Bruce Louie and Marty Townsend;

Bill Coleman and SunIntegration Services™ for permission to use the material on the Sun tools in Appendices A-F;

Riley Jackson for his work on the Data Center architecture and on disaster recovery;

Tom Thomassen and SunService™ for use of the material in Appendix H, "Service Level Agreement."

Special thanks and appreciation to Karin Ellison, our SunSoft Press editor, for reformatting and editing the rough drafts, and for her tenaciousness in getting this book to publication.

Special thanks and appreciation to Phyllis Eve Bregman, our Prentice Hall editor, for pulling all the loose ends together so quickly and getting this book to publication in time.

Special thanks to Astrid M. Julienne for developing and producing the final published version of this book.

Thanks to Cathy Melior-Benoit, Dina Hendry, and Nancy Sullivan for their administrative support as well as their help with files.

Thanks to Ron Ledesma, Will Shelton, and Diane Yee for their keyboard wizardry in converting some of the figures.

Thanks to Kelly Johnson for proofreading the entire manuscript several times and to Shelby Corey for scanning numerous documents.

— *Randy and Harris*

About the Authors

Harris Kern, formerly Sun's Data Center and System Administration Manager in charge of the East Bay Campus, Milpitas, California, now supports marketing and sales on a worldwide basis.

Mr. Kern joined Sun in August 1988 as the Technical Support Manager responsible for establishing and supporting a mainframe production environment known as "Sunbeam." From 1989 to 1993, he implemented the tools, processes and procedures to support Sun's first 24-hour, 7-day-a-week UNIX production environment for mission critical applications, and, without any new headcount, he successfully transitioned his mainframe organization to support UNIX while maintaining their legacy environment.

Between 1984 and 1988, Mr. Kern worked at Fujitsu as the Manager of Computer Systems, responsible for worldwide data communications, the HP data center, and over 400 IBM-compatible personal computers. While at Fujitsu, he developed, documented, and implemented systems, standards, procedures, and an organizational structure encompassing all systems operations. He also established performance guidelines, measurement tools, and other management controls to ensure optimal service and support. Prior to Fujitsu, Mr. Kern spent 10 years at GTE Inc. as a Senior System Programmer and 2 years at Gould Inc. as a Technical Services Manager responsible for mainframe technical support and computer operations. He also designed and implemented their first data center.

Randy Johnson is a full-time rightsizing consultant. In 1994, he established R & H Associates to specifically deal with the rightsizing issues that are addressed in this book. [R & H Associates, 185 Oakwood Lane, Boulder Creek, CA 95006, tel: (408) 338-6727.]

Prior to becoming a full-time rightsizing consultant, Mr. Johnson held two key positions in Sun Microsystems' IT department. During the first two years, Mr. Johnson was responsible for implementing Sun's Wide-Area Network (SWAN). Later, he took over management of Sun's Corporate Data Center and was responsible for integrating client/server operations with the existing mainframe operational standards.

Before joining Sun, Mr. Johnson held various positions related to networking and data center management in mainframe environments. At National Semiconductor Corporation he was Director of their worldwide SNA network. Prior to National, he was Director of

Computer Operations at Braniff Airlines. Mr. Johnson also worked at Federal Express Corporation where he was part of the team that implemented their package-tracking system. Overall, Randy has over 25 years of experience in the high-tech industry.

Preface

Our definition of rightsizing is getting the right information to the right people in order for them to run their business using distributed client/server technology. *Rightsizing the New Enterprise* is intended for the Chief Information Officer (CIO), IT (Information Technology) director/manager, and technical support personnel who are facing these challenges.

There have been many books and articles written about rightsizing and/or client/server distributed environments. Many say it will increase support costs. Many say it can't be managed. Many say you need a new support paradigm. Many say the cost of ownership increases and training costs increase. Many say the system management tools and processes are too immature. Many say a distributed server environment is not as secure as the mainframe, and that you cannot maintain high reliability, availability, and serviceability (RAS). We decided to dedicate our time and efforts to disprove these *fallacies*! It took us 1-1/2 years to document the *proof*!

As we travel the world speaking to customers and potential customers, one important fact is always made clearly apparent to us: Customers do not care which vendor has the "newest hardware with the most MIPS" — they want a vendor who will support them, guide them through their rightsizing nightmare, and show them the tools and processes that will help them manage their new distributed environment.

The hardware, tools, processes, and the technology are here today. The know-how is contained in this book in which we share our experiences *but not the pain*! We have successfully rightsized a global Fortune 100 company. We've done it.

Read this book, and *get the facts!*

Rightsizing the New Enterprise

The Message for a Smooth Transition: Don't Reinvent the Wheel

We have both worked at Sun for over five years — the extent of our UNIX background. Before that, our careers spanned a combined 35 years of IT experience with mainframe systems. We understand what the requirements are to support running mission critical systems with our systems, data center, and IT management backgrounds. But running mission critical systems in a UNIX distributed environment?

How can the same operational management controls be put into place to support UNIX distributed systems? We were just as skeptical five years ago as you probably are now. No way can we put in the processes to support reliability, availability, and serviceability (RAS) in this new environment! Well, we did it at Sun. We lived through the experience (and pain) over the last five years, and that's why our motto is, "Don't reinvent the wheel!" We will share our experiences with you.

This chapter details the new processes and methodologies we developed to support UNIX systems in a fully distributed environment...without adding headcount! And we mean new! One new process, called the UNIX Production Acceptance (UPA), is the key. We first developed this to support and implement distributed systems with mainframe disciplines!

Other keys to a smooth transition are centralized control and integration. We've found that as we moved systems from mainframe to UNIX distributed environments, there must be integration tools to provide for a smooth transition! We initially had a difficult time selling management on the need for integration tools. But once developed and implemented, management saw the importance of these new tools. However, we had no proof until they actually worked!

Another key to success, and one of the most important, is the network. Supporting distributed systems (and integrating with mainframes) can only be done effectively if the enterprise-wide or global network topology is in place to support it. We were able to implement such a global topology at Sun while being very cost effective! The network has become a competitive advantage!

Remember, you can't just throw away the legacy systems and controls you have implemented on mainframes; you need to migrate over time by taking one step at a time and providing for a gradual smooth transition. And we can help! If you have an existing data center (i.e., glasshouse) environment, half the battle is won because mainframe disciplines will help you be successful in the new distributed environment. Read on...and we'll show you how.

— Randy and Harris

Doing Business in the 1990s

Most companies today are not wondering whether or when to rightsize, they are wondering *how* to rightsize. The first step toward leaving the mainframe "security blanket" starts with confidence — the confidence that rightsizing can be done. *Rightsizing the New Enterprise* defines the how-to of rightsizing based on real experiences; for example, implementing UNIX distributed client/server production systems and supporting distributed mission critical business applications.

We certainly do not have a crystal ball to predict what the future might bring in terms of business issues and the IT organizations that support them. However, we will give you our views for the remainder of the 90s based on what we have seen and experienced.

First, let us take a look at "big" business — the Fortune 100 to 500 companies. Before the 90s, the IT organizations tended to be structured like the overall corporate model it supported: large, central environments. The corporate model of the 90s is *to diversify and decentralize*. Big business is becoming many small businesses under one corporate umbrella; each small business is a highly productive, independent unit *focused* on one particular market with its own profit and loss (P&L) statement.

Sun started its reengineering in the early 90s, establishing several business units each of which focuses on a particular segment of the market (such as hardware, software, connectivity, and technology). Each business unit is responsible for its own requirements, implementations, and cost issues; each business unit must justify the cost and capital that impacts its own P&L statement.

Each business unit has its own business system requirements, and IT needs to respond to these requirements. To support this new business model, Sun aligned application development groups with each business unit. In this new paradigm, changes happen quickly. The IT organization within each business unit must understand the unit's business and implement cost-effective solutions in a very timely manner. Projects that span years to complete are no longer tolerable or viable: If the project cannot be completed in six to eight months, the system will be obsolete before it is put into production.

If the business units control IT application development, what does the remaining IT organization do? The IT organization should be responsible for what is called *utility services*. Utility services can be classified as the network, data center, and system administration services. These services are standard for all business units worldwide and should continue to be centrally controlled. Central control allows IT to negotiate network costs, desktop software licenses, and overall productivity improvements more effectively. We believe this organizational structure can support the business model for the 90s and adapt to change very quickly.

Now, let us look at the systems model for the 90s: getting the right information to the right people.

The Systems Model for the 1990s

We define the systems model for the 90s by using the four R's:

1. The **R**ight information

2. To the **R**ight people

3. At the **R**ight time

4. For the **R**ight price

Client/server distributed computing supports this model and the reengineered business model of the 90s. But how do we support the corporate umbrella if all systems and data are decentralized? A centralized data dictionary (also called *centralized data depository*) or centralized data warehouse (also called *enterprise-wide database*) is needed.

Centralized Data Dictionary

One solution is to implement the centralized data dictionary technology. While all data and systems are being decentralized, one enterprise-wide data dictionary will define the data, who owns it, and where it is located.

This solution is effective but may require some new developments to support it. One new technology that is being considered is a model called the *Information Highway*. This technology is based on broadcast technology. Broadcast technology dictates that data will be sent across the information highway (that is, the network); it is the responsibility of receiving systems to capture the data they require. Decision support tools are then used to provide a corporate-wide view of the data.

Centralized Data Warehouse

Another possible solution to supporting vast corporate-wide business functions without duplication of information is through the centralized data warehouse. The centralized data warehouse is the master data warehouse; it is where any decentralized system updates or extracts data and downloads to decentralized systems.

This solution requires a data center or corporate file server; either using a mainframe or a data center-sized UNIX server as the central file server machine. Data center-sized servers are effective. To make a full transition, the data center server is the optimum choice because the server not only satisfies the need for centralized control but also supports new business requirements as they arise.

Keys to Rightsizing

There are several keys to rightsizing:

- *The network*
  This is perhaps the most important key. Supporting distributed systems (and integrating with mainframes) can only be done effectively if the enterprise-wide or global network topology is in place to support it. We implemented such a global topology at Sun.

- *Centralized control and decentralized operations*
  These keys are extremely important in managing a distributed environment. Centralized control ensures that disciplines are maintained; decentralized operations ensure timely implementation based on user requirements and business needs.

- *The UNIX Production Acceptance (UPA) Process*
  We developed this key process to support and implement distributed systems with mainframe disciplines.

- *Mainframe disciplines* and *integration tools*
  These two keys will provide a smooth transition. You need the same controls to support mission critical systems regardless of the platform on which your system is running.

- *Transitioning mainframe personnel to the UNIX environment*
  Keeping existing staff is an important key to a successful rightsizing endeavor because they understand your business requirements and have the disciplined background that provides high reliability, availability, and serviceability (RAS).

- *Personalized communications*
  Another key is the personalized communications we now have with our internal customers. In our distributed paradigm, we are no longer only in the Data Center and are, instead, working closely with our internal customers, understanding their business issues and requirements. This is quite a different situation from the old mainframe paradigm, where we were always segregated from our user community, and the only contact would usually be only by telephone when a problem arose.

Some people say that business units in the new distributed model should have complete control. Our model suggests more initial communications between IT and the business units IT supports. These communications are especially important for supporting high reliability, availability, and serviceability — which is what IT knows how to do. The business units should, instead, concentrate on running their businesses.

1

The Proof

Although *Rightsizing the New Enterprise* is a step-by-step account containing enough specifics and examples to convert even the greatest of skeptics, how does our work qualify as the proof, not the hype?

Well, we have established priorities, and we address all the pertinent issues from maintaining business functions to dealing with important staffing questions. Throughout the process of developing an enterprise-wide client/server environment, it is important to reemphasize the fact that the change is completed *without additional headcount*. To be successful in accomplishing this development without additional headcount, it is necessary to develop a checklist such as the one shown in Table 1-1 to support this new environment.

Table 1-1   Rightsizing Checklist

The Network	Develop a global network architecture statement
	Develop a network management strategy
	Develop a worldwide network topology
	Establish centrally controlled network design
	Implement the WAN and the LAN
	Decentralize network operations
	Develop productivity tools
	Establish centrally controlled network security
The Data Center	Develop a data center architecture statement
	Develop a data center infrastructure
	Meet the data center staffing requirements
	Implement the data center
The People	Transition existing mainframe personnel to UNIX programming
	Develop the training curriculum
	Address Human Resources (HR)issues (such as threat of job loss, morale, and involvement)
The Tools	Software distribution — SunDANS™
	Remote Application Interface — SunRAI™
	Distributed report viewing tool — Sun® Paperless Reporter™
	Remote system administration — Sun® ConsoleServer™
The Process	UNIX Production Acceptance (UPA) — The key process and the number one priority for implementing and supporting a mission critical distributed environment

Rightsizing the New Enterprise discusses each of the items on our checklist in detail.

Architectural Concepts 2

Why Leave a Mainframe Environment?

A common tendency in implementing a rightsizing program is to throw out the concepts used in the mainframe environment and start over in the distributed computing world. However, many of the mainframe concepts are worth saving, such as enterprise data, controlled user access, and thirty years of production disciplines.

Before the mainframe, information was maintained at a departmental level. The mainframe brought the concept of enterprise data and controls to manage it. With the centralized mainframe environment, only one enterprise data file was needed. This eliminated the inconsistency associated with having the data files in different departments. The mainframe also provided control of the software. To protect the integrity of the central processor, all software running on the mainframe was maintained under the tight control of the IT organization. We have implemented this same architecture to support mission critical systems in a distributed environment. With effective controls, reliability, availability, and serviceability (RAS) are maintained and provide the structure to improve business productivity and the potential to lower IT costs. It is important when designing a distributed computing environment to retain the mainframe disciplines.

So how did we leverage our expertise in mainframe disciplines to support UNIX systems that today operate the global SWAN (Sun Wide-Area Network) network? Let's step back for a moment and tell how we got started on the rightsizing paradigm. We were actually hired at Sun to implement the network and a mainframe business systems environment. Yes, there were mainframes at Sun. Why? Because five years ago the technology wasn't available to support running mission critical systems on a UNIX platform (but, we can say emphatically that it is here today!).

Back in 1989, all Sun business systems were running on 14 midrange computers in our data center, handling all manufacturing, order entry, and financial processes. Sun was approaching a $1 billion company, and we began to have capacity problems. Our ability to enter orders, ship products, and close the books was being impaired. So, we went to management and said we needed to install mainframes to support the business. Although our long-term strategy was to run Sun on Sun, the technology was not there to realize this goal immediately. Therefore, we installed a mainframe environment with MVS, VM, and an IDMS database. After we put the systems into production (which, by the way, was the only losing quarter at Sun), management issued a directive not to spend another dime on mainframe capacity. Any new business function that we *supported needed to be in a distributed environment. Also, we had to off-load processing from the mainframe to maintain performance for existing mainframe transaction systems that supported the business growing from $1 billion to almost $4.5 billion by 1993. Our transaction volume tripled during that timeframe, going from a peak of about 250K per day to over 650K per day. Without adding mainframe capacity? Yes!*

This book details the processes and tools put in place to support this heterogeneous environment of midrange, mainframe, and UNIX distributed systems. How we did it begins with this chapter. The network and data center environments are managed to 100% availability with goals set at 99.9%. (We managed to 100% availability to meet the performance goal. Remember, this is what we are paid to provide — high RAS. And, there is good news about implementing the mainframe — we can implement and support RAS. The bad news is that our customers (Sun's end-users) will accept nothing less...but now it's fully distributed!)

We support high availability regardless of the platform. And, our UNIX distributed systems meet business needs better and support improved business processes. Yes, implementing distributed client-server systems, suggests reengineering business processes. And, that's how it all started, in the spring of 1989.

— Harris and Randy

The Mainframe Environment

The mainframe environment arose out of the need to maintain control of the RAS for mission critical systems that support business requirements. Data processors created and implemented this concept of tight centralized control. Business functions could be managed from one location, which not only improved productivity but also allowed for easier access in times of change or problems. The mainframe brought about the information age during which IT became critical to supporting business requirements.

The mainframe introduced the concept of enterprise data and the controls required to manage the data. A centralized data file replaced the many (inconsistent) data files that were formerly kept in different departments. The mainframe also provided control of the software. To protect the integrity of the central processor, all software running on the mainframe was maintained under the tight control of the IT organization.

However, new problems arose as businesses expanded: application backlogs increased; implementation times and the cost of business computing increased; and software costs increased. Hardware and labor costs also continued to increase due to the high level of skill required to support the centralized data.

The new client/server distributed environment answers these problems while allowing for improved productivity and reduced costs.

Mainframe Concepts

Mainframe concepts include enterprise data, controlled user access, and production disciplines. When you design your distributed computing environment, it is important to retain the mainframe disciplines. A common mistake is to throw out the concepts used in the mainframe environment and to start new in the distributed computing world.

Mainframe concepts can be leveraged in two main areas: network and data center infrastructures. While the specifics of these two infrastructures will be discussed in detail later, it is relevant to emphasize a few disciplines that are retained:

- Security standards — On-line access, backup, maintenance, and response time are more efficient under centralized control.

- Continuous service — Customers are insured uninterrupted access. Operations are maintained 24 hours a day, 7 days a week.

- Network connectivity and capacity — The ability of the structure *not* to dictate limits on the business functions is essential.

- Hardware and software control — The business can implement standards for control because the hardware and software are installed at key hubs worldwide.

Three important reasons for maintaining these mainframe concepts are costs, easy transition, and a superior ability for the current state to maintain functions. The distributed model that maintains these concepts will, therefore, utilize the best aspects of each system: central control through the mainframe disciplines and decentralized operations through the network to the local level.

The Distributed Computing Environment

Controlling Software

To control the software for mission critical systems in a distributed environment, implement the same architecture as the mainframe. That is, to protect the integrity of the central processor, maintain the software under the tight control of the IT organization. Reliability, serviceability, and availability can be maintained, and the controls provide the structure to improve business productivity and the potential to lower IT costs.

Hardware Architectures

Two basic hardware architectures can be employed in a distributed computing environment: PC LANs or client/server systems running UNIX. These two architectures are often used together in one distributed computing environment.

Note – PC LAN systems are not discussed in this book.

The systems are robust, reliable, and can support any mission critical business functions.

Software Availability

The biggest advantage of the UNIX approach is the availability of good application software products capable of meeting the needs of large businesses. New UNIX applications are being written or converted by companies already established in the marketplace. Many of the same quality off-the-shelf products that were once available only for PCs are now more and more available for UNIX and client/server environments.

Rightsizing Infrastructure

Setting Up the Infrastructure

Some of the most frequently asked questions concerning the infrastructure include:

- How do you organize IT (e.g., equipment, staff) to support this new distributed model?

- Do you organize to support a distributed or a centralized infrastructure or both?

- Do you hire a system administrator for every remote location that has a server?

- Can you use existing staff to support the new distributed environment?

A good starting point is to organize your departments from the corporate CIO down to the systems level. Figure 2-1 shows the basic groups involved.

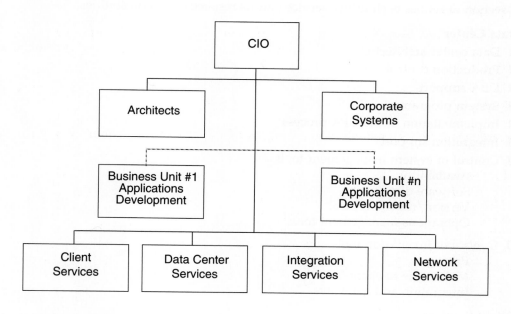

Figure 2-1   *Company Infrastructure Organizational Chart*

Chief Information Officer

The Chief Information Officer (CIO) is responsible for all departments down to the desktop. This organizational structure is the most effective way to deploy standards, provide the best possible customer service, control the end-user environment, and support the implementation of distributed systems. This approach also allows the enterprise to understand all IT costs because IT is under one "umbrella" (that is, the CIO).

Architects

The Architects are responsible for developing a 3- to 5-year architecture plan for each utility service (such as the data center, client services, network and integration services). Depending on the size of your infrastructure, you will have one to four architects, one of whom will have the position of Chief Architect. The Chief Architect is responsible for developing the overall IT technology architecture.

Utility Services

This section describes each utility service and its respective responsibilities.

- ◆ **Data Center**
  - ❑ Data center architecture
  - ❑ Production control
  - ❑ DBA support
  - ❑ System programming
  - ❑ Implementation of the UPA process
  - ❑ Integration support
  - ❑ Control of system management tools
    - Availability
    - Software distribution
    - Version/release control
    - Operations management tools

  - ❑ Control of integration tools
    - Pricing
    - Mainframe to client/server
    - Integration and gateways

- ◆ **Client Services**
  - ❑ Desktop architecture
  - ❑ LAN management
  - ❑ End-user services
  - ❑ Third-party vendor negotiations and licensing

- ❏ End-user desktop support
- ❏ End-user Service Level Agreements (SLAs)
- ❏ Change management
- ❏ Third-party desktop software (Lotus, Excel, etc.)

♦ **Network Services**
- ❏ Network architecture for wide-area (WANs), metropolitan-area (MANs), and local area networks (LANs)
- ❏ Implementation of network routers and gateways
- ❏ Network performance and metrics
- ❏ Network management
- ❏ Second-level support for LAN management

♦ **Integration Services**
- ❏ Integration architecture
- ❏ Responsibility for identifying technical solutions for business issues
- ❏ Interface between business units and utility services
- ❏ Project lead for implementing distributed business solutions
- ❏ User/owner of the UPA process
- ❏ Definition of technology solutions for business problems

Corporate Systems

Corporate Systems includes all business applications that affect the company as a whole entity (such as Finance and Human Resources). For example, some of the financial applications would include General Ledger and Fixed Assets. Applications in the Human Resources area would include payroll, personnel, and an on-line employee directory of services, compensation, and benefits.

The size of the Corporate Systems staff depends on the size of the company. The group consists of Application Developers and Business System Analysts who are chartered with defining and developing systems that affect the entire corporation.

Applications Development

Applications Development is the *only* organization that should reside in the business unit and have a dual reporting structure, reporting both to their respective business unit and to IT. This group is chartered with implementing business system solutions specific to the business unit they support.

Architecture Definition

Network Architecture

The network design, implementation, and management are essential to distributing application systems anywhere in the enterprise. The network architecture defines the enterprise-wide networking design to support these requirements. Refer to Chapter 4, "The Network," for specific information about networking and its architecture.

Data Center Architecture

The development of the enterprise-wide data center is a key to distributing application systems anywhere in the enterprise. The data center infrastructure provides the supporting environment for your company's mission critical business processing systems (including standards, procedures, operational controls, and reporting metrics) that must be implemented to maintain reliability, availability and serviceability. Once the architecture statement is defined, the next step is to evaluate the existing infrastructure to determine if it will meet the needs of the new client/server environment. For example, should you keep your traditional IT data center support infrastructure intact, or should you reorganize to support a client/server distributed model? Because of the effectiveness of its existing structure, we concluded that the existing data center organization was more than capable of handling the distributed environment.

The data center provides the environment for mission critical business functions within the framework of the key productivity goals. First, the data center provides the reliability essential to maintaining business applications and customer satisfaction. Many of the services relate to the security standards on which so many businesses focus to avoid data loss should a crisis occur. For instance, our Data Center provides backup and recovery and software distribution services for all customers who use the Data Center services. Potential problems and necessary recovery steps are anticipated through contingency planning, which is critical to providing uninterrupted services even in the event of weather and utility problems and/or disasters.

The data center also provides continuous service to customers and users. One important function relating directly to the decision to keep the existing infrastructure intact is its ability to maintain client-server hardware and software. It supports not only standard workstation operating environments but also distributed applications for processing mission critical and customer data. Another important function is the maintenance of the continuous backbone connectivity and network capacity that we developed through the network management strategy. The data center also ensures on-line access performance and availability.

Finally, the data center provides services for maintenance and updates of the system as business and information increases. This maintenance and updating is accomplished by several services: database administration, capacity planning, hardware and systems software maintenance, and software processing control.

2

Outline of a Data Center Architecture Statement

The following outline represents the topics to consider in writing an architecture statement for the data center.

Architectural Overview

- Definition of the Data Center
- Definition of the Data Center Architecture
- Data Center Services
  - RAS (Reliability, Availability, Serviceability) Services
  - Business System Processing Services
  - Database Administration Services

- Data Center Components
  - Data Center Hardware
  - Data Center Software
  - Data Center Staff and Procedures
  - Data Center Facilities

Standard Architecture

- Architecture Standards
  - Data Center Hardware Standards

- Operational Standards
  - Service-level Agreements
  - Production Acceptance
  - Change Control
  - Problem Management
  - Performance Goals, Metrics, and Service-level Reporting
  - Backup and Recovery
  - Report Distribution
  - Batch Processing
  - Software Security
  - On-site Support Staff
  - Documented Standards and Procedures

- Facilities Standards (for Server Rooms)
  - Location in Building
  - Size and Shape
  - Raised Floor
  - Physical Security

- Heating, Ventilating, and Air Conditioning (HVAC)
- Electrical Power
- Miscellaneous Standards

- Database Standards
  - Configuration Standards
  - Procedural Standards

Organizational Architecture

- Organization by Function
  - Operations
  - Technical Support and Production Scheduling
  - Systems Support
  - Database Administration
  - Hardware Planning and Support

- Sample Organization: Full-service Data Center

Processes and Procedures

- Operational Procedures
  - Change Control
  - Software Development
  - Source Management
  - Problem Management
  - Performance Reporting
  - Shift Turnover Reporting
  - Backup, Recovery, and Contingency Planning and Testing
  - New Data Center Implementation Process

- Database Administration Procedures
  - Database Procedures Standards
  - Database Development Support

- ISO 9000 and ANSI/ASQC Q90 Standards Considerations

UNIX Operations Systems Configuration Standards

- Operations Processing Servers
  - Server Configuration
  - Connecting the Sun ConsoleServer
  - Sun Unbundled Software — Setup
  - Security
  - Man Pages — UUCP
  - Symbolic Links
  - Accounting
  - Automount — NIS+, Email

- Naming Conventions
- Documentation of System File Changes and Evolution
- Kernel Configuration Standards
- Sybase Standards
- File Changes
- Local Administration Files
- File Systems
- Man Pages
- Disk Labels/Partition Maps
- Default Files for Root

IT Technical Support Services Support Agreement

- Technical Support
  - Production Environment
  - Development Environment
  - Migrations

- Assistance Center
  - Trouble Ticket Resolution

Rightsizing Tools and Methodologies

UNIX Tools Increase End-User to System Administrator Ratio, 125:1

A common fallacy noted by IT executives is that "UNIX lacks disciplines." This phrase is used in three key areas: system management, controls, and security. Effective tools and disciplines are keys to success in these areas.

When we started rightsizing at Sun, our goal was to implement, in the UNIX environment, the same types of data center management tools that were running our mainframe systems. Our mainframe system programmers assisted us in this area. It was their fundamental understanding of the requirements of business information systems that allowed us to successfully build tools to run Sun's mission critical applications on UNIX systems.

What helped us to develop hundreds of UNIX tools was an understanding of the fundamental difference between mainframe and UNIX systems:

- *The mainframe uses integrated system management utilities. Its strengths are the availability of highly integrated system management tools and well-defined administrative procedures. However, the ability to modify and customize system management tools is generally limited.*
- *The UNIX system allows the user to construct powerful tools that meet the needs of large businesses. Its strengths are its lack of centralized applications and its wealth of software building blocks that can be integrated quickly to create powerful custom environments and applications. However, with the ability to customize comes a dearth of defined system management policies, which can lead to ad hoc and unreliable system management.*

By maximizing the ability to quickly and easily customize UNIX tools, we focused early on choosing and/or developing tools to help the productivity of system administrators. The results: We saw our employee-to system administrator ratio increasing from 50:1 to over 125:1 with a 3-year roadmap to increase the ratio to 300:1.

An important consideration in choosing software tools at the local-area network level is to examine the type and number of clients to be supported on each local area network. By using some of the newest technologies available, we found that approximately 60 clients per local area network provided effective performance. Connectivity from one local area network to another should be accomplished through gateway or bridge connectivity rather than subnetting or physical connections between them. This is another important performance-level consideration and productivity tool for systems administrators because they will spend less time on performance issues and more time on proactive customer support.

— Randy and Harris

Investing in Rightsizing Tools

One of the most important aspects of providing a smooth transition from mainframe to distributed client/server systems is an investment in rightsizing tools. Rightsizing tools are procedures, processes, and systems that not only improve productivity during the transition but allow effective integration with mainframe systems.

When we started the process of integrating distributed applications with mainframe applications, our IT group saw the need to provide automated software tools that allowed interoperability between heterogeneous environments. *Integrate* is the key word to effect a smooth transition: as long as enterprise-wide databases and mission critical data still reside on the central mainframe, you must interact with them and implement tools that allow integration. A good example is the Sun Remote Applications Interface (SunRAI), which we used for the implementation of our Product Distribution Center (PDC) in Europe to support interaction between third-party RDBMS systems and our mainframe IDMS systems. Other key rightsizing tools offer the ability to distribute software automatically anywhere in the enterprise and the ability to distribute reports anywhere in the world and to allow end-users to view those reports on-line.

Software Distribution

Users need application software as well as access to the finest workstations and UNIX operating system to help them do their job: Spreadsheets, publishing software, database managers, and business system access mean the difference between productivity and frustration.

The *Distributed Administration of Network Services (SunDANS)* tool is the most important tool developed by our IT organization. A standard utility through which software is distributed across the network through other servers, SunDANS provides the ability to distribute software from a central location to anywhere in the worldwide network. The software can either be desktop tools or business applications.

This system enables a small staff to provide enterprise-wide simplified installation and access to a large body of disparate software applications. Both users and their desktop support person gain access to new software applications (such as revisions and bug fixes to existing releases) automatically. Applications are delivered on demand over the network, ready to run, without disrupting users. SunDANS allowed us to achieve our extremely productive user-to-system administrator ratio of 125 to 1 in our end-user environments.

See Appendix A, "SunDANS," for a more detailed description.

Remote Application Interface

The *Sun Remote Application Interface (SunRAI)* tool is a connectivity tool that enables heterogeneous databases to communicate with one another as well as with mainframe databases.

We developed this tool during our UNIX production inception in 1989. At that time, the sales order entry system for our European manufacturing systems was a UNIX product called MFGPRO with a Progress RDBMS. Users keyed in orders first on this system and then rekeyed the same order into our mainframe IDMS database.

SunRAI eliminates dual manual entry of orders and keeps sales orders in sync between the remote and mainframe systems. The tool allows the order to be keyed in once in the MFGPRO system and then automatically performs a real-time update to our mainframe database.

See Appendix B, "SunRAI," for a detailed description.

Distributed Report Viewing Tool

The first rightsizing tool we developed was the *Sun Paperless Reporter,* an on-line report distribution and viewing tool. This tool provides a generalized data distribution mechanism and a report viewing tool.

Users can either view reports (in compressed ASCII format) using the Sun Paperless Reporter or access them via standard UNIX commands. Users view the reports from their workstation and print only the sections of the report they require to their local desktop printer.

Note – This tool saves Sun millions of printed pages per year, and its use has earned the corporation an ecology award for saving trees.

See Appendix C, "The Sun Paperless Reporter," for a more detailed description.

Rightsizing Methodologies

A very critical methodology issue for client/server systems is the integration of new UNIX applications with existing mainframe "legacy" systems. Business productivity improvements are seen early when mainframe data is extracted or downloaded to the UNIX environment while legacy systems are being converted.

The process calls for downloading data from a global mainframe database to a "localized" database. The localized database is, for example, division level, group level, or department level. End-users access the localized data with GUI front ends on a local RDBMS such as Sybase's RDBMS.

Two key business indicators at Sun that improved when this process was implemented were:

1. Yearly inventory cycle turns improved to over 11.
   The competition was at 5 to 6 — a two-fold increase.

2. Quote-to-collect time was reduced to an average of 100 days.
   The number of days previously averaged 257 — a 150% return.

We only supported file downloads from the mainframe to the UNIX environment; we did not support file uploads from UNIX databases to the mainframe. Updates and changes to the mainframe database were made through mainframe applications or SunRAI.

Figure 3-1 is an example of a decision support process for Human Resources (HR) systems. The HR personnel support divisions such as sales, manufacturing, IT, and engineering. Each night extracts are taken from the global HR database and downloaded to the local HR database (in this case, a division).

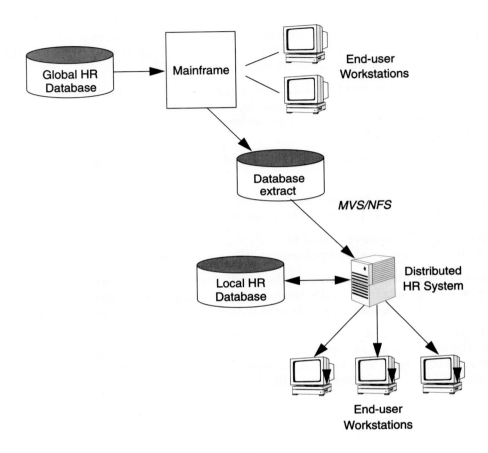

Figure 3-1   Decision Support Tools

Alternate Strategies

You can also install MVS/NFS to integrate UNIX platforms with MVS systems. MVS/NFS is a mainframe subsystem that permits users to access MVS files as if they are UNIX files on the user's desktop machine. Created by J. Frank and Associates, MVS/NFS is an emulation of Sun Microsystems' industry-standard Network File System (NFS®).

Another alternate strategy is to use TCP/IP on the mainframe for FTP functionality or other MVS/NFS-type products.

The Network   4 ☰

The Network Is the Computer™

As we travel the world and present to thousands of customers, we always spend a good deal of time talking about the importance of the network in supporting client/server or peer-to-peer computing in a distributed environment.

The network is the key infrastructure in the new rightsizing model. What do we mean by new model? Simply stated, it is getting the right information (data) to the right people at the right time for the right price to successfully complete the job function and give more effective tools to improve business processes. This is what client/server peer-to-peer is all about — improved business processes! And, the right enterprise network topology can become the competitive advantage that supports your critical business requirements!

Network design, implementation, and all the issues related to cost and justification continue to be the real concerns of our customers. Because of the centrally controlled "glasshouse" environment implemented to support commercial business systems processing over the last 20 to 30 years, networks tended to support centralized computing. In other words, networks were inclined to be centralized (i.e., controlled by the mainframes) and terminated in the data center where access to critical data was available. If service was provided by a mainframe, access was usually supplied by "dumb" terminals or PCs on the desktop and was supported by proprietary network protocols from the mainframe. All networks ended (terminated) in the mainframe.

Over the years other nonhomogeneous networks began to spring up throughout the enterprise to support additional computing requirements like CAD, CIM, word processing, and email. Because they were justified by local departmental requirements, many IT groups lost control of the networks and were unable to manage them. Problems began to occur when departments wanted to interface these networks for access to common data or systems, that is, email. Who should they turn to? The IT director most often had to solve the problem. The successful IT department took the leadership role and implemented the required interconnectivity with additional hardware and software. This supported interim requirements, but long-term problems were related to operational costs and support. This example is fairly typical of the commercial environment that we see in every city around the world today. With the network being the key infrastructure to support client/server, peer-to-peer, what does the IT director do given the example stated?

When we came to Sun in 1988, people had ASCII terminals on their desktops, supporting access to midrange systems, email, and simple text editors such as vi. The network was X.25, and there was no global connectivity. Then the work environment changed, and workstations were placed on the desktop. People were reluctant to use the new desktop tools like Lotus, Interleaf™, and FrameMaker®. They thought the vi editor would continue to fill their needs (especially the die-hard UNIX programmers). Once people started learning these new tools, they really became excited about the new functionality available. They went overboard on creating documentation and presentations. Everyone tried to outdo each other! After standards were developed and implemented, we began to help control the environment and improve productivity. Even the UNIX gurus became converts and the services sold themselves!

We were very fortunate at Sun. The company was young, and we were able to define a network vision and strategy before any networking problems occurred. We implemented a full TCP/IP network with a topology that provided for growth and the ability to support distributed, peer-to-peer computing as well as a key business function, email. The Sun network also supported connectivity to our mainframes with access through TCP/IP without the requirements of proprietary networks like SNA. The topology consisted of wide-area, metropolitan-area, campus-area, and local-area networking support with ring and spoke design. For example, the United States backbone was a full ring connecting various network hub cities. Connections were provided from the nearest hub city (for example, Dallas) to each sales office (for example, Denver). Every office where employees were located was connected to the network, providing full email and distributed computing capability. The decisions for client/server systems became a business division issue rather than a network issue. For once IT was not the bottleneck in implementing systems that supported business requirements! With TCP/IP installed and our ring topology, the network provided further support with redundancy and resiliency! All this was done while keeping the network costs to a minimum. The network became a competitive advantage for Sun!

In summary, the network is the computer. It is the key infrastructure that supports distributed computing. Distributed computing can lower IT costs and improve business processes at the same time — a win-win for the IT department and the business it supports! And, our experience shows that our network model reduces costs. A phased implementation approach can be used while providing interfaces to the old mainframe architecture until these assets are fully depreciated. The more homogeneous your environment, the more productive your IT staff will be while also reducing IT expenses.

— Harris and Randy

Developing the Network Infrastructure

The first step in developing the rightsizing infrastructure is enterprise-wide networking. Productivity improvements and information at the local (work group) levels are the most important strategies to rightsizing. The network design, implementation, and management are key to distributing application systems anywhere in the enterprise. If there are network limitations, there are limitations on distributing the computing environment. The right network infrastructure allows the business to decide where to distribute application systems; for example, we implemented network connectivity to every domestic sales office. (The geographic locations included in the Sun Wide-Area Network — known as SWAN — are shown in Table 4-1).

Table 4-1   Worldwide SWAN Sites

Location	Number of Sites
South America	2
Canada	5
Europe	52
Pacific Rim	19
United States	90

This connectivity allowed us to implement a fully distributed sales office application on a server in each location, putting information and improved productivity in the hands of the sales staff.

The network is implemented effectively through the use of centralized control with decentralized operations. We accomplished central control with one group, called the Enterprise-Wide Network Design and Development Group (ENDDG). The ENDDG was responsible for completing the architecture[1]; implementing the appropriate wide-area, metropolitan-area, campus area, and local-area networking topologies; and defining the network management strategy. Network testing and prototyping of new technologies was also done by this group.

Once quality assurance is completed on the new technology, implementation is done at the local level. The implementation of Sun's wide-area network routers is a good example. Every router has a standard hardware and software configuration. All the hardware and software are received into the centralized network testing lab. The network

---

1. The network architecture was defined by a team consisting of the architecture group and the ENDDG.

routing software, security processes, firewalls, and any other standard software (or daemons) were installed on standard hardware. Once installed, the routers were tested, quality-assured, and production-readied, then boxed up and shipped to the appropriate site. At the local site, the router is unboxed, powered up, and connected to the network by local personnel. All network upgrades are then automatically distributed over the network to all routers.

This chapter discusses the importance of developing a solid infrastructure for the network and outlines the three stages of developing an enterprise-wide network: *architecture*, *management*, and *topology*.

Topics discussed in this chapter include:

- Networking in a distributed environment
- Developing an architecture statement and contents
- Developing a network management strategy
- Function and importance of worldwide topology
- Network implementation and operations
- Centralized control
- Decentralized network operations
- Network security
- Terminal access

Note – There are two critical technical infrastructures required to support a rightsizing effort. These infrastructures are related to enterprise-wide networking and data center operations. See Chapter 5, "The Data Center," for information about data center operations.

Networking in a Distributed Environment

The network plays the most important part in supporting client/server or peer-to-peer computing in a distributed environment.

Network design, implementation, and all the issues related to cost and justification continue to be real concerns for customers. Sun defined a network vision and strategy in its early years, implementing a fully TCP/IP network with a topology that provides for growth and the ability to support distributed, peer-to-peer computing as well as a key business function, email. It also supports connectivity to Sun's mainframes with access through TCP/IP — without the requirements of proprietary networks such as SNA.

Defining a Network Architecture

The first step toward gaining control of the network is to define its architecture. To define the network architecture, you need to develop an *architecture statement*. An architecture statement is a 3- to 5-year plan of how the network will evolve based on business requirements, changes, and developments. To help understand the evolutionary requirements, the architecture statement also indicates the current state of the network.

Developing an Evolutionary Plan

Current assets cannot simply be thrown out to make room for new technology. To support the requirement of utilizing current assets, an evolutionary plan must be developed and implemented. For example, if the current network standard is proprietary and/or mainframe-based, the architecture statement defines this current state *and* then further states that any new implementation will be based on the new standard (such as TCP/IP) with the understanding that interconnectivity is required until all existing networks are replaced. This architectural approach can at least point to proactive involvement in meeting business requirements for client-server systems and provides a documented, approved design for the future.

Defining a Network Management Strategy

The most important part of the architecture is defining a network management strategy. This strategy is essential to determine how the network infrastructure will look, including staffing requirements. Sun's network management strategy enabled us to implement centralized control with decentralized network operations. We chose a network management tool that supports the network from any network hub location; that is, the network management tool owns and manages the network wherever it is located. The product, SunNet Manager™ (SNM) from SunSoft, was placed in strategic hub locations. Full operational support is allowed from any one of the locations. In addition, SNM also includes interfaces to other networking products so that it can support the evolutionary architectures.

Developing an Architecture Statement

As mentioned earlier, the first stage of defining the enterprise-wide network is through the architecture statement. It outlines the design to implement the topology and define the network management strategy. This plan is essential to make a smooth transition to client-server production systems.

The architecture statement contains the following kinds of information:

♦ **Overview Statement**

Briefly defines the contents of the document.

♦ **Current State of Network**

Defines the state of the network today (as a basis for its evolution). Issues to consider include:

❑ What is the topology?

❑ What is the inventory of existing network assets?

❑ What are the protocols?

❑ How is it managed?

❑ Is the documentation accurate and complete?

❑ Can it be audited?

♦ **Definition of Requirements**

Defines the business requirements, including network security and the network management strategy, related to the network over the next 3 to 5 years. Issues to consider include:

❑ What tools are available that can be supported anywhere in the enterprise?

♦ **Target State**

Note – We use the term *target* to indicate that the architecture is evolutionary. The *target state* is the direction in which the architecture is expected to evolve, but the architecture must be able to change as the business changes.

Defines how the network architecture will evolve over the next 3 to 5 years and details the final outcome. Issues to consider include:

❑ Will the topology support any kind of distributed computing environment or will it impose limits on business units?

❑ Can the architecture evolve with the business as the business changes?

♦ **Organizational Architecture**

Defines the organizational architecture. Issues to consider include:

❒ How do we organize the network development and support group to meet the target state?

❒ Will the organization be based on centralized control with distributed management and operations?

❒ Can we organize to meet a centralized control/decentralized management model?

♦ **Processes and Procedures**

Details implementation phases, costs, procedures, and operational standards. This section may also include implementation requirements to support distributed applications. Issues to consider include:

❒ What are the first distributed client/server applications that will be implemented and where will they be located?

❒ What are the systems to be implemented that will provide the best ROI (return on investment)?

♦ **Expected Changes in Technology**

Documents technology that is expected to change (such as network topologies and hardware and software standards). Issues to consider include:

❒ Can we look at future business requirements?

❒ What new networking technologies are becoming available that will impact this topology (e.g., ATM, CDDI)?

Once an architecture is approved, it becomes the "stake-in-the-ground" (that is, basis) from which all network decisions are made.

Developing a Network Management Strategy

The architecture must include the *network management strategy*. This strategy will determine organizational issues as well as address whether you implement methodologies such as centralized control and decentralized operations. It helps define the tools, structure, and protocol that directly relate to the cost of the network. The network management strategy also provides the guidelines for making the transition through the various stages of development and will have a direct impact on the services provided. By implementing an effective network management strategy with emphasis on RAS, you can support mission critical application functions distributed throughout the network.

The steps to defining the overall management strategy are:

1. Identifying and evaluating the network viewpoint.

2. Finding network management tools that support the network view that can be supported anywhere in the enterprise and meet the requirements of the architecture statement.

3. Defining the kind of protocols that will be supported.

Viewing the Network

The first step in defining the overall management strategy is to identify and evaluate the network viewpoint. There are two kinds of strategies to view the network:

1. View the network from the *inside out*.
An inside-out strategy typically views the network from a mainframe-based centralized network management that looks out to a network node.

2. View the network from the *outside in*.
An outside-in strategy views the network from a tool *outside of the network* that is able to manage the entire network from any hub location and looks in from any network node.

We recommend the outside-in view for the network management strategy. This strategy is more effective because it allows the mainframe — or any other client/server computing environments — to become just another node on the network. Systems can be placed anywhere on the network and be accessed by anyone. Users of the service do not need to know where the systems are located. It also allows you to have multiple executions of the network management tool at more than one network hub, so that you can fully distribute and decentralize network management. If there is a problem on one hub or node of the network, the rest of the network stays intact and can be managed by other hubs.

Network Management Tools

The next step in defining the overall management strategy is finding network management tools based on the network viewpoint and centralized control/decentralized operations methodology versus a fully centralized model. These tools must meet the requirements of the architecture statement. If a heterogeneous (multivendor) network is already implemented, the network management tool must not only interface and manage the existing network, but it must also support future directions. There are several network management tools available in the market today.

Proactive Network Management

Today's network management tools can actually perform the network operations function (called a *proactive approach* to network management).

A proactive approach means the network management tool can recognize events that are happening in the network and take action to rectify the situation. This functionality eliminates the need for network operations staff to monitor network screens and take manual action each time a problem occurs, which reduces the overall labor costs of the network and improves RAS.

An example of a network management tool that uses the proactive approach is the SNM tool, which we chose to support our network. This tool proactively monitors network events over the wide area. If a problem occurs, it pages the on-call network support person who can log in to the system from home or office to correct the problem. We implemented SNM to manage a worldwide network of over 180 locations with more than 23,000 workstations and servers (nodes) attached. It is installed in multiple locations, and any location can view or monitor other locations.

Using Third-party Network Vendors

An effective network management tool also allows you to include many third-party network vendors in network support. For example, you can use third-party telecommunications vendors to manage all or some parts of the network or to manage circuits. The network management tool can be located at their site, and they can support the network or circuits based on agreements or contracts. Third-party vendors can help your company's distributed network management and also reduce labor costs. For example, third-party vendors — trained by Sun to use SNM — manage networking functions in Europe and the Pacific Rim.

An Open Systems Approach to Defining Protocols

The next step in defining the overall management strategy is defining the kind of protocols that will be supported. TCP/IP, for example, is now becoming a *de facto* standard.

We recommend an *open systems* approach for protocols and network routing; that is, the protocol and network routing is nonproprietary — which means that *any* vendor equipment attached can function without special consideration. They should be able to support different kinds of bandwidth speeds and protocols. Once you implement an open environment, it is easy to support business requirements for connectivity around the enterprise.

There are several vendors that provide open routing functionality through hardware, software, and open gateway functionality that make it easy and effective to support the kinds of heterogeneous equipment that may already be in place; for example, a network that will support PCs, workstations, servers, and other desktops. This functionality will allow you to preserve existing assets while you implement functions that will meet the needs of the business over the next 3 to 5 years.

As the assets become outdated, they can easily be replaced with new architecture requirements. Make sure your third-party vendor can support your future as well as current needs; for example, you currently require your vendor to support bandwidths of 56/64 Kbytes but anticipate a future need of a T1 or T3 speed.

We recommend TCP/IP as the protocol with gateways in place to support, for example, X.25, X.400, X.500, IPX, and SNA. If you use fiber-optic (for metropolitan area or campus area) and twisted-pair Ethernet (to the desktop), you will be able to support future technologies such as 100 megabit Ethernet or ATM. You can also use FDDI if you need the bandwidth requirements (for example, in engineering).

We use TCP/IP corporation-wide with twisted-pair ethernet for most corporate users and FDDI for engineering. If a circuit is lost, TCP/IP automatically reroutes the packet. In addition, the packet is routed on the least-used route (referred to as *load sharing*). This implementation allows for very efficient connectivity between major hubs with access to every business location and provides the highest performance and response available.

Worldwide Topology

The final step in defining the overall management strategy is to implement the topology at the enterprise-wide/global level. Management of the entire system can be supported from any hub location. For example, the architecture we implemented for networking connects all locations worldwide. This topology allows us to implement fully distributed applications around the world, based on business requirements and high availability.

Sun's worldwide network topology supports two key business functions:

1. Sales order processing through new rightsizing tools
   SunRAI allows transactions to be automatically "played" against any two different database systems. Sales orders entered in Europe are automatically transferred and updated in the mainframe. See Appendix B, "SunRAI," for more information about this tool.

2. Decreased inventory and liability through a Product Distribution Center (PDC)
   Products are centralized at the PDC in Holland. Each plant ships product to the PDC, which then ships to the customer. The network in place and the functionality of SunRAI allow inventory transactions in the PDC to be automatically updated in the mainframe.

Sun's topology consists of wide-area, metropolitan-area, campus-area, and local-area networking support with ring and spoke design. Figure 4-1 is an example of the campus/building- and local-area network topology; it also shows responsibility separation between local and wide-area networks.

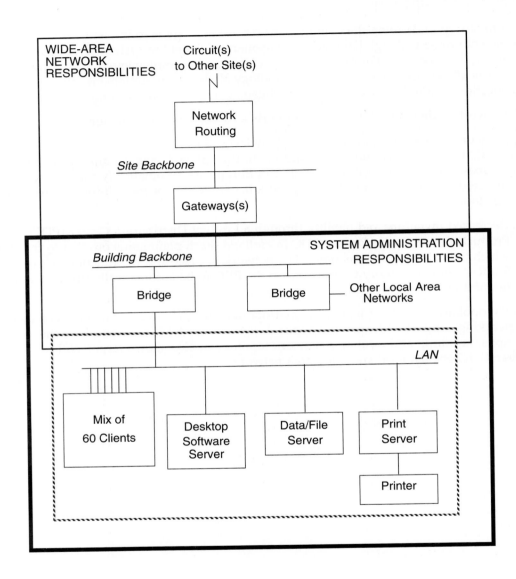

Figure 4-1   Local-Area Network Topology

Sun's network topology provides voice, video, and data services throughout the world. Each Sun location defines its voice and video requirements; the total bandwidth requirements at each location vary according to these requirements.

Note – The term *network* may include voice and video as well as data; however, only data is discussed in *Rightsizing the New Enterprise*.

Domestic Network Topology

The United States topology is a full ring connecting various network hub cities, as shown in Figure 4-2. Connections are provided from the nearest hub city to each sales office where employees are located. Each office is connected to the network, providing full email and distributed computing capability. It provides support with redundancy and resiliency — and network costs are kept to a minimum. Backup service for each sales location is currently provided by dial backup.

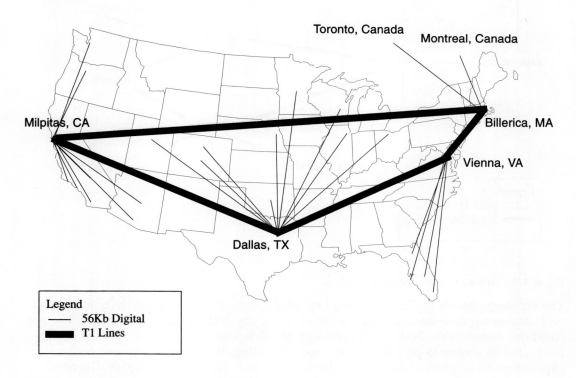

Figure 4-2   SWAN Topology (United States)

European Network Topology

A key element in developing an efficient business network is the European network topology. Figure 4-3 shows Sun's European network topology. The Network Management Center (NMC) is located at the British Telecoms facility in London. We installed three different connections to the U.S. backbone: one connection from the NMC to Vienna, Virginia, one connection from the NMC to Boston, Massachusetts, and one connection from Grenoble, France to Dallas, Texas.

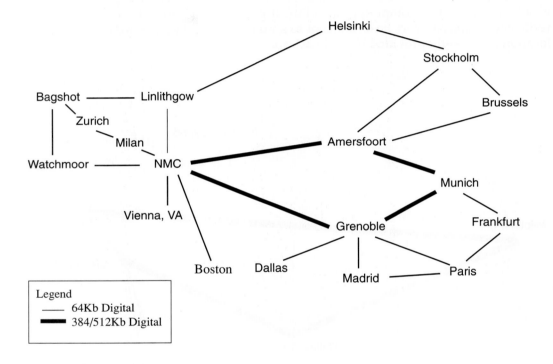

Figure 4-3   Sun's European Network Topology

The topology shown in Figure 4-3 is a logical topology. Because connectivity was based on business requirements, it does not indicate the physical topology for Europe. The real backbone connects the NMC to Amersfoort, Munich, and Grenoble. Other locations are connected as shown to provide full redundant routing. We learned from our earlier experiences in implementing the U.S. backbone which did not provide this diversity.

Pacific Rim Network Topology

Figure 4-4 shows an example of Sun's Pacific Rim network topology.

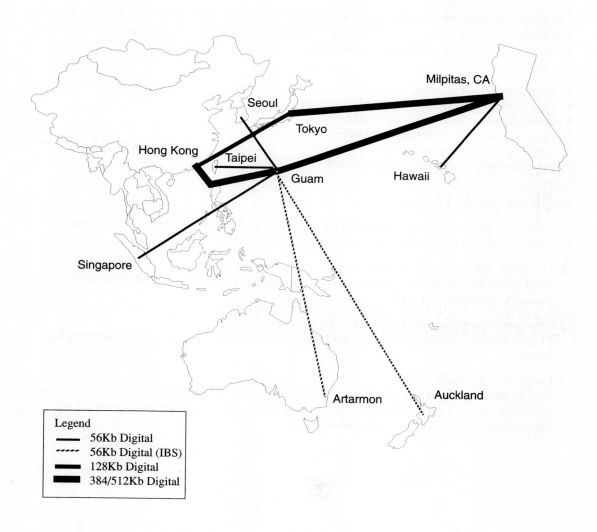

Figure 4-4   Sun's Pacific Rim Topology

The Network

4

Network Implementation

Once the architecture statement has been defined, the specifics of the implementation must be planned. The overall implementation plan must be related to the business. If this methodology is used, the architecture implementation phases can be based on the overall requirements for the 3- to 5-year architecture and will meet short term requirements for implementing a required client/server solution that supports business needs.

The ultimate result of this plan will be efficient networks (such as WANs, MANs, CANs, and LANs) with access to the entire system at the desktop. This section addresses how to actually begin the installation process using the tools developed. Important topics discussed are:

- Implementation phases
- Hardware/software deployment
- Centralized control of equipment
- Decentralization of network operations
- Security at mainframe levels
- Recommendations for terminal access

Implementation Phases

To begin the process of implementing the network and ensuring the most efficient transition, use the top-down approach. The recommended priorities are:

1. The wide-area network backbone
   Establishes the backbone hub locations and connectivity and allows deployment of the network management tool.

2. Campuses or metropolitan areas
   Establishes connectivity between buildings and/or offices in a common geographic location.

3. Local area network
   Can be implemented simultaneously with campuses or metropolitan areas, based on priorities to meet business needs. Local area networks should be implemented to support up to 60 clients or 60 workstations.

Deploying Functions Across the Network

The next logical question is:

If there is a central network group and centralized test and implementation, how do we deploy functions out across the network?

To deploy functions out across the network:

1. Make sure the hardware and software are functional before deployment.
   This function is essential in making a smooth transition and preventing any system delays. Central control tests, quality-assures, and packages. Implementation is handled at the local level.

2. Determine how to handle maintenance from both a hardware and software point of view.
   The best way to implement maintenance or changes is from a central point with centralized change control by an automated process that allows full network-wide distribution of any change on the network. This control ensures that standards and versions are maintained on software and hardware and that each networking hub and location is running the same release levels.

Centralized Control

Network design from a central point is a key reason for success in efficiency; that is, only one Network Management Support Group controls:

- Testing for quality on a timely basis
- Decreasing labor costs through the use of one location
- Simplifying problem determination
- Negotiating costs with third-party vendors

Note – Networking people are still required at strategic hub locations for local operational support and decentralized network management.

Once the architecture hardware for routing, software for routing, and the topologies are defined, it is easier to implement from a central point of view. In addition, if equipment is brought to a central point, the standards for hardware and software can be implemented on the equipment, tested, quality-assured, and deployed into the network as required. In this manner, the support is easily attained and the labor costs can be minimized because the standard set of hardware and software implementations are known.

Simplifying Problem Determination

It is easier to identify problems with centralized control because the standard sets of hardware and software installed throughout the network are known. Also, by implementing a paging tool on top of SNM, network support personnel are automatically paged.

Negotiating with Third-party Vendors

A centralized network development group can also negotiate with third-party vendors on overall cost of equipment, hardware, and software.

Decentralizing Network Operations

The recommendation for defining network operation activities includes decentralizing network operations as far to the local-area network level as possible.

Decentralized network operations (with centralized control) allow full network-wide distribution of any change on the network— guaranteeing that standards are maintained on software and hardware and that each network hub and location is running the same release levels. This type of function support means network RAS requirements are kept high, costs are kept low, and the network can be managed proactively. With the network management tool at the forefront of the process, efficient connectivity exists throughout the entire enterprise.

For example, a typical scenario could be:

- Third-party vendor delivers networking hardware and software to the central location.

- The central network group implements the routing functions in a central testing area and simulates how the functions will run over the wide-area network.

- The central network group then packages the equipment and ships it to the remote location.

- Local personnel install the equipment.
  If a proactive network management system is installed, the equipment can be connected to the network and will be automatically recognized by the network management tool.

To decentralize the network as far down to the local level as possible, divide it into two operational areas: the *wide-area network* and the *local area network*.

Wide-Area Network Operations

From a wide-area perspective, extend the control/operations (and the view from the network management tool) to the network router level only (that is, to the hub connectivity between cities, campuses, and/or buildings). Decentralize operations and management of the network to each major hub location level (*if* the network management tool is placed in each major hub location). Sun's network management tool of choice (SNM) owns and manages the entire wide-area network and is installed in each major hub. We also located network support personnel at each hub. They manage operations to those locations connected to the hub (that is, the regional area) as well as manage the wide area network (as depicted in Figure 4-2 on page 37).

Local-Area Network Operations

Decentralized network operations allow you to provide local support at the local-area network and desktop level, typically through the system administration function; that is, they should manage the local area networks. Connectivity from one local area network to another local area network should be through a gateway or bridge connectivity (instead of subnetting or physical connections between the networks). This connectivity allows you to better define the number of clients that can be supported per local area network. The newest available technologies provide effective performance that allow approximately 60 clients per local-area network. The system administrators also use SNM to manage local area networks.

Benefits of Decentralized Network Operations

Benefits of decentralized network operations include:

- The ability to provide local support for the local-area network and desktop levels through the system administration function.

- Data and desktop software servers improve productivity and customer service. Data servers store data for the desktop (desktop hard disk drives are used only for performance); desktop software servers contain the standard sets of desktop tools needed to perform business functions.

- The ability to provide contingency planning allows another location to take over network operations in the event a problem occurs at a major hub. This means that the network can continue to function with minimal interruption. Contingency planning can prevent loss of information, revenue, and customers.

For example, Sun benefited from its decentralized network operations during the Bay Area's 1989 earthquake. The damage caused by the earthquake caused many problems for Sun's Mountain View campus. Network people in the Bay Area (central location) were unable to physically get to the facilities, and, because telephone lines were down, remote login was not possible. The network operations staff at the Dallas, Texas hub automatically took over management of the wide-area network — and the network continued to function for the rest of the world during a very critical period.

Note – We recommend that the system administration function report to IT, not to the business units. This way, standards can be implemented and supported down to the desktop level. Support for distributed environments can also be controlled and disciplined.

Network Security

Network security is another critical factor to consider when developing the new network. The increased availability to the desktop level and the distribution of critical applications across the network makes this an even more important issue.

Network security is a function that includes the network routers and gateways, the desktop, and implementing other security measures such as securing access to public networks. The levels of security are described in Table 4-2.

Table 4-2   Levels of Security

Level	Area Controlled	Description
1	Desktop	Determines whether the user has authorized access to the desktop.
2	LAN / building gateway	Blocks packets in and out of LANs and/or buildings.
3	Security gateways	Limits access to engineering network.
4	Dial-in modem pools	Provides dial-back access to employees.
5	Firewalls	Limits access in and out of networks (that is, the Internet). Monitors incoming packets for viruses.

Requirements

Many of the networking products available today include a security function; however, there are certain security requirements that may be unique to your company. These unique requirements can easily be developed internally and will enhance the purchased network product.

Authentication of Users

The first-level security access to the network comes from the desktop. The desktop operating system contains authentication of users and passwords. Implement guidelines and processes to indicate how often the password is changed and number of characters contained in the password (including examples of passwords commonly used that can potentially be broken) and an automated process that requires password changes every *x* number of days. You can also implement processes that "edit" each new password so that the password used (a) has not been used by this desktop for *xx* number of password changes and (b) does not contain characters that are easily or commonly broken by remote break-ins.

Building and Local-Area Network Security

The second-level security access to the network comes from the local area network or buildings. If third-parties access the network (such as through Internet, third-party vendors, or customers), we recommend that only one gateway be available to each based on protocol (such as X.25 or X.400). For example, we implemented internally developed security processes (scripts) on each gateway. These processes, which we called a *firewall*, allowed each network packet to be monitored and detected any unauthorized access or entry or potential virus.

In addition, we also implemented security software at the building/local-area network level to block packets in and out of a building or local area network.

Limiting Access to Engineering Network

We placed security gateways between the corporate-wide and engineering network backbones to limit access to the engineering network. In most cases, the only access available to the engineering backbone is for email traffic.

Dial-back Access

Dial-in access to the network is always a potential threat to security. One way to control access is through controlled dial-in *modem pools*. A modem pool is a server with modems attached (up to 32) and a rotary of telephone access numbers. The security system on each modem pool requires dial-back access to the employee. Once logged into the system, employees can access their own desktop machine.

 Caution – For security reasons, define a separate modem pool for consultants and contractors working for your company; for example, we define a separate modem pool that allows contractors and consultants to send/receive email only.

4

Terminal Access Recommendations

Terminal access to mainframe applications from workstations can be controlled along with the other network management functions. This strategy provides the necessary controls to implement access and standardize security processes on a network-wide basis.

For example, to support Sun's heterogeneous processing environment of HewlettPackard machines, mainframe, and UNIX production systems, a methodology to support access from workstations was implemented. Because TCP/IP was not implemented on the mainframe, a 3270 terminal emulation at the desktop was selected to allow access to the mainframe. We then utilized the security systems on the mainframe and HPs to control access to applications and data implemented on them. Each channel gateway to the LAN provided for up to 250 virtual sessions and looked like a 3270 bisync terminal to the mainframe. The emulation software that runs on the workstation to provide access to the mainframe is called SunLink™ Software -(TE3270, CG3270); the hardware to support the channel-attached gateways is called a *Chat Board*.

Figure 4-5 shows how this solution is implemented.

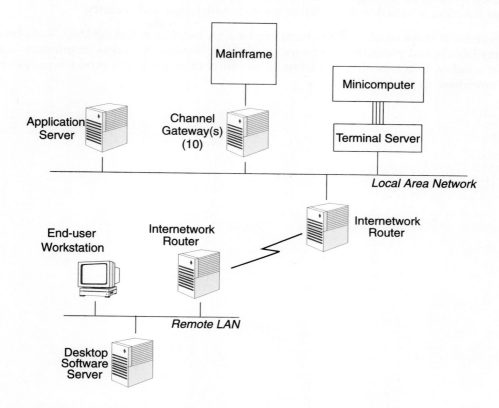

Figure 4-5   Terminal Access to the Mainframe

In Figure 4-5, a Sun server (gateway) is channel-attached to the mainframe with a board that fits in the server. It is similar to, and is defined as, a local bisync 3270 and does not require SNA support. Each server supports up to 250 virtual 3270 sessions. Ten servers are attached to the mainframe to support up to 2,500 simultaneous users. To access the HPs, a terminal server allows window access from a workstation. At the desktop are two terminal emulation products from Sun: a black and white 3270 version (TE3270) and a color 3190 version (CG3270).

We also implemented a resource manager that resides in two small servers between the channel-attached servers and the network. The resource manager has two primary functions: session login management and session termination.

- *Session login management* allocates each new 3270 session (from a workstation) to the least-utilized channel-attached server. This function utilizes all gateways by equally dividing sessions among them.

- *Session termination* terminates a 3270 session that has been idle for 30 minutes or more. This function is valuable for effective resource utilization and security.

The benefits of these emulation products can be seen running at the desktop: tools (such as spreadsheets and publishing software), an icon or window to access mainframes, an icon or window to access HPs, and icons or windows to access UNIX production systems from anywhere in the world.

The Data Center 5 ≣

To Centralize or Not to Centralize?

During 1991 and 1992, Sun went through a major company reorganization, creating multiple business units and decentralizing everything. The biggest and most costly mistake we made was to decentralize our utility functions (networking, data center, and system administration). We separated every function within the utility services group by geography. We now had a set of utility functions for the Pacific Rim, another for Europe, and a third for the Americas. Everyone was implementing their own standards and configurations for networking, the data center, and system administration. We let this new organization run for about a year and a half. What we found was that each geography was deploying whatever it wanted; there were no standards. Connectivity issues were immediately apparent. Duplication of effort was everywhere. No one was communicating when selecting a new technology. In 1993 we put all the utilities back under the same management structure and imposed some worldwide standards for the infrastructure.

Another example of centralized versus decentralized groups occurred in 1991. One centralized mainframe/UNIX Data Center supported a majority of the Sun business units. However, there were pockets of independent support groups that supported several business units. Each of these groups resided fully decentralized at its respective facilities. Each unit was self-contained with its own System Programmer, Database Administrato,r and Production Control personnel: usually a group of about five people and one manager.

In 1992 there was a reorganization at Sun that affected both the centralized mainframe Data Center as well as one of these independent support groups. As part of the reorganization, the central Data Center assumed responsibility for the small support group, and the headaches began. The small support group was vociferous in opposing the reorganization because they feared that they would be pulled into a centralized paradigm. The opposition was so loud that we did not know whether incorporating them into the Data Center was a good idea. So, we chose to leave all groups intact, as they were. The Data Center supported most of Sun; this independent support group took care of a very large business unit.

What happened?

While the Data Center maintained availability at 99.9%, the support groups did not even measure availability. Change control to them was nonexistent. If two people were out (for example, one was on vacation and one was sick), they were in trouble. If this situation arose, they would ask the Data Center for additional headcount to cover their activities during these periods. After dealing with these issues for a year, we folded this independent support group into the centralized Data Center. This change was also important because while there were few-to-no career options in the smaller groups, the data center infrastructure supported many career opportunities.

In summary, there is much discussion about decentralizing support for mission critical applications, that is, eliminating the Data Center. Our experience indicates that the existing data center infrastructure is critical to supporting this new environment. If you have an existing data center that provides high RAS, half the battle is won for supporting distributed environments.

— Randy and Harris

Developing the Enterprise-wide Data Center

The second step in producing the rightsizing infrastructure is development of the enterprise-wide data center. The data center is the major hub of information and business processes; it is essential to develop the most efficient infrastructure with the ability to maintain and upgrade hardware and software, provide foolproof security with minimum information loss, and house employees who are not only trained but also adaptable to new situations. The right data center infrastructure will support any kind of distributed computing environment and will not impose limits on business units; for example, backup times. In a mainframe environment, backups are done at times dictated to the users; in a distributed environment, servers can be backed up based on business or user requirements. Specific topics discussed in this chapter include:

- Developing an architecture statement and contents
- Evaluating the existing infrastructure
- Implementing the data center
- Centralizing control
- Meeting staffing requirements
- Managing databases in a distributed environment

Other key issues to resolve for the data center include:

- Productionalizing and supporting mission critical distributed systems
- Implementing effective system management tools
- Managing personnel issues (such as transitioning and retraining staff, new hires)

These topics are discussed in Chapter 6, "Implementing and Supporting Distributed Applications," Chapter 8, "System Management Tools," and Chapter 7, "Transitioning and Training Staff."

Note – There are two critical technical infrastructures required to support a rightsizing effort. These infrastructures are related to enterprise-wide networking and data center operations. See Chapter 4, "The Network," for information about the network.

Developing an Architecture Statement

The data center infrastructure provides the computing environment for your company's critical business processing systems, standards, procedures, operational controls, and reporting metrics that must be implemented for these systems to maintain RAS.

The first stage of defining the enterprise-wide data center environment is through an *architecture statement*. An architecture statement gives the company a definite plan of the changes, requirements, and developments to take place over the next 3 to 5 years. It is designed to implement the support infrastructure, management tools, processes, standards, and procedures. The architecture statement contains the following kinds of information:

◆ **Roles and Responsibilities**

Defines specific roles and responsibilities; for example, the database structure, performance, and operating system maintenance. Issues to consider include:

❐ What should the organization look like?

❐ What are the definitive rolls of each function?

❐ Will the data center be chartered to support mission critical distributed systems?

◆ **Functions Supported**

Discusses all operational support for any production application — regardless of where the application is located or the platform on which the application runs — including support for applications down to, and including, the server level. This section contains information on functional support for desktops. Issues to consider include:

❐ What is the difference between system programming and system administration in this new environment?

❐ Will the business units be allowed to support their own client/server systems?

Note – To gain a clear agreement between different architectures of exact functional definitions and roles of each architecture, it is important to define the roles and responsibilities and the functions supported.

♦ **Organizational Structure**

Defines the organization to support the target state. Issues to consider include:

❐ Should the database administrators be part of the data center organization, or should they be decentralized into the business units?

We recommend the structure shown in Figure 5-1 because it is best suited to implement our new productionalization process. (See Chapter 6, "Implementing and Supporting Distributed Applications," for detailed information about this process.)

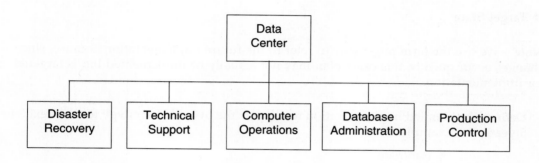

Figure 5-1   Organizational Structure for the Data Center

♦ **Current State**

Documents the current (that is, existing) infrastructure. For example:

- Hardware
  - HP3000 (3 machines)
  - IBM-compatible mainframes (2 machines)
  - SPARCservers™ (200 machines)

- Software
  - MPE
  - MVS
  - Solaris®/SunOS™

- Operational Management Tools
  - CAUnicenter (MVS)
  - UNIX third-party software (such as Online: Backup™, Online: DiskSuite™, ProWorks™/Teamware), Networker, AutoSys
  - Maestro™ (HP)
- Operational Support
  - 24 x 7
  - 24 people and 4 shift supervisors

Issues to consider include:

❐ Is the infrastructure thoroughly and accurately documented?

♦ Target State

Note – We use the term *target state* to refer to the future implementation because, since changes occur quickly, this exact plan may not actually be implemented but is targeted for implementation.

Defines the planned implementation to support the overall IT strategy for the next 3 to 5 years. For example:

- Hardware
  - All SPARCservers
- Software
  - Solaris
- Operational Management Tools
  - Selected third-party tools that run under Solaris and support heterogeneity (Networker, AutoSys)
- Operational Support
  - Lights Out operations with a minimum of 5-7 people supporting 24x7 operations and network-wide production control

Issues to consider include:

❐ Will job scheduling be centrally controlled?

❐ Will a complete "lights-out" operation be in effect?

❐ Will we back up any mission critical systems over the WAN?

♦ **Operational Standards and Procedures**

Defines the detailed day-to-day processes and support requirements, such as change control requirements, operations standards, escalation procedures, problem management, and adherence to the UPA document. Issues to consider include:

❑ Are daily, weekly, and monthly processing schedules planned?

❑ Are service-level agreements required?

❑ How can we best utilize the UPA process? (See Chapter 6, "Implementing and Supporting Distributed Applications," for a definition of the UPA process.)

❑ Do we use all of the same mainframe processes and standards, or do we customize and automate?

❑ Will we continue to use our existing support infrastructure?

❑ What role does Production Control play in this new environment?

♦ **Hardware and Software Standards**

Defines the hardware and software standards required for all productionalized applications and hardware. Also defines standard practices performed for all supported applications and hardware. Issues to consider include:

❑ Who is responsible for capacity planning (both new and ongoing)?

❑ Who is responsible for performance and tuning?

Once the architecture statement is defined, the next step is to evaluate the existing infrastructure to determine if it meets the requirements of the new client server environment.

Evaluating the Existing Infrastructure

The data center must provide the environment for critical business functions within the framework of the key productivity goals (RAS). For example, we concluded that Sun's data center was more than capable of handling the distributed environment because of the effectiveness of its existing structure. The services of Sun's data center show a textbook example of how to provide for the necessary environment:

1. The data center provides the *reliability* essential to maintaining business applications and customer satisfaction. Many of its services relate to the security standards. For example, the data center provides backup and recovery and software distribution services for all customers who access the data center environments.

   The data center also provides physical security for equipment and data, and physical plant and support systems such as cooling and power. These maintenance steps are critical to providing uninterrupted services even in the event of weather and utility problems or disasters.

2. The data center satisfies *high availability* standards and focuses on the ability to provide continuous service to customers and users.
For example, the data center maintains client-server hardware and software. It supports not only standard workstation operating environments but also distributed applications for processing mission critical and customer data.

In addition, the data center maintains the continuous (data center) backbone connectivity and network capacity developed through the network management strategy; that is, it monitors the standards and efficiency of the data center network on a regular basis. To provide the best service possible, staff and operations are maintained 24 hours a day, 7 days a week.

3. The data center provides *serviceability,* such as maintenance and updates of the system as business and information increases.

Several services provide the disk and tape media with adequate capacity to handle all functions: report distribution servers, database administration, capacity planning, hardware and systems software maintenance, and software processing control. The databases and their software are maintained and data is downloaded to distributed processing centers regularly. In addition, inquiry access is ensured to authorized users worldwide. The data center also supports the development of business system processing applications and provides a showcase data center environment.

Once the existing architecture has been evaluated, the final step is to develop a plan for implementing the architecture.

Data Center Implementation

Once the architecture statement has been defined and approved, the specifics of the implementation must be defined. The plan to implement the data center architecture needs to include:

• How to implement new or additional functions using the architecture
• A phased approach to upgrade or replace existing architectures

For example, Sun's data center organization is responsible for supporting servers around the world. The data center and server rooms throughout Sun were reclassified as Production Server Rooms (PSRs). There were two types of PSRs, as described in Table 5-1.

Table 5-1   Types of Data Centers

Type	Description
24x7 production server room	The user owner is provided the following services: 24 hours a day, 7 days per week on-site support; nightly incremental backup to tape with off-site retention; weekly or monthly full dump backups to tape with off-site retention; system administration support; DBA support; air conditioning; UPS; halon; generator backup; disaster recovery.
12x5 production server room	The end-user is provided the following services: 12 hours a day, 5 days per week on-site support; nightly incremental backups to tape with off-site retention; weekly or monthly full dump backups to tape with off-site retention; system administration support; DBA support.

Note – For the purposes of this book, we have referred to the 24x7 production server room as a data center.

Many different Sun machines (such as the SPARCserver 490 or the SPARCstation® 2) function in data centers as servers, as network connections, and as processors for databases and applications software. These machines, described in Table 5-2, are commonly referred to as *Sun servers* or *Sun workstations*.

Table 5-2   Data Center Machines

Server Type	Commonly Called	Description
Network connectivity servers and workstations	Gateways or routers	Provides network backbone connectivity hardware, software, and data storage service to connect Sun networks into the Sun Wide-Area Network (SWAN).
Workstation-support servers	Client servers	Provides business office support software and data storage services to client machines.
Production-application servers	Production servers	Supports critical application software processing and databases.

Centralized Control

As with the network, developing the data center from a central point is a key reason for success in supporting existing business applications and new application environments. Centralized control in the data center environment has been in place for more than 20 years. This concept of central control, called "the glasshouse" by data processing groups, means that mainframes and midrange systems are housed and controlled in one or more data centers. By extending the glasshouse out around the worldwide network, the same controls and operation management tools can be utilized to support mission critical business systems in the new client-server model.

At Sun, there is now more activity in supporting application environments which are *not* in a traditional glasshouse setting but, rather, in the distributed server rooms. This work is accomplished by utilizing the system administration staff in other facilities for some hands-on duties and coordination of DBA type functions. This means that the UNIX Database Administrators (DBA) and Technical Support (TS) staff reside in the data center support infrastructure. The data center support infrastructure is responsible for all production servers, regardless of location. In addition, the DBAs and Technical Support staff implement the software on all new production servers before the server is delivered to the appropriate server room. In some cases, the DBAs and Technical Support staff "contract" with the local system administration group to provide on-site support.

DBA Responsibilities

The DBA handles all new database releases and is the contact for third-party vendors for problems and bug patches. The DBA also owns security and is responsible for database integrity regardless of where the production server is located for all mission critical systems that are supported by the data center infrastructure.

Technical Support Responsibilities

Technical Support (known simply as system programming, tech support, or TS) owns *root* authority and coordinates all system administration functions for the production servers including upgrading the operating systems, applying bug patches, installing third-party management tools, and performing backups for all mission critical systems that are supported by the data center infrastructure.

Production Control Responsibilities

The Production Control group is responsible for coordinating the productionalization of new business applications and implementing new releases to existing applications. They are also responsible for scheduling processes and handling tape management, integrity, and installations. These responsibilities affect all mission critical systems that are supported by the data center infrastructure.

Computer Operations Responsibilities

Computer Operations handles the physical operation of the servers, including tape mounting, problem escalation, and facilities maintenance and support.

Database Administration in a Distributed Environment

Database administration typically carries two meanings:

1. The design, definition, and support of the *logical* database.

2. The design, definition, and support of the *physical* database.

In the mainframe environment, both roles were filled by a single person or a single staff. This was facilitated by the hierarchical design of databases where relationships between objects were defined in a parent-child structure. This encouraged a centralized computing environment with a centralized staff. As the technology moved from glasshouse computer room environments to distributed server room installations, database administration has changed.

The distributed computing environment (as well as emerging object-oriented technology) created databases that conform to a relational database (RDBMS) model. An RDBMS allows design and definition issues to be an integral part of application development. As such, the logical database administration tasks fall within a development group, and the physical database administration tasks belong to an operations (support) organization.

In a distributed database environment, information that is critical to the success of a given organization is located as close to the actual user group as is physically possible. This allows the production environment to be more reliable due to the removal of multiple points of failure. For example, if the user community that is primarily responsible for the data is located in Boston and the server is in Colorado, the users have to traverse a myriad of network connections in order to play their transactions. This means that if a network connection fails in Chicago, the transaction will either be queued or rerouted through a less expedient path. In the event of a lack of redundancy for every network connection, the user will most likely get a message of failed transactions, which will have to be replayed at a later time. For environments that involve a high number of user transactions, a remote location could involve network saturation and a high rate of collisions. This would also affect the response time to the user, which could be detrimental to business success.

It is important that production environments adhere to basic configuration standards and that every distributed server follow a minimum set of requirements. This will ensure the highest DBA-to server ratios. In the event of database outages or errors, the DBA will be able to quickly access the machines, navigate through the file system structure, and obtain information necessary to take quick corrective action. If no guidelines are enforced, there will be an increased delay in problem diagnosis and resolution.

Data Server Guidelines

The following guidelines are recommended for dataserver environments:

- The home environment should be located under the /home file system.

  For example, the file system for a Sybase RDBMS would be /home/sybase; for an Oracle RDBMS, it would be /home/oracle, etc.

- All RDBMS partitions should be owned by RDBMS user login and should not be readable by group or world.

- RDBMS software should reside in its own subdirectory.

  For example: Sybase version 4.9.1 software would be found in /home/sybase/4.9.1; Oracle version 7.0.15 would be found in /home/oracle/7.0.15.

- Database dump files (required for disaster recovery) would be located in a dbdump directory under /home.

- No database partitions would be allowed on the system disk. (This will allow technical support personnel (or OS system administrators) to recover from system disk failure without the involvement of database administrators.)

- Administration utilities would be distributed from a centralized development group and would be found in a subdirectory with the RDBMS home environment.

  For example, utilities for administering a Sybase system would be distributed to /home/sybase/dist.

- Localized utilities and parameters would be defined and located in a subdirectory within the RDBMS home environment.

  For example, log files that reflect utility processing for Sybase would be found in /home/sybase/local/log.

- Database administration tasks would be routinely run through cron programs and the program names and schedule would be found in the crontab file for the RDBMS user login (e.g., sybase, oracle).

Database Administration Utilities

Table 5-3 describes the standard database administration utilities that were developed to manage our environment.

Table 5-3   Database Administration Utilities

Utility	Definition and Functions
Installation	An automated process to install programs, documentation, required directory structure, and necessary devices within the dataserver environment.
Error checking program	A regularly run program that analyzes information in various log files and notifies support personnel of errors as they occur.
Database consistency checking	Regularly scheduled programs that validate when index and data pages are correctly linked; indexes are in properly sorted order; all pointers are consistent; all page offsets are reasonable; pages are correctly allocated; no data page is allocated while it is unused.
Database recovery scripts	Regularly scheduled programs that provide full and transactional snapshots of database activity. These snapshots are usually written out to a UFS and then backed up to tape as part of routine file system backups. This suite of programs also includes necessary automation to extract data on a row-by-row basis, using either bcp or export/import functions.
Database capacity programs	Regularly scheduled programs that provide analysis of database growth patterns. This information is critical to database administration since capacity needs to be tracked carefully.
Disaster recovery utilities	Automated programs that can be run either routinely or on demand and that will collect information necessary to create the production environment on another server in the event of a physical disaster. These programs develop the actual device- and database-created syntax necessary to install the environment on another machine and to load from off-site backup tapes.

All of the above utility programs should be run on a routine basis to ensure that the database administrator has the necessary environment for support and recovery. Error notification can be done either through email or through an auto-page agent as required by system criticality. The commitment to regular schedules of database maintenance and analysis is critical to the health and recoverability of the production system.

5

The role of a database administrator includes responsibilities in the areas of performance and tuning. Although most performance gains are found in the process of application and logical database design, there are tuning procedures that can be done by the DBA which optimize the performance across the physical resources of the production server. For example, allocating data space and index space across separate devices and device controllers can remove the potential of processing bottlenecks. In order to accomplish this tuning function, the DBA needs access to programs and routines that can collect performance statistics on an as-needed basis.

Implementing and Supporting Distributed Applications

Supporting Mission Critical Distributed Applications

Our number one priority (and our biggest concern) when we started our rightsizing adventures was how we would support mission critical distributed production applications when it had never been attempted before. How do you take an application from design and development, through the different testing phases (alpha, beta, pre-production) and productionalize it? How would you set up the support paradigm? Who would we turn to for help when no one in the world had ever done this?

It was a difficult situation because UNIX distributed applications were rapidly being developed all over the world, and we did not have a process in place to manage this new environment. We also had another problem: our mainframe environment never slowed down. Month-ends and quarter-ends were just as hectic. The business was not going to wait for us to get our infrastructure together to support this new way of doing data processing.

So, we let the process evolve as we and key members of our staff literally camped out in a conference room for weeks to design this new tool. We wrote down everything you could possibly think of that would be required to support this new environment. The document we produced was 200 pages long.

We then needed to pilot our plan on a distributed application, but we could not use a mission critical one that would upset our business flow. We spent the next three years refining our methodology; it was a painful, cumbersome process. Today, the process is streamlined and efficient; and, the template is only seven pages long!

What is the UPA process?

- It is a methodology...a set of standards and procedures...a discipline for supporting mission critical distributed applications by a centralized data center staff.

- It identifies the processes to implement service level agreements between the distributed application users and the data center.

- It defines standard hardware and software configurations to ease ongoing support (RAS) issues.

- It promotes upfront communications and teamwork between the users of distributed applications and the central support staff.

- *It is* the key *to implementing and supporting distributed applications that meet business requirements.*

Once the process was designed, we had to sell it to the user community (i.e., application developers and user owners). To them, it was a mainframe type of discipline. And, they were right; it was *based on the mainframe disciplines. Most of the community would not adopt it. The process was lengthy, and, at Sun, all of these developers were now comfortable in the UNIX world. They did not want to deal with any mainframe rules and restrictions. Most did not even deal with the support process; they elected to support their own applications on their own workstations and small LANs. They quickly realized that they were not chartered for support and, therefore, could not maintain availability as we could with the data center infrastructure. We began to work with several different groups who were friendly to our cause. They helped us streamline the process and championed our methods throughout Sun. But, it was a very slow and painful evolution.*

This tool/process was our number one priority. It is our bible for production implementation and support. Without it, we would have failed.

— Harris and Randy

Supporting the Production Environment

A major problem the Data Center immediately encountered was the question of how to maintain our original production environment (which consisted of 80% mainframe systems running manufacturing systems and 20% HP systems running financial systems) while "productionalizing" the new UNIX systems — *without* increasing our personnel headcount. Some of the questions we asked ourselves included:

> *How do we take an application from design and development, through the different testing phases (alpha, beta, pre-production) and productionalize it?*
>
> *How do we set up the support paradigm?*
>
> *To whom do we turn for help when this process has never been done before?*

In the new distributed computing environment, our data center did not dictate assignments such as availability requirements, database backup schedules, or batch job schedules; instead the business unit responsible for the application defined these assignments based on their business requirements. These issues were the basis for the development of the UNIX Production Acceptance (UPA) process, which we then piloted with one of our own internally developed and supported tools called the Sun Paperless Reporter.

The Sun Paperless Reporter was perfect for our pilot program because it was a distributed system, and, more importantly, it was developed and supported by a group of UNIX gurus who initially wanted no part of our process. However, once they discovered they could not adequately support the tool themselves, we were able to negotiate a support agreement with them in which they, in turn, would help us streamline the UPA process. We spent the next three years refining our methodology; it was a painful, cumbersome process.

Once the process had successfully completed its pilot program, we had to convince the user community (that is, application developers and user-owners) to use it. At first, most of the user community was not interested in adopting our process. To them, it was a mainframe type of discipline — and they were right: The process *was* based on the mainframe disciplines. The process was lengthy, and Sun's user community, comfortable in the UNIX environment, did not want to deal with *any* mainframe rules and restrictions. Eventually several different groups realized that they were not chartered for support and, therefore, could not maintain the availability that we could with the data center infrastructure. We began to work with these groups, and they helped us streamline the process and championed our methods throughout Sun.

The UPA is a negotiated service-level agreement between our user owners and the data center infrastructure. The UPA is a set of standards and guidelines (discipline). But most importantly, a personalized communication vehicle. We found that communication is more important in this new environment. In the mainframe paradigm, data center personnel were isolated from our user community. Today, with the UPA process, we work with our business units to understand their computing needs to reengineer their business, while they have a better understanding of how our support paradigm works. It also bridges the communication gap between mainframe data center personnel and UNIX development staff.

Today, the process is very streamlined and efficient, and the document is now only seven pages. In addition, the UPA process has become Sun's standard for production implementation and support.

The General Process

The UPA was specifically developed to support and implement distributed systems with mainframe disciplines. It is a guideline to work with developers to productionalize their applications and is the key to implementing mainframe disciplines to support systems running around the world.

When a new application is developed, a three-member team (consisting of a Database Administrator, a System Programmer, and a Production Control Analyst) is assigned to the project. This team works directly with the developers or project lead (user-owners) during their application development cycle, including alpha, beta, pre-production, and production cycles. Once the application is productionalized, the product team and the data center infrastructure team sign off on the process, and security becomes owned by the data center, regardless of where the server is located. Root access is then controlled by the System Programmers.

Tracking the UPA Process

Another process, called the Production Implementation Process (PIP), is used in conjunction with the UPA process to track the application through its entire development process (for example, both the alpha and beta cycles). The PIP process is an on-line graph that maintains the status of each UPA process.

Multiple UPA processes are handled at any given period of time. The PIP process tracks which phase of its UPA process each application is in and lists the outstanding critical issues pending before productionalization. The Production Control staff is responsible for maintaining the PIP process.

The Detailed Process

To productionalize UNIX applications, a team consisting of a Database Administrator, a Production Control Analyst, and a System Programmer is assigned to work with the developers or project lead (user-owners) during their application development cycle. The team is a communications vehicle for both organizations: it provides Operations with a better understanding of how to support the new application, and it provides the developers with a clearer understanding of our support levels. The team provides guidance to the developers in regards to performance issues and sizing of hardware, along with any other issues related to implementing and supporting their new system.

In addition, each group within the Data Center organization provides the following functions to complete the UPA process:

- Production Control (PC) is the focal point of the process.
- Database Administration (DBA) sets up the database.
- Technical Support (TS) sets up the hardware and systems software.

Note – We recommend that the development groups make contact during the project design review phase. All new releases of the UPA process are communicated to our business units via email.

The UPA report is a very detailed document used to support the application. The support groups encompass Computer Operations, Production Control, Database Administration, and the Assistance Center. The team works together to complete a template that contains pertinent information for the various groups. The UPA template consists of the sections described in Table 6-1.

Table 6-1   The UPA Template

Section	Information to be Completed	Used by
System Configuration	Provides hostname location, model, power, swap, memory, and system functions.	Technical Support
Disk Configuration	Provides number and type of controllers, quantity and type of disk, and disk partitioning layout.	Technical Support
Peripherals	Includes (as applicable) modem, number of printers, tape drive, and CD-ROM.	Technical Support

Table 6-1   The UPA Template (Continued)

Section	Information to be Completed	Used by
Database Configuration	Describes the design of the database(s), initial size, and placement of the database; also includes specific logins used by applications, batch jobs, support staff, initial sp_configures, Sybase devices, sys_usages, dataserver name, version of the RDBMS, copy of /etc/fstab with RDBMS partition marked, and copy of the run file.	Database Administration
Software Tools	Describes the system software (such as operating system, windowing system, and compiler).	Technical Support
Other Software Tools	Describes top-level application structure including any third-party software (e.g., MVS/NFS).	Technical Support
Storage Management	Schedule for incremental and full backups; defines whether stored data needs to be retained off-site.	Technical Support; Computer Operations
Error Messages	Describes problems to be fixed or escalated.	Technical Support; Computer Operations
Interdependencies	Describes the interdependencies (such as environment, applications, tools, information flow in/out, data flow diagram, entity relation diagram, and transition document).	Production Control
Capacity Planning	Describes estimated disk space including future growth, growth projections by month, existing controls to manage the plan, and a list of performance characteristics of certain key transactions.	Database Administration; Technical Support
System Availability	Defines system availability and the aliases to which to announce machine downtime.	Production Control
Test Plan	Describes the alpha and beta test plans.	Database Administration; Technical Support; Production Control
Training	Describes training that has been provided to the Assistance Center, Operations, Production Control, Technical Support, and Database Administration.	

Table 6-1   The UPA Template (Continued)

Section	Information to be Completed	Used by
Database Configuration	Describes the databases; for example, the description of a Sybase database would include the database configuration, database size, raw devices, SQL processes, and Sybase version.	Database Administration
Administration Guide	Describes job/batch processing and monitoring scripts as well as restart procedures.	Production Control
Capacity Planning	Describes the projected growth of the application to anticipate disk capacity and database increase.	Technical Support; Database Administration
Disaster Recovery Procedure	Describes the recovery procedures (if applicable).	Technical Support; Database Administration; Production Control
Documentation	Installation Guide — Describes installation procedures. Reference Guide — Provides reference material. User's Guide — Describes design concepts and discusses how to use the application.	Technical Support; Database Administration; Production Control

It takes between 2 weeks and 6 months to productionalize an application. The length of time depends on how well the application is developed. Each new application is taken through four phases before it is supported by the data center:

Phase I   Gathering information
Phase II   Resource planning
Phase III   Implementation
Phase IV   Production cutover

There is also a post-UPA phase, which defines the responsibilities for the application once the cutover is completed.

Phase I: Information Gathering

During the information gathering phase, developers and project leads (user-owners) contact the production control department within the data center infrastructure. They assign an Operations Analyst to be the focal contact point and to work with the project lead during the entire process.

To start the process, the project lead must provide some general information about the project. Example information provided by the pre-PIP questionnaire includes:

- Project name
- Development group
- Project description
- Project owner
- Project lead
- Does the application contain a database?
- Hardware requirements
- What kind of coverage is required?
- Location of users
- Is the application accessed in a front-end or rlogin?
- Is Assistance Center support required?
- What are the target dates for server installation, alpha test, beta test, production freeze, software distribution, UPA signoff, and production date.

The estimated time of completion for Phase I is one month.

Phase II: Resource Planning Phase

During the resource planning phase, the Operations Analyst uses the information on the pre-PIP questionnaire to add the project to the PIP planning status list. Phase II tasks include:

- Adding new projects to PIP planning status list
- Working with Technical Support to define the cost for chargeback
- Emailing the UPA template to the project lead
- Working with Technical Support to obtain footprint for the hardware[1]
- Creating an alias which includes Production Control, Database Administration, and Technical Support
- Assembling the UPA committee[2]

---

1. During Phase II, the project lead orders the equipment , based on feedback from Database Administration and Technical Support.

2. The UPA committee is made up of representatives from each organization within the data center infrastructure. These members review the documentation that is provided by the project lead to support the application.

Phase III: Implementation Phase

During the implementation phase, the Operation Analyst adds the application to the Auto-Paging System for support escalation. This system tracks which Technical Support and Database Administration staff supports the application and also tracks daily production problems. Phase III tasks are described in Table 6-2.

Table 6-2   Phase III Tasks

Responsible Person or Group	Task Description
Technical Support	Install the hardware and/or software Install all utilities on the server Inform tape librarian to create tapes and labels for backups Install UNIX tape backup tool
Database Administration	Work with developer on database design Work with Technical Support on disk partition information Receive database creation scripts Install RDBMS and execute object creation scripts Install utilities for production support
Project Lead	Complete the UPA document Schedule technical overview with Database Administration, Technical Support, Operation Analyst, and operations staff
UPA committee	Review UPA document for approval

The estimated time of completion for Phase III is one month.

Phase IV: Production Cutover

Phase IV is the production cutover. The time frame for this phase is as long as necessary to ensure that the application can run in a production environment. Before an application can pass the UPA process, it must meet the following technical support standards:

- Root access is limited to Technical Support
- Setuid programs and non-UNIX login shells have been approved by Technical Support
- Passwords are not hardcoded
- Information about the setup for end-user access has been provided
- Permissions for files after installation has been listed
- Store procedure that allows user-owners to add logins has been developed

This phase is considered complete when the application is able to run in a production environment. Table 6-3 describes the tasks involved for this phase.

Table 6-3   Production Cutover Tasks and Responsibilities

Responsible Person or Group	Task Description
Operation Analyst	Add the application to relevant reports.
Technical Support	Add the new system to applicable utilities to communicate special requests and notify operations of new application releases.
	Add the UPA and all related documents to the Technical Support Production server.

Post-UPA Phase

Once the UPA document is complete, Technical Support maintains it and updates the systems portion; Database Administration updates the database portion.

After the application is in production, each group in the data center infrastructure has specific responsibilities to support the application, as described in Table 6-4.

Table 6-4   IT Organization Responsibilities after UPA Implementation

Group	Responsibilities
Assistance Center	Provides a single point of contact.
Database Administration	Maintains the database, upgrades RDBMS software, and makes changes as required to the RDBMS system (such as adding dump devices, increasing db sizes, analyzing and reconciling maintenance script error messages including resolving problems with database dumping, and analyzing/resolving RDBMS error log messages).
Production Control	Manages job scheduling function, restarts to the application, and performs crontab changes.
Technical Support	Maintains the operating system, hardware, and systems software. Formats and repartitions disks, installs unbundled software, maintains and configures system security, and maintains network services.

Production Standards and Procedures

Another key to successfully implementing a UNIX production environment to support critical applications is to develop — and adhere to — standards and procedures that are comparable to those used in the mainframe environment. The following list includes some of the standards and procedures our staff developed for Sun:

- Minimum hardware requirements for production servers
- Operating system configuration
- System software sizing
- Disk layout
- Third-party and in-house developed software installation
- Tape Management installation
- SunNet Manager installation
- Change Management installation
- Morning Report installation
- Security
- Disk check
- ckreboot installation
- System Monitoring Script installation
- Preventive maintenance installation
- Automount
- MVS/NFS

Open Systems versus a Disciplined Environment

The UPA process consists of two parts:

- The actual 7-page template

- A productionalization guide that addresses standard configurations

Both parts are *key* to keeping the infrastructure support costs down.

In developing the UPA process, we encountered many issues regarding the openness of UNIX versus the disciplines of the mainframe environment. The UNIX side did not want to have the type of controls used to manage critical mainframe applications placed on their environment. They thought that the UPA process was a waste of time because *"it is too cumbersome for the UNIX environment," "UNIX is more wide open than the mainframe environment,"* and *"mainframe disciplines will never work in a distributed environment."* Gradually, even the most skeptical UNIX users found their applications could not maintain the same availability and reliability as those applications that were under the control of the UPA process.

From the start, we believed in the UPA process. We argued the concept that "a production system is a production system is a production system," regardless of the platform or the environment. As former mainframers, we also had to learn not to be so focused about how something worked with mainframes. A good example of the open-mindedness we had to learn is the issue of standard naming conventions: In the mainframe environment, standard naming conventions are necessities; in the distributed environment, we gradually realized we could manage the environment no matter what names were used. We, therefore, allowed the user owners and developers to select their own names.

Note – The UPA process will be made available to Sun customers in 1994 through SunIntegration Services. The UPA process is *not* hardware-dependent. It supports distributed environments regardless of the hardware platform.

Transitioning and Training Staff   7 ≡

Transitioning Those Mainframers to a UNIX Environment

An important consideration in retraining our mainframe staff is to get them involved as early as possible in the day-to-day running of the Data Center. This ensures high employee morale. We learned this important Human Resources (HR) lesson earlier when we transitioned Sun's business systems from HP3000s to the mainframe in the late 1980's. At that time, we had brought in mainframers to implement the environment, and it had a negative impact upon the HP3000 staff who felt that their jobs were in jeopardy. They felt left behind, and, consequently, morale was extremely low. We began to develop training programs to transition HP3000 staff over to supporting the mainframe. We put together many hands-on courses, including how to write and execute clists and JCL, and morale was instilled back into our environment. These same practices can be used to establish training materials for transitioning mainframers to the UNIX environment. Providing the opportunity to everyone from the computer operator all the way up to senior technical staff is key to maintaining morale in your organization.

Our mainframe to UNIX retraining program consisted of classroom courses, hands-on group projects, and homework and reading assignments (done by employees on their own time!). Our first training course curriculum consisted of three courses, which were offered to every staff member in the data center:

- *System Administration Essentials (a 3-day class)*
- *System Administration (a 5-day class)*
- *Shell Programming (a 5-day class)*

Shell programming was included in our core set of courses because it allowed staff members to write shell scripts (very similar to clists in the mainframe world), thereby getting them involved in projects for the Data Center. In addition to the above-mentioned courses, our senior technical staff members had access to additional courses on C++ programming, advanced system administration, OS internals, device drivers, and system interface programming.

However, the single most important program that we developed was a 1-day "get acquainted with the hardware" class. We used three SPARCstation 2s and three 4/490 servers destined for production use. This hardware class consisted of a half-day classroom session depicting the differences between SBus and VME. The second half of the class was hands-on practice in the Data Center. Teams of three to five staff members (i.e., a Database Administrator, a System Programmer and a Computer Operator) were encouraged to take the hardware apart and then put it back together. (We eventually used this brand-new equipment to run our production applications.)

The present-day curricula is more elaborate and is discussed in detail in this chapter.

— Randy and Harris

Managing the Open Systems Environment

Moving to client/server and distributed systems does require that you train the existing staff to use the new technologies.

Note – We recommend that you retrain existing staff rather than restaff to support the new technology whenever possible; however, if it is necessary to restaff, we recommend that you hire experienced UNIX personnel to support this new distributed environment.

It is important to maintain the same data center infrastructures and mainframe disciplines in the new open systems, client/server environment; centralized control for distributed production systems is critical to success and controlling costs. In addition, it is also very important to transition the mainframe staff to the UNIX environment rather than bring in additional people who have UNIX experience. Why? Because, in this centralized control model, the most important aspects for the data center environment are the disciplines of supporting RAS for critical systems *regardless* of the platform on which they run. (Mainframers knew how to support mission critical environments. When a system crashed, they responded immediately.) We also found that it was easier to train the mainframe people about the UNIX environment than it was to train UNIX people on the mainframe disciplines; this was key to our support paradigm.

We had two primary objectives:

1. Reducing the cost of the data center

2. Implementing a "lights-out" environment

Transitioning our mainframers was essential to meet these objectives. For example, who knew tape management, security, and disk management better than the mainframers? Their knowledge was a key factor in selecting and implementing the System Management tools required to support our mission critical systems.

The Primary Challenge

The primary challenge in supporting business applications from the mainframe platforms to the UNIX environment is retraining the staff.

- While members of the staff may have transferable organizational and administrative skills, they must learn the new UNIX technology.

- A lack of adequate tools in the UNIX environment requires the operations staff to receive more technical training in order to support the UNIX environment. Functionality exists in the mainframe environment that allows the operations staff to better diagnose problems and plan for growth; although much work is being done by

RDBMS vendors and third-party software companies to provide toolsets, this functionality in the UNIX environment is not yet as mature as in the mainframe environment.

Key Points for a Successful Transition

Some of the key points for making a successful transition are:

1. Maintain data center staff as a single group to keep objectives in alignment.

2. Keep existing personnel and develop their UNIX expertise.

3. Initially involve senior members of the mainframe operating system software group to gain support and alleviate skepticism.

4. Train and develop UNIX skills while continuing mainframe activities.

5. Allow all staff members the opportunity to learn the new system. Do not exclude *anyone* from the training.

6. If you lose a mainframe support person, always backfill with UNIX expertise. A balanced mix of UNIX and mainframe personnel is extremely important.

This chapter discusses:

- The importance of mainframe disciplines
- The importance of transitioning existing staff
- The education and training curriculums required for transition
- Staffing requirements
- Job descriptions for transitioning staff
- The importance of establishing a support agreement within your support organization
- Controlling morale
- Maximized training with minimal cost

Importance of Mainframe Disciplines

The mainframe environment uses integrated system management utilities. Its strengths include the availability of highly integrated system management tools and well-defined administrative procedures; however, the ability to modify and customize system management tools is generally limited.

The UNIX environment allows you to construct powerful tools. Its strengths are its lack of centralized applications and its wealth of software building blocks that can be integrated quickly to create powerful custom environments and applications; however, the ability to customize means that system management policies are not well defined, if at all.

When we first started Sun's rightsizing effort, we felt that the pivotal point to making it a successful venture was to implement the same types of data center management tools that were running our mainframe systems. This same rigor and discipline transitioned Sun from mainframe to network computing — while leveraging the productivity aspects of the new technology. In addition, the IT staff's fundamental understanding of the requirements of business information systems enabled them to perform the same extensive analysis in our new UNIX environment, which ensured the same required level of integrity. We believe these mainframe disciplines helped to successfully establish our support paradigm in running Sun's critical applications on UNIX.

Importance of Transitioning Existing Staff

The long-term success of your organization in a UNIX distributed environment depends on the right employee skill set. An organization can use two approaches to acquire the skills necessary for rightsizing: either hire new people with rightsizing skills or retrain existing personnel.

We recommend retraining existing personnel and developing UNIX expertise from within the organization for several reasons, including:

- The mainframe staff members can still maintain and support your legacy systems, running the business.

- The mainframe staff members have experience in supporting a controlled and well-managed environment, and it is essential to bring this type of mind-set into your new paradigm. It is equally important to have the mainframe staff involved in planning the implementation of the new distributed computing environment.

- Circumventing morale issues. If the existing staff feel that their jobs are in jeopardy, morale will be extremely low — low morale will make it even more difficult to implement the new distributed environment.

It is important to choose the senior people of the mainframe operating system software group to be the UNIX experts. Failure to bring the mainframe system software leadership into the rightsizing program will result in initial skepticism, then opposition.

We asked our most senior MVS System Programmer to be the first to participate in our training programs while continuing to support mainframe activities. Three months later, he was supporting our UNIX environment as well as the mainframe. Once the top MVS person completed the training curriculum, other staff members were eager to take the training, too.

Of course, everyone may not want to transition to the UNIX environment. In Sun's case, two out of ten system programmers and two out of ten database administrators opted to remain with the mainframe — completely aware that they would need to be retrained once the mainframes were turned off. The rest accepted the new challenges of working in the UNIX environment — and acknowledged that they were now twice as marketable because they knew both the UNIX and the mainframe environments.

To avoid major Human Resources (HR) conflicts during the transition to support UNIX, our data center organization rewrote job descriptions (keeping the same job titles) to encompass our data center support paradigm. For example, system programmers supported both the mainframe and UNIX, including installing operating systems for both environments, managing third-party program products, and debugging problems. Production Control personnel performed the same functions for both environments including scheduling, production problem resolution, and maintaining report distribution.

Education and Training Curricula

When we started Sun's rightsizing efforts in 1989, the most common cry was:

> *What is going to happen to my job?*

To avoid major morale issues, we invested heavily (in time, including our own personal time, and not in dollars) in training. The training required maximum involvement; the entire staff was involved with the transition. The key points to our training program were:

- Provide opportunity and participation to everyone — do *not* exclude anyone.

- Solicit upper-management commitment.

- Do not send people to classrooms without getting them involved in work projects, homework assignments, and reading.

- Use your lead MVS System Programmer as the first person to go through training programs.

- Develop curriculums that were specifically geared towards mainframers.

- Make sure all curriculums are based on hands-on assignments.

Management commitment was overwhelming, from the VP level on down. Not only were the executives extremely supportive, but they had our entire management staff establish training metrics to be tracked daily and submitted with our monthly status reports. It was so important to management that performance goals were established to meet training commitments.

We feel that training played a major role in our successful transition primarily because morale was always extraordinarily high. By providing the opportunity for training to all staff members, we found there were no morale issues to deal with. People were not wondering if they had a job from one day to the next and, once involved, they really supported the implementation of the new environment. They actively participated in creating the new environment!

Curricula Developed Professionally

The following curricula were developed by our company's professional training curriculum services organization, (SunService):

- System Administration Essentials
- System Administration for Solaris™
- Shell Programming

These courses were provided to our Data Center Staff: System Programmers, Database Administrators, Production Control Analysts, and Computer Operators.

Other specific courses were available for the System Programmers, Database Administrators, Applications Programmers, and Networking staffs. Topics were defined for each job function such as OS internals, C and C++ programming, and advanced system administration.

Internal Courses, Projects, and Homework Assignments

It was important to get everyone directly involved in developing tools for the new environment as soon as possible. Along with professionally developed curriculums, we developed some internal courses and many hands-on group projects, as described in Table 7-1.

Table 7-1   Internal Courses and Projects

Course or Project	Description	Attended by or Assigned to
Weekly Seminars	"Everything you wanted to know about UNIX but were afraid to ask." These seminars were tailored for beginners. Homework was assigned after each lecture to measure the seminar's success rate.	Mainframe Operators, Production Control, Database Administrators, System Programmers, and Application Programmers
Hardware Class	Required participants to disassemble and then reassemble hardware, including three servers andthree workstations. Our "UNIX guru" first gave a lecture on the hardware platform and then assisted class participants through the entire project. This course was extremely helpful in breaking down the barriers and myths and prompted teamwork throughout the Data Center. This class was also the most important because it helped deal with morale issues.	Mainframe Operators, Operation Analysts from Production Control, Database Administrators, and System Programmers
Special Projects	Included developing shell scripts to help manage the production Data Center environment and a project to measure system availability. Assigned as the first set of professional classes were completed. Note: The shell scripts projects were the single most critical factor of our successful transition: the HP3000 computer operators would not write clists as part of their homework during the transition from the mainframe, but these same operators would write shell scripts.	All Data Center personnel

Internal Courses

It was extremely important to implement training programs that would break the barriers between mainframe and UNIX environments.

Without a doubt, the single most important program we developed to accomplish this goal was a 1-day "Get Acquainted with the Hardware" class. This class consisted of a half-day classroom session depicting the difference between Sbus and VME and a half-day hands-on workshop in the Data Center.

Four hours were spent in a classroom getting to know the peripherals inside a server and workstation. After the lunch break, the next four hours were spent in an area of the Data Center, where three servers and three workstations had been set up specifically for this workshop. A team of five to six persons was assigned either a server or a workstation to disassemble.

The servers and workstations were brand-new (still in the crates!) and were to be used for housing our mission-critical systems. We had negotiated with the user-owners — who had purchased the hardware during their UPA process — to bring the servers and workstations into the data center the day before (without telling them why we wanted the machines early).

Once the disassembly was completed, the team had to reassemble the server or workstation *and* make sure it worked properly. When the machines were put back together again, they were running mission critical applications.

The investment in this class was minimal, but the payback was tremendous.

Group Projects

One of the projects, called the "Morning Report," was developed to provide us with an on-line automated report depicting server availability during a 24-hour period. This script — and others developed during our initial transition training — are still used today to manage our environment. See Chapter 8, "System Management Tools," for a detailed description of this system availability report.

Homework Assignments

Homework, completed on the employee's own time, was assigned with all of the courses. In addition, the completion of homework was also tracked as part of our training metrics. Why were these training metrics so important? They served as a criteria to help resolve any HR-related issues that might occur if, for some reason, a technical staff member could not make a successful transition to the UNIX environment. For example, if a staff member complained that proper or adequate training was not provided, these records were reviewed to determine if training was indeed an issue.

Related Books

In addition to the training curriculums, the transitioning staff was allowed to purchase books related to their job functions, including books on the following UNIX topics: operating system, system administration, programming, network topics, security, database administration, and C programming language. See Appendix J, "Recommended Reading," for a list of these books.

Measuring Success

We measured each employee's performance once a month in our status report.

Staffing Requirements

In order to support our infrastructure, the staff was divided into four groups: Computer Operations, Technical Support, Production Control, and Database Administration. Table 7-2 summarizes the staffing requirements necessary to support the data center infrastructure.

Table 7-2   Data Center Staff Requirements

Position	Responsibilities	Training Required
Computer Operations (CO)	Physical operation of the servers: - console monitoring - tape mounting - problem escalation	UNIX end-user skills including ability to read email and navigate through UNIX file system (for example, use cd and ls commands) entry level system administration, including shell scripts
Technical Support (TS)	Provide systems support including maintaining the operating system and utility software for all computer platforms.	Senior system administration skills, including ability to diagnose error messages from the network, UNIX, unbundled software packages, and data server requirements
Production Control (PC)	Manage production resources, schedule production workload, coordinate operator training, and implement new production applications.	Good communication skills, UNIX end-user skills, entry-level system administration skills, SQL inquiry level transactions, and ability to comprehend business requirements for the production application

Table 7-2   Data Center Staff Requirements (Continued)

Position	Responsibilities	Training Required
Database Administration (DBA)	Installing, upgrading, monitoring, and performance tuning the RDMSs to support business applications.	Strong knowledge of RDBMS, strong UNIX skills, shell scripts, good systems analyst skills, current hardware technology knowledge, and understanding of the current business needs that the systems fulfill

Job Descriptions for Transitioning Staff

This section discusses job descriptions that were created for mainframe staff (specifically System Programmers in Technical Support) who were the first group being transitioned to the UNIX environment.

System Programmer

The basic functions of this position support Sun's IT Group by providing reliable mainframe and UNIX system software. This function includes base operating systems and associated program products in one or more of the following UNIX and mainframe environments: Solaris, OpenWindows™, MVS/XA, VM/SP, and VM/XA. Table 7-3 describes specific duties and responsibilities, qualifications, and competencies requirements.

Table 7-3   Requirements for System Programmer

Specific Duties and Responsibilities	• Assist in the installation and customization of mainframe and UNIX operating systems to meet Sun's business requirements. • Install related program products and support levels.
	• Produce clear and concise operations and assistance center procedures. • Provide operational user support as required.
	• Resolve intermediate user problems regarding the UNIX operating systems, program products, and network environment.
Qualifications	Typically requires a B.S. degree in Computer Science plus 2-4 years in mainframe/UNIX software installations, customization, and support.

Table 7-3   Requirements for System Programmer (Continued)

Competencies	

	• Basic understanding of the following:
	   • operating system fundamentals (reentrant code, control blocks, kernel, multitasking)
	   • operating system (UNIX, MVS, VM) externals
	   • one or more high-level computer languages (C, C++, COBOL, C-shell, or Bourne shell)
	   • UNIX system administration
	
	• Working knowledge of networked Sun environment, including Solaris and Sun services (for example, NFS, NIS, NIS+, or DNS)

	• Basic understanding and experience with Sun system administration (such as dump/restore and disk configuration) • Basic understanding of a distributed computer environment

	• Familiarity with:
	   • 370 assembler and C language (that is, ability to read and understand the code)
	   • operating system customization and I/O configuration
	   • program product installation
	   • access methods
	   • C shell and Bourne programming skills

	• An understanding of the software installation process • Ability to coordinate work and interface with other groups For example: work closely with DBA group to aid in IDMS, UNIX database support and problem determination; work with Operations to train, develop procedures, and improve the operation; work with System Administration to provide a user-friendly and responsive environment; work with the Assistance Center to develop effective problem determination and resolution procedures; work with Applications Development staff to improve and support the development environment.
	• Ability to analyze and track system- and application-oriented problems via, for example, error logs and dumps

System Programmer II

The basic functions of this position support Sun's IT Group by providing reliable UNIX and mainframe system software. This includes base operating systems and associated program products in one or more of the following environments: MVS/XA, VM/SP, VM/XA, Solaris, and OpenWindows. Table 7-4 describes specific duties and responsibilities, qualifications, and competencies requirements.

Table 7-4   Requirements for System Programmer II

Specific Duties and Responsibilities	• Install and customize UNIX and mainframe operating systems to meet Sun's business requirements. • Install related program products and support tools.
	• Produce clear and concise operations and Assistance Center procedures.
	• Provide operational problem determination and support as required.
	• Provide internal training to Operations, Assistance Center, DBAs and System Administration as required.
	• Measure system/network performance; then recommend and implement performance improvements.
Qualifications	Typically requires a B.S. degree in Computer Science, Mathematics or Business, and formal vendor training (for example, IBM, Amdahl, or Sun), plus 5-10 years in UNIX/mainframe system software installation, customization, and support.

Table 7-4   Requirements for System Programmer II

Competencies	• Requires an understanding of the following:
	• operating system fundamentals (reentrant code, control blocks, kernel, multitasking, UNIX processes)
	• operating system (MVS, VM, UNIX) externals
	• one or more high-level computer language (COBOL, C-shell or Bourne shell, C, C++, FORTRAN)
	• operating system customization and I/O configuration
	• system administration functions
	• program product installation
	• access methods
	• operating system internals (one or more: UNIX, VM, MVS)
	• 370 assembler coding
	• reconfigure kernel, communication protocols (SNA, VTAM, Ethernet, TCP/IP)
	• software monitors (such as SunNet Manager, Omegamon, or Resolve)
	• microcode relationship to software and hardware
	• system exits (SMF, operating system, etc.)
	• third-party system software
	• Ability to independently make decisions For example: choose proper options and parameters when installing/initializing/configuring software; determine data set planning and kernel configuration for optimal performance.
	• Ability to analyze and solve problems For example: read problem program dump, error logs to determine failure, resolve error; isolate system problems to determine if caused by failing hardware or software; read and analyze an operating system dump or core dump; code in 370 assembler language or C for UNIX; recover from system failures (such as disk failures, damaged system catalogs/file systems, Jes2 failures, faulty parameters, and alternative boot procedures). Ability to troubleshoot hardware and software problems in a distributed environment.
	• Ability to coordinate work and interface with other groups For example: work closely with DBA group to aid in IDMS support and problem determination; work closely with Network Support and integration development in Management tool support; work with application programming staff to improve and support the development environment; coordinate bug reporting, patches and upgrades.

Table 7-4   Requirements for System Programmer II

Competencies (Continued)	• Excellent understanding and experience with Sun system administration (such as dump/restore and disk configuration).

Advisory System Programmer

The basic functions of this position is to support Sun's IT Business Operation Group by providing reliable mainframe system software. This function includes base operating systems and associated program products in one or more of the following Sun and mainframe environments: Solaris, OpenWindows, MVS/ XA, and VM/SP. Table 7-5 describes specific duties and responsibilities, qualifications, and competencies requirements.

Table 7-5   Advisory System Programmer

Specific Duties and Responsibilities	• Install and customize the Solaris kernel and mainframe operating systems to meet Sun's business requirements. • Install related program products and support tools.
	• Produce clear and concise operations and Assistance Center procedures. • Provide operational problem determination for unique and most complex problems and support as required.
	• Provide internal training to Operations, Assistance Center, DBAs, Application Development, and System Administration, as required. • Measure system and network performance, then recommend and implement performance improvements.
	• Evaluate new products and recommend solutions. • Perform capacity-planning studies and identify capacity shortages.
Qualifications	Typically requires B.S. degree in Computer Science, Mathematics, or Business (MSCS desirable), plus 8-10 years UNIX kernel installations and system software installation, customization and support. Formal vendor training desirable (such as IBM, Amdahl, or Sun).

Table 7-5   Advisory System Programmer (Continued)

Competencies	• Requires an understanding of the following:
	  • operating system fundamentals (reentrant code, control blocks, multitasking, UNIX processes)
	  • operating system (MVS, VM, UNIX) externals
	  • one or more high-level computer languages (COBOL, C-shell or Bourne shell, C, C++, FORTRAN)
	  • operating system customization and I/O configuration
	  • system administration functions
	  • program product installation
	  • access methods
	  • operating system internals (one or more: UNIX, VM, MVS)
	  • 370 assembler coding
	  • reconfigure the kernel, communication protocols (SNA, VTAM, Ethernet, TCP/IP, NFS)
	  • software monitors (i.e., SunNet Manager, Omegamon, Resolve)
	  • microcode relationship to software and hardware
	  • system exits (SMF, operating system, etc.)
	  • third-party system software

	• Familiarity with TP monitors (IDMS/DC, CICS, IMS, etc.) and databases (IDMS, Sybase, DB2) • Ability to independently make decisions For example: choose proper options and parameters when installing/initializing/configuring software and determine data set planning and kernel configuration for optimal performance.
	• Ability to analyze and solve problems For example: read problem program dumps, error logs to determine failure, resolve errors; isolate system and network problems to determine if caused by failing hardware or software; read and analyze an operating system dump or case dump; code in 370 assembler language or C for UNIX; recover from system failures. Ability to troubleshoot hardware and software problems in a distributed environment.
	• Ability to coordinate work and interface with other groups For example: work closely with DBA group to aid in IDMS support and problem determination; work closely with Network Support and integration development on Management tool support; work with Application Development staff to improve and support the development environment.

Technical Support Manager

The basic functions for this position direct Data Center Production activities including computer job scheduling, operating systems programming and maintenance, DASD management, input/output control, data set and library maintenance, job control language, software installs, and routine production failure analysis and resolution. Table 7-6 describes specific duties and responsibilities, qualifications, and competencies requirements.

Table 7-6   Requirements for Technical Support Manager

Specific Duties and Responsibilities	• Direct the Technical Support function, including worldwide scheduling, software installations, job control language, production acceptance procedures, and routine production failure analysis and resolution.
	• Direct the DASD management function, including space management, disk library maintenance, software installation, and capacity forecasting.
	• Direct the UNIX system programming function, including all aspects of technical support plus the development of operational software tools and server installation.
	• Ensure the proper scheduling of all IT production systems to support a 24-hour, 7-day operation with users located worldwide.
	• Serve as the liaison with the IT user community and application programming staff to ensure a smooth implementation and continual system assurance for production services.
	• Provide information to management in defining policies and procedures in the production support areas.
	• Negotiate with diverse groups of worldwide users to arrive at optimum production schedules to meet Sun's business requirements. In addition to regular schedules, manager must negotiate and develop special scheduling and processing such as month-end, quarter-end, and year-end physical inventory as well as special-run requests.
	• Develop a long-term strategy to meet corporate business demands while continually shifting processing loads from the mainframe to UNIX platforms.
	• Ensure worldwide policies and procedures are established and adhered to in accordance with Sun's goals.
	• Define and enforce standards.

Table 7-6   Requirements for Technical Support Manager (Continued)

Specific Duties and Responsibilities (Continued)	• Provide application development environment for programming staff. • Ensure accomplishment of assigned goals and objectives.
	• Ensure that the staff is informed of Sun policies and actions, including corporate communications, inter-/intraorganizational coordination, commitments, and decisions. • Recruit, train, discipline, motivate, and evaluate staff. For example: recognize accomplishments; set and clarify performance expectations and objectives; approve leaves; identify staff members for promotion or reassignment; and implement Sun's Affirmative Action policies.
	• Manage group's resources. For example: handle the assigned budgets; assign responsibilities; ensure quality of end results; promote creativity, technical excellence, productivity, and teamwork; implement Sun's policies.
	• Assist manager in developing new administrative initiatives, strategic plans, policies, and operational procedures. Develop group's plans, budgets, and objectives in support of IT goals.
Qualifications	Typically requires a BS/BA degree or equivalent plus 5-8 years of computer production experience with 3-5 years in management.
Competencies	• Understanding of MVS facilities and production control tools (such as JCL check, report archival, scheduling, and data management) • Understanding of a networked UNIX environment • Excellent communications skills • Strong negotiation skills • Strong leadership abilities; ability to plan, organize and motivate others to achieve objectives • Ability to make sound judgments that lead to timely and accurate decisions • Understanding of Sun's product strategy, ability to deploy resources wisely and to make decisions that benefit Sun's business
	• Strong human resources management and interpersonal skills. Ability to attract, motivate, and develop the right people, ability to correct substandard performance; skill to confront and resolve conflicts immediately without major disruptions to the work flow or to existing relationships.

Table 7-6   Requirements for Technical Support Manager (Continued)

Competencies (Continued)	• Ability to adjust performance to meet changing circumstances such as reorganizations, reassignment of priorities, alterations in strategic direction, and shifting customer needs
	• Ability to communicate with specific groups of people at their level (i.e., users, DBAs, System Programmers, Applications Development staff, upper management, and all levels of corporate users)
	• An understanding of MVS concepts, facilities, and architecture
	• Ability to conceptualize the overall business needs and develop a global scheduling plan
	• Ability to identify department processes and acquire software tools to improve operations
	• Ability to monitor and report on DASD capacity and recommend solutions
	• Basic competency in all technical support software tools (JCL check, CA-dispatch, CA-scheduler, ASM2, TMS, TSO/ISPF)
	• Understanding of UNIX concepts, facilities, and architecture and connectivity to mainframes
	• Strong negotiation skills and ability to deal with a major cross section of corporate users

Establishing a Support Agreement

A Support Agreement within the data center organization was documented because it was essential for us to know what everyone's new job responsibilities were. We had just introduced UNIX into our "glasshouse," and it was necessary to have a clear understanding of everyone's support role in the Data Center.

This agreement established a commitment between the Data Center groups as well as an escalation procedure. The goal is to solidify and clarify each groups' expectations and to build efficient and timely service between the groups.

Since we were breaking uncharted ground with our new UNIX production environment, the Support Agreement was a way of communicating our support paradigm within the entire organization.

See Appendix I, "Internal Support Agreement for the Data Center," for more information about this type of agreement.

7

Rightsizing the New Enterprise

System Management Tools 8 ≡

Our Biggest Fear!

As we started down the path to implement and support this new distributed environment for the Data Center, we had two objectives at all times:

1. Reduce the cost of running the "glasshouse" (i.e., the Data Center)

2. Implement a "lights-out" (no computer operator intervention) environment

And, of course, everything we implemented was based on mainframe functionality.

When we were given the assignment to start supporting mission critical distributed applications, there were a couple of little issues to deal with:

* *We were not given any new headcount*

* *Our working environment (i.e., the mainframes and the HPs) did not slow down for us to implement and support these new mission critical distributed applications which were rapidly being developed around the world*

But our biggest concern, and our biggest fear, was that there were no UNIX system management tools! We were accustomed to those good old mainframe tools that are very robust and have been around for at least two decades, such as tools for tape management, disk management, and security. How can you run a production operations for a multibillion company without these tools? It was a nightmare!

Another issue was that Sun's management could not relate to these system management tools because they did not yet exist for the UNIX world. Oh, the times were tough!

The tools we discuss in this chapter are:
* *System availability*
* *Tape management*
* *Change control/management*
* *Problem management*
* *Monitoring performance and capacity planning*
* *Database utilities*
* *Auto-paging*
* *Preventive maintenance*

8

- *Job scheduling*
- *System resource management*

— Harris and Randy

System Availability Reporting

In addition to UNIX programming classes, we knew that it was important to have our staff involved in the planning and implementation of the new distributed computing environment. The mainframers had experience in supporting a controlled and well-managed environment, and it was essential to get them involved early in projects for the Data Center. So we put together many hands-on courses, including how to write and execute clists and JCL (eventually these clists were used in our daily mainframe production support processes).

One of the first projects that our staff developed during the mainframe-to-UNIX transition was called the "Morning Report." The Morning Report provided us with an on-line automated report delineating server availability during a 24-hour period. It was written as a csh script (C-shell) by our computer operations staff and showed the servers we supported around the world, the applications which resided on these servers and their uptime availability hours. (We did not dictate when the servers were going to be backed up; each Sun business unit made that decision.) The Morning Report showed when we had an outage on a particular server. It tracks all production servers, regardless of location, and is automatically delivered every 24 hours (through email) to interested parties and data center management. The information provided by the report on a daily basis includes server name, application name, uptime availability hours, outage notification, and outage description. It also provides an incremental metric on the total number of days the server has been available without an outage and the number of days since the last time an outage occurred. The format of the report is similar to:

```
Day/Hi    System     Application      Uptime          Percent     Outage
0/148     Driven     Fixed Assets     07:00-20:00     99.4        1
Explanation of outages:
          1. Driven - (system rebooted)18:40 - 18:47(7 mins)
```

where the server *Driven*, on which the *Fixed Assets Application* resides, had *one* outage the night before between 6:40 pm and 6:47pm. *Day* indicates the number of days since the last outage (zero indicates an outage occurred the previous day); *Hi* indicates the highest number of consecutive days the server was available (this server has been available 148 consecutive days without an outage); *uptime* indicates the application is available from 7:00 A.M. to 8:00 P.M.; and *percent* indicates this server was available 99.4% during the past 24 hours. This same report is used for all platforms that have production systems, including mainframe, HP, and UNIX servers. We found that the same controls can be used for distributed systems; however, the processes should be automated.

The availability is tracked by various in-house-developed scripts that were written by our computer operations staff. These scripts comprise two programs:

1. The outage reporting mechanism
   This program consists of ten C-shell scripts that work in conjunction to track server availability. The program outputs a list of hosts (contained within a Master Host List) into one of two categories: *Available Server List* or *Unavailable Server List*. The program determines the total downtime of any server that falls into the Unavailable Server List. It tallies the time the server went down, the time the server came back up, and the total downtime of the server. All of the outage information is stored in an error directory for retrieval at a later time.

2. The format program
   When this program is invoked, it begins to format the availability report. It first calculates and formats a site summary, showing all the servers for a particular location, and then lists the duration of any outages. Finally, the script formats the summary matrix section, which lists every server within a particular site, denoting the server on-line history. Once the report is formatted, the script automatically mails it to the respective site managers.

The mainframe and HP3000 statistics were also in the Morning Report, along with detailed information on each mission critical application, such as average response times and number of application and system transactions. The report was extremely valuable for us to maintain high availability. Our goal was to maintain 99. 9% availability for all 200 servers worldwide; this was how we measured ourselves.

The Morning Report script, which started as a class project during our transition period, is still in use today.

With mainframe systems programming, data center management, and networking backgrounds, we had a good idea of what it would take to implement the first of its kind UNIX production environment supporting mission critical applications. We constantly kept the following concepts in our thoughts:

- Maintain system availability at 99.9%, as we did with the mainframe environments

- Provide analysis on system management tools

- Provide the same functionality as mainframe tools

- Reduce current costs

- Implement a "lights-out" operations environment

As we started down the system management path, we knew that our goal was to deploy the tools that would help us maintain our system uptime availability at 99.9%.

See Appendix E, "An Example Morning Report," for an example report.

Tape Management

One of our top three priorities for UNIX production was a Tape Management System (TMS) which met the same stringent functionality requirements as our mainframe product.

There were only four products available in the market in the fall of 1989. We performed extensive analysis — similar to the type of analysis you would perform when selecting mainframe tools — and determined none of the four tools provided the mainframe functionality we wanted.

What does *mainframe functionality* mean for Tape Management? In the mainframe world, you *cannot* accidentally write over a production tape — this is called standard labeling. For example, if you accidentally mount the wrong tape, tape management functionality ejects it. Another example of mainframe functionality is called *off-site retention criteria* — daily, weekly, and monthly tapes are stored in a vault off-site for disaster recovery purposes.

We eventually chose a Sun product called On-line: Backup and incorporated some additional functionality (such as shell scripts) to meet our tape management requirements.

The original components and features of On-line: Backup included:
- Dump, restore, recover, on-line database recording of all dumped files
- Dump configuration and execution system
- electronic label, expiration date, dump level (supports all UNIX dump levels plus true increments)
- Dump devices: local/remote, multiple
- Network monitoring utility
- Utilities for database maintenance
- Tape initialization
- Dump active file systems (on-line in multiuser mode)
- Perform faster dump/restore/recover
- Perform on-line restore
- Dump multiple file systems on one tape
- Verify tape label
- Monitor dump throughout the network

We developed shell scripts that allowed us to provide the same functionality as was available for the mainframe. The administration scripts we developed to enhance the product included:
- Operator backup notification (time for backups/mount tapes)
- Standard tape-labeling maintenance (conforming to standards)
- Error notification

- Error recovery (standard format)
- Status report (completed/failed)
- Data center tape-retention standards

This tool has been in full production status for more than three years. One tape librarian performs all HP, mainframe, and UNIX tape management. All backups are performed automatically by these shell scripts based on division business requirements; incremental tape backups are completed nightly; full dump backups to tape are done on the weekend.

Below is a list of the functionality we were seeking when looking for a Tape Management System.

♦ Weight

Extremely Critical	1.0*
Critical	0.8-1.0
Desired	0.4-0.7
Wish List	0.1-0.3

♦ Analysis

Functionality	Weight
Compatibility with the Previous, Current, and Next OS Level	1.0
Compatibility with Current System Architecture	1.0
Easy to install, configure, and expand: Setup/Install Procedure Configure/Customization Process Automation of System Administration Central System Administration Ability to Expand/Add/Delete machine	 0.8 0.8 0.9 0.9 0.9
Training Availability	0.7
Documentation: Clarity Completeness	 0.8 0.8

Functionality	Weight
Full/Incremental Backup Capabilities:	
Full/Incremental to Single Local Device	1.0*
Full/Incremental to Multiple Local Devices	1.0*
Full/Incremental to Single Remote Device	1.0*
Full/Incremental to Multiple Remote Devices	1.0*
Full/Incremental of Single Server/File System	1.0*
Full/Incremental of Multiple Servers/File Systems	1.0*
Full/Incremental of Multiple Volume Dumps on Local and Remote Servers/File Systems	1.0*
Supports Distributed Device Host	0.7
Ability to Exclude Filesystems	0.8
A Hook Before/After a Backup Runs	0.7
On-line Backup Database (File Database):	
Ability to Query/Locate Files	1.0
Ability to Modify	0.9
Media (Volume) Management (Media Database):	
Ability to Index/Label Tapes	1.0
Ability to Customize Labels	0.9
Ability to Create Tape Library	0.9
Ability to Initialize Remote Media on Local Device	1.0
Ability to Add/Delete Media to/from Library	0.9
Ability to Incorporate Media Bar Codes in Media Database	0.7
Integration of File Database with Media Database	1.0
24-hr Accessibility of File Systems:	
24-hr System Availability	1.0*
Guaranteed File Integrity	1.0
On-line Restore Capabilities:	
On-Line Restore Capabilities for 35 days	0.8
Ability to Restore Single File	1.0*
Ability to Restore Directory	1.0*
Ability to Restore File System	1.0*
User-invoked Restore Capability	0.9
No System Administration Intervention Required for User Restore	0.7
Unattended Backups	1.0*

Functionality	Weight
Reliability:	
Media	1.0*
Fewer Points of Fail	1.0
Software Reliability	1.0
Reliability of On-line Backups	1.0
Security:	
Standard UNIX File Security	1.0
Added Security for File Restores	0.9
User-invoked Restore from User's Point of View	0.9
User-invoked Restore with Exclusion by Export	0.9
Report Generation:	
Media Reports	0.7
System Reports	0.7
Ability to Archive	1.0
Ability to Migrate	0.7
Ability to Handle Standard Supported Backup Devices:	
8 mm Tape Drives	1.0*
Different Disk Types	1.0*
TTY Interface:	
Command-line Interface	1.0
Curses-based Interface	0.8
GUI Interface:	
For Users	1.0
Motif-based GUI	0.8
COSE-Compliant GUI	0.5
Acceptable Capacity vs. Optimal Performance:	1.0
Dump Completion within its Allotted Time	

Functionality	Weight
Disaster Recovery:	
Ease of Local Recovery	0.8
Ease of Recovery Across the Network	1.0
Movement of Dump Server to Different Machine	0.9
Time to Recover a Single File	0.8
Time to Recover Multiple Files	0.8
Time to Recover a Filesystem	1.0
Time to Recover an Entire Disk	1.0
Hardware Device Failover	0.8
Multiple Server Recovery Procedure Recommended by Vendor	0.7
Compatibility with Previous Backup Software Versions	1.0
Use with Optional (Destination) Storage Media:	
8 mm Jukeboxes	1.0
Higher-Speed Robotics Support	0.9
Ease of Operability:	
Clear, Concise Error Messages	0.7
"Wrong Tape Loaded" Error Message	0.7
"Device Not Ready" Error Message	0.7
"Multiple Commands to Device" Error Message	0.7
"No Tape Loaded" Error Message	0.7
Ability to Restart Jobs:	
Ability to Resume Failed Job	1.0
Ability to Restart Single Job	1.0
Ability to Restart Multiple Jobs	1.0
Ease of Verification of Dump Success	1.0
User Database Backup:	
Ability to Dump Raw Partitions	1.0*
Ability to Interface with Database Vendors Dump Utilities	0.9
Ability to Dump Tables and Incremental DB	0.8

Functionality	Weight
Internationalization:	
Level One (8-bit Clean ASCII)	1.0
Level Two (Date-Time Collation)	1.0
Ability to Run under Localized OS	1.0
Vendor Support:	
Bug Fix Availability	1.0
Bug Fix Turnaround	1.0
Customer Service Telephone Support	0.8
On-site Response Time	0.8
Vendor Screen	1.0
International Distribution	0.9
International Support	0.9
Cost:	
Software License	0.8
Service Contract	0.8
Internal Support	0.7
Installation	0.7

Change Control and Notification Management

Effective control and notification of change is an important part of data center services. The data center must have a standard procedure for reviewing, scheduling, and advising customers of upcoming changes. We accumulate changes and email these changes to our customer base on a biweekly basis.

First, let us explain how change control and notification management is done in the mainframe environment: If you are a System Programmer and you want to make a change to the operating system, you use the change control process to notify everyone affected two weeks prior to making the change. Then, from a centralized location, you document the change for your peer System Programmers. However, this process in the mainframe has a fault: A System Programmer on the mainframe or a System Administrator in the UNIX environment had the authority to make a change to the environment at any time. Many times changes would be made without the System Programmer using the change control process, or (even more commonly) neglecting to document the changes that were made.

Did we really want to have this type of change control process in a distributed environment with production servers all over the world? Could we authorize System Programmers and System Administrators to make changes at any time they determined to do so? How could we manually document all these changes?

We needed a foolproof, secure, automated way of tracking all the changes made to our distributed environment.

Our change control and notification management process is a checks-and-balances system. We do not stop change — we *monitor* every change. The process that we developed was based on our UPA process, which included standard configurations. When a server goes through the UPA process, we know exactly what the configuration of that server is, (for example, the third-party products, including version and release, residing on the server and how a disk is partitioned). In addition, we have a shell script that tracks our inventory and another process that takes a "before and after" snapshot of the server each morning. This process is even *more secure* than that of the mainframe.

A System Programmer or a System Administrator *cannot* make a change to any server without our knowledge or proper authorization — every system level change that has been made is automatically recorded. In addition, each System Administrator and System Programmer is responsible for specific servers in a geography; any changes made without using the change control process are documented on their yearly review.

The change management process is a series of shell scripts written by one mainframe system programmer, a UNIX guru, and two mainframe computer operators. This program was developed to address the growing needs of UNIX system configuration control and management for a client/server distributed environment. This process achieves the following:

- Provides the Database Administration group with disk partition information for Sybase installation maintenance

- Provides server information that is utilized by SunNet Manager to construct its list of monitoring servers

- Provides up-to-date inventory of all production server configurations worldwide

- Automates processes that manage and track server configurations and changes

- Detects unauthorized and/or inadvertent changes being made to servers

- Uses SQL technology to provide on-line queries and generation of customized reports

- Serves as the central configuration information databook that facilitates related processes inside or outside the organization

With this experience in mind, we developed a weekly change control report that describes upcoming changes that are scheduled, so that our customers can plan their work around possible production interruptions. This same process has been used without any modification, regardless of hardware and software technology evolution.

With over 200 servers, change management is the tool used by the UNIX system programmers to keep track of every change. This proactive approach enables UNIX support personnel to support and control the production environment 24 hours per day 7 days per week, regardless of location.

In addition, this process played a large role in establishing the first "lights-out" UNIX production environment supporting mission critical applications.

Problem Management

Each problem must be documented and tracked to make sure a solution is developed, installed, and verified. The data center must have standard procedures for recording and reporting problems and for tracking progress towards their resolution. SunIRS (Sun's Incident Reporting System) is a tool used in the Data Center for problem management. SunIRS is used primarily for three functions:

1. To locate on-call personnel in the event a problem needs to be escalated.
   This function is a key element in Data Center Operations because Operations is goaled to escalate any problem within 15 minutes.

2. To help isolate recurring problems.
   This function allows us to perform trend analysis on any mission critical server/application. For example, we can look up a history of each server/application for a given period of time by simply entering the server/application name.

3. To escalate trouble tickets.
   This function allows us to close trouble tickets within a 24-hour time frame. Every time a problem occurs, the Operations staff assigns a trouble ticket to that problem. This trouble ticket is then escalated to the on-call support person and his/her manager.

The tool is also useful in ongoing trend analysis.

To bring up SunIRS, you would first enter the following command in a shelltool window:

```
sunirs &
```

Next, enter the password into the password window, and press Enter. If the logon is successful, the main menu is displayed, as shown in Figure 8-1.

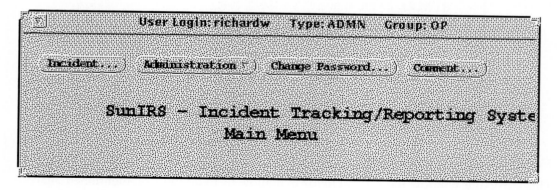

Figure 8-1   SunIRS Main Menu

SunIRS Selection Window

This window is utilized via the Operations staff in order to perform a history on any server or application that has been deemed mission critical.

By using this window, we are able to perform a trend analysis on servers in order to pinpoint recurring problems with our production servers.

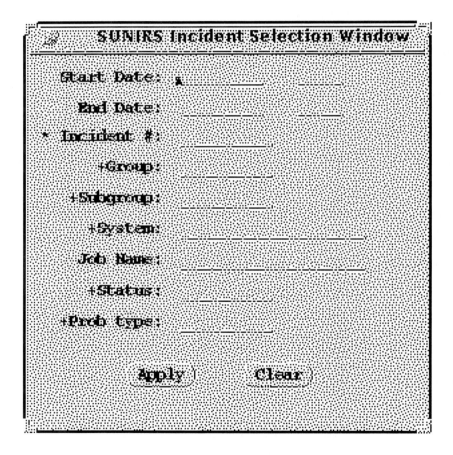

Figure 8-2   SunIRS Incident Selection Window

This particular window has several fields that allow us to do the aforementioned analysis. Table 8-1 contains a brief description of each field.

Table 8-1   Field Descriptions in SunIRS Selection Window

Field	Description
Start Date	Enter the starting date from which you want the system to begin the sort.
End Date	Enter the date you want the system to terminate the sort.
Incident #	Enter the trouble ticket number, if known, to see the current status of the ticket.
Group	To browse the database by group only, enter the group within this field.
Subgroup	To browse the database by subgroup only, enter the subgroup within this field.
System	To view the trouble tickets that have been issued for a specific server or application, enter the server or application name within this field.
Job Name	To view all trouble tickets that have been issued for an application, enter the application name within this field.
Status	To view the status for any trouble tickets, enter either Open, Closed, or Follow-up within this field. For example, to see all open trouble tickets, enter Open within this field. At this point, the system will scan the database for applicable matches.
Problem Type	To browse the database by problem type, enter the problem type within this field.

You can use one or any combination of these fields in order to sort the database.

SunIRS On-call Lookup Window

This is the window that Operations uses to browse the Sybase database for on-call personnel. You search through the database by using one of two search keys. You can go through the database by an on-call person's name or by a server/application's name.

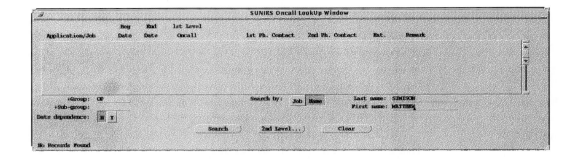

Figure 8-3   SunIRS On-call Lookup Window

Table 8-2 contains a brief description of each field.

Table 8-2   Field Descriptions in SunIRS On-call Lookup Window

Field	Description
Group	To find people within a specific group, enter the group name within this field.
Subgroup	To find people within a specific subgroup, enter the subgroup name within this field.
Date Dependence	To find people who are on-call for specific date range, enter the date in this field.
Search By	To sort through the database, use one of these two keys.
Job	To scan the database by a job name or server name, enter the information within this field.
Name	If you know the support person's name, but not the phone number, enter the person's name within this field.

Once you have entered the information, you press the search key to begin the sort of the database.

SunIRS Trouble Ticket/Incident Report Window

Figure 8-4 shows the standard template that the Data Center Operations staff use in order to issue a trouble ticket for a problem within the Data Center. The basic purpose of this window is to open lines of communication between Operations and the Support staff. Every time a trouble ticket is created, it is automatically sent to the support person and the support person's manager. Our goal is to have any ticket resolved or closed within a 24-hour time frame.

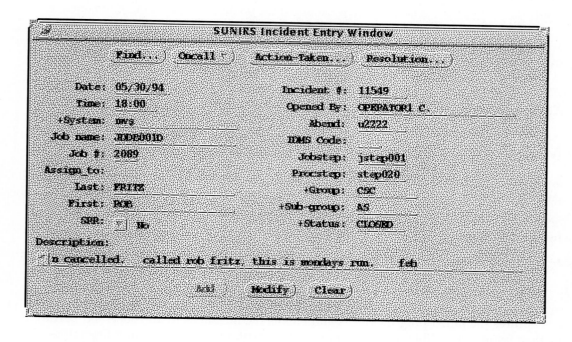

Figure 8-4   SunIRS Trouble Ticket/Incident Report Window

Table 8-3 contains a brief description of each field.

Table 8-3   Field Descriptions in SunIRS Trouble Ticket/Incident Report Window

Field	Description
System	The name of the system that has had a problem.
Job Name	The application name that has encountered a problem.
Description	A brief description of the actual problem.
Action Taken	The steps taken by the operations staff to fix the problem.
Add	Once you have completed the trouble ticket, click the Add button to add the trouble ticket to the database and email the support person and manager of the actual trouble ticket.
Assign To	Used in conjunction with the Oncall window to assign the trouble ticket to a support person.

All other fields will be automatically updated by clicking the add button.

Monitoring Performance and Capacity Planning

To monitor system availability, disk I/O, paging and swapping, volume of Ethernet packets, network load (output packet collision), we installed SunNet Manager (SNM).

SNM is installed on a SPARCstation 2 with multiple monitors. IT performs several key functions for production servers.

• For monitoring production servers, the SNM console periodically emits *ping* messages to all the systems. Based on the ping responses, SNM determines system availability on our production servers. The primary console is set to capture any ping failure messages and blinks their corresponding icons on the screen; the secondary console captures the failed ping messages and emails the messages to all concerned parties. It then issues an audible message to draw the attention of the Computer Operators.

• For monitoring CPU and disk utilization events, SNM periodically emits requests to all remote systems and requests its client agents to collect system information. When the predefined threshold is encountered, the primary console blinks the corresponding icon while the secondary console issues email and audible messages.

SNM is also set up to collect Ethernet, TCP/IP, network packet size, and response time monitoring status. SNM polls its remote client agents every 15 minutes for information.

This tool provides data on a daily basis. The data is stored and analyzed by a third-party product (SAS/CPE from SAS Institute) that performs trend analysis and capacity planning. Figure 8-5 shows a sample report.

```
Legends: high-  highest value of the sampling list
         low-   lowest value of the sampling list
         avg-   average value of the sampling list
         norm-  average value after removing both the highest
                and lowest values from the sampling list

data representation:data from each category is represented in the
            xxx(cc) form; where xxx is the value of the category and cc
            is the quantity of such value from the sampling list

Server:     "cascade"
```

CPU utilization statistics

	high	low	avg	norm
cpu%	99(6)	0(308)	6.88	14.48(206)

ethernet traffic (input) statistics

	high	low	avg	norm
ipkts:	103360(1)	49(8)	707.12	647.58(505)
oerrs:	225(1)	0(443)	0.87	3. 17(70)
ocolls:	20177(1)	0(3)	186.95	149.22(510)
odrops:	0(514)	0(514	0.00	0.00(0)

protocol layers statistics

	high	low	avg	norm
ip	151871(1)	13460(1)	43074.13	42920.67(516)
udp	124142(1)	11623(1)	33661.36	33528.72(516)
tcp	54514(1)	347(1)	8910.07	8838.28(516)
icmp	18464(1)	17(1)	579.56	545.99(516)

network packet layers statistics

size groups	high	low	avg	norm
60-241	627088(1)	2179(1)	296300.81	295634.16(55)
242A23	373085(1)	45(1)	66912.75	- 62561.76(55)
424-605	94501(1)	13(1)	13079.39	11836.56(55)
606-787	11310(1)	10(1)	3706.32	3635.27(55)
788-969	7555(1)	10(1)	3706.32	3635.27(55)
970-1151	4442(1)	4(2)	1591.95	1597.98(54)
1152-1333	2668(1)	3(1)	992.63	998.31(54)
1334-1514	2461(1)	0(1)	619.82	597.62(55)

Figure 8-5   Sample Report to Monitor Performance

Database Utilities

Based on our mainframe experience, another key area was tools to support relational databases (RDBMS). Our DBAs developed standard database administration utilities for Sybase® and Oracle® to provide the same functionality in the UNIX environment as we had for the mainframe database management systems.

Sybase Scripts

The first set of Sybase scripts included:

- Automatic installation of programs
- Man pages
- Directory structure
- Documentation and creation of Sybase devices within the data server
- Automatic check for errors that are written to the Sybase error log
- Notification of the necessary support personnel via email
- Automatic dump of Sybase databases
- Automatically dumps Sybase transaction logs
- Automatic execution of database consistency checkers and storage of space information in a Sybase database for trend analysis of disk usage

The second set of Sybase scripts included:

- Enhancement to daily database dumps and transaction dumps
- A utility to identify the well- being of database server
- A utility to automate recovery of a database from the database and transaction dumps
- A set of tools to provide a snapshot of the database (e.g., to identify who is using which objects or has what locks)
- Alert tools to interface with SunNet Manager for paging and other non-email facilities
- Enhanced utilities to track growth of database
- A set of tools to analyze data server performance
- Auditing tools to gather statistics on who is accessing the system and number of connections made

- Utilities to capture information needed for disaster recovery of a database on another server in a remote site.

Table 8-4 provides a more detailed description of each utility.

Table 8-4   Sybase Database Utilities

Tool		Description
Sybase Utilities Release 1.0	Installation Script	Automated way to install programs, man pages, directory structure and documents, and to create Sybase devices within the data server.
	Error-checking Script	Automated way to check for errors that are written to the Sybase error log and to notify the necessary support personnel via email.
	DBCC Script	Standard automated way to execute database consistency checkers and store space information in a Sybase database for trend analysis of disk usage. Also calls error program in the event of DBCC errors.
	Database Dump Script	Standard automated way to dump Sybase databases.
	Transaction Dump Script	Standard automated way to dump Sybase transaction logs.

Table 8-4   Sybase Database Utilities (Continued)

Tool	Description
Sybase Utilities Release 2.0	Enhancement to daily database dumps, transaction dumps, checking error logs, reporting disk space usage, and so forth
	Utility to identify the well-being of database server.
	Utility to automate recovery of database from database and transaction dumps.
	Tools to provide a snapshot of the database (e.g., who is using which objects, has what locks)
	Alert tools to interface with some type of SNM for paging and other non-email facilities.
	Enhanced utilities to track growth of database.
	Enhanced utilities to track growth of individual database objects.
	Tools to analyze dataserver performance.
	Auditing tools to gather statistics on who is accessing the system, number of connections made, and so forth
	Generic utility to allow others to add login to Sybase server without giving system administrator password.
	Automating installation and configuration of new servers and utilities.
	A database similar to AnswerBook™ that can be accessed by novice DBAs to get answers to frequently occurring problems and how to resolve them.
	Utilities to capture information needed for disaster recovery of a database on another server in a remote site.

Oracle Scripts

The first set of Oracle scripts included:

- A backup script for automated database backups (both hot and cold) to disk

- A restore script that generates UNIX commands necessary for automated database restores from the last backup

- An automated way to verify that the process is functioning properly and local users can connect

- An automated way to verify that the concurrent manager(s) are connected to the instance(s) and restart concurrent manager; generic scripts for compressed export and/or import of Oracle databases

- A way to generate the necessary database creation scripts from the current configuration

- Generic scripts to capture necessary statistics for performance evaluation.

The second set of Oracle scripts included:

- A set of tools to provide a snapshot of the database (for example, to identify who is using which objects or has what locks)

- Tools to interface with SunNet Manger for paging and other non-email facilities

- Tools to gather statistics (for example, who is accessing the system or the number of connections made)

- Enhanced utilities to capture information needed for disaster recovery of a database on another server in a remote site.

Table 8-5 provides a more detailed description of each utility.

Table 8-5   Oracle Database Utilities

Tool	Description	
Oracle Utilities Release 1.0	Backup	Automated way to backup databases (both hot and cold) to disk.
	Restore	Generates UNIX commands necessary for automated database restores from last backup.
	Check Oracle Server	Automated way to verify that the orasrv process is functioning properly and that local users can connect.
	Check Concurrent Manager	Automated way to verify that the concurrent manager(s) are connected to the instance(s) and restart concurrent manager as required.
	Export/Import Scripts	Automated, generic scripts for compressed export and/or import of Oracle databases.
	Build/Create DB Scripts	Automated way to generate the necessary database creation scripts from current configuration.
	Capacity Monitoring	Automated way to measure capacity of database objects. Analyzes data segments, backup directory structures, Oracle usage of raw partitions, ufs, and composite partition maps and calculates space requirements for database objects.
	Statistics	Captures necessary statistics for performance evaluation. Currently includes hit ratio, physical reads/writes per I/O device, Oracle system-level statistics and block-level wait statistics (both cumulative and interval values).

Table 8-5   Oracle Database Utilities (Continued)

Tool	Description
Oracle Utilities Release 2.0	Support of RDBMS 7.0 Enhancement to daily database dumps, transaction dumps, checking error logs, reporting disk space usage, and so forth Tools to provide a snapshot of the database (e.g., who is using which objects, has what locks) Enhance Alert Tools to interface with some type of SNM for paging and other non-email facilities. Auditing tools to gather statistics on who is accessing the system, number of connections made, and so forth. Automating installation and configuration of new servers and utilities. A database similar to AnswerBook that can be accessed by novice DBAs to get answers to frequently occurring problems and how to resolve them. Enhanced utilities to capture information needed for disaster recovery of a database on another server in a remote site.

Preventive Maintenance

The concept of preventive maintenance came from our mainframe environment. MVS provided a tool called *erep* which proactively alerts system personnel of potential hardware problems. Once erep notified us of a potential problem, we could *schedule* system downtime (what a novel idea!) and, thereby, not impact our availability. Based on this concept, we developed a key tool for maintaining reliability in a distributed environment.

The preventive maintenance script runs daily to monitor our production servers, checking the system for various entries that record hardware errors. The script will only look for entries recorded for that day. Any errors tracked by the script are emailed to personnel on a recipients list for evaluations and preventive maintenance scheduling.

This preventive maintenance script (called *prevent_maint*) is available to Sun's customers and potential customers through SunIntegration Services. So what is wrong with mainframe concepts and processes!

Table 8-6 is a description of the services provided by the preventive maintenance script.

Table 8-6   Preventive Maintenance Program

Service	Description
Clean system	A System Administrator will clean the server and inspect the condition of the card cage. If the card cage requires cleaning, the system boards will be removed and the card cage will be cleaned.
Check voltage	A System Administrator will check the 5VOC, -5.2VOC, -12VOC, 12VOC voltages, and ac ripple for compliance within specifications.
Install FCOs	System will be checked to see if all mandatory FCOs are installed. If a mandatory FCO is not installed, the System Administrator will schedule the installation.
Inspect card cage	The card cage will be checked for missing parts, loose cables, and properly seated boards. If the system requires downtime to reseat the boards, the System Administrator will schedule the procedure.
Check fans	System fans or blowers will be checked for proper operation.
EEPROM/NVRAM	The system's EEPROM/NVRAM parameters will be checked for proper settings and corrected if necessary. The system will be programmed to reboot itself quickly in the event of a system crash.
Check and clean peripheral devices	The system's tape and CD-ROM drives will be tested and drive heads cleaned, if present.
Check disk drives	The system disks will be checked by diagnostic software and evaluated for a pass/fail condition.
Check memory	The SunDiag™ utility will be used to test the main memory of the system.
Check log table	The System Administrator will evaluate the contents of the system log files for indications of system maintenance requirements.

Auto-paging

One of the more recent technologies we have implemented is an automated paging service to automatically page the on-call systems programmer. When our automated paging tool detects a problem, this process bypasses computer operator intervention and automatically pages the on-call system programmer.

Auto paging provides the following services:
- Automatically pages the on-call support person based on selected events
- Provides an on-line on-call schedule that defines support personnel and event relations
- Logs all paging requests
- Generates weekly reports

These services provide an effective and prompt way to communicate system events to support personnel. This early communication enables our staff to address problems at the earliest possible stage, bypassing the need for operator or help-desk intervention.

We did not see a need for a computer operator to sit in front of the master console, waiting for a problem to occur — then look up a number to call someone. For us, always trying to improve our availability numbers was a number-one priority. Think of the wasted minutes from the time a server goes down. What if the operator were not sitting there at that moment? The operator would then look up a phone number, call, or escalate if necessary. Why not have the mechanism in place so when a server goes down, someone is paged (by beeper) automatically — completely bypassing Computer Operations — and you want Technical Support on the problem immediately. We have done that by using an auto-paging tool found on one of the Internet bulletin boards. We did, however, customize it for our environment. We have a System Programmer (Technical Support) on the problem before the Help Desk knows about it.

Job Scheduling

Automated job scheduling is a must for a production environment supporting mission critical systems, especially in a distributed environment with production servers attached to your wide area network all over the world. A network-wide batch scheduling system is essential for this new environment. Can you imagine coordinating jobs and processes in a distributed world without such a tool? And what happens if there were resource failures somewhere along this global network? How would you recover?

Our current solution for data center scheduling is done using the standard UNIX utility called *cron*. This utility does not meet the data center's job scheduling requirements. Since seven of the eight critical requirements are not met by cron, this solution is considered unacceptable. The missing critical requirements (which cron does *not* provide) are:

- Check on job status
- Notification when jobs complete
- Automated job restart
- Resource dependency support
- Completion of job if system is down when scheduled to run
- Job dependency support
- Distributed dependency support

For the mainframe, we use a product called *CA Scheduler*. When looking at a UNIX scheduling system, much of the functionality that was available for the mainframe was used in picking a similar type of system for this new distributed environment. One very critical piece that was missing from the mainframe product that is most important is networking functionality, in order to manage servers on a network-wide basis. To give you an idea of the functionality we were seeking in a scheduling product, we have listed in Table 8-7 the functionality required.

Table 8-7   Job Scheduling Requirements and Evaluations

Desirable Functional Requirement	Weight[‡]
Start and stop jobs at specified date and time	1.0*
Check status on jobs	1.0*
Notify users and administrator when jobs do and do not successfully complete	1.0
Restart jobs that do not complete successfully	1.0

[‡] Weight = Extremely Critical:1.0*; Critical:0.8-1.0; Desired:0.4-0.7; Wish List:0.1-0.3

Table 8-7   Job Scheduling Requirements and Evaluations (Continued)

Desirable Functional Requirement	Weight[‡]
Queue jobs until a specified resource becomes available (e.g.. file transfer, machine, network fixed)	1.0
Complete jobs if system is down when scheduled to run (unlink cron)	1.0*
Associate dependencies between various jobs and whole schedules of jobs	1.0*
Security: Master schedulers to control all schedules and schedulers, with one group responsible to run schedule and another where people can run only their own schedule	0.8
Ability to cross time zones	0.8
Fiscal and calendar year scheduling	0.8
Distributed scheduling: Coordinate with resource on another machine	1.0
Error notification flexibility (e.g.. email, SunNet Manager)	0.8
Global change (e.g., change quarter-end to Sunday from Saturday)	0.8
Execution prioritization to ensure that most important work completes first	0.8
Variable parameter substitution to define jobs and cycles that can run under different circumstances	0.6
Support fault tolerance to eliminate single point of failure for scheduling	0.9
Automatic archival of production log files, reports, and transaction data files	0.8

[‡] Weight = Extremely Critical:1.0*; Critical:0.8-1.0; Desired:0.4-0.7; Wish List:0.1-0.3

Table 8-7   Job Scheduling Requirements and Evaluations (Continued)

Desirable Functional Requirement	Weight‡

Management Reporting:
  Critical Reports:
    Pre-production schedules
    Post-production schedules
    Resource statistics
    Dependency listing
    Resource profile reports
    Schedule delay impact analysis metrics (failures, errors, average run times, etc.)
    Schedule optimization recommendations
    Security (access and change logging)
	0.8

Wish List Reports:
    Job details
    Prompts calendar
    Parameter
    Job/cycle history
    Report distribution
    Planned production
    Actual production
    Job/output analysis
    Control/reconciliation
	0.3

cron Conversion:
  Initial installation conversion support
  Ongoing conversion via a utility
	0.9
	0.7

Dynamic Scheduling	1.0*
Queue Management, future support	0.8

‡ Weight = Extremely Critical:1.0*; Critical:0.8-1.0; Desired:0.4-0.7; Wish List:0.1-0.3

System Resource Management

During our five years of implementing distributed computing at Sun, system resource management was not on the top of our priority list. As previously mentioned, tape backup and security were. We have only now started looking at the tools available in the marketplace. The functional requirements we are seeking along with their importance is outlined in Table 8-8. The products we are looking at will allow us to perform analysis of Data Center resources, including hardware operating system and database performance data. We are also looking at performance awareness products to capitalize and play back application transactions.

Table 8-8   System Resource Management Functional Requirements

Desirable Functional Requirement	Weight[‡]
CAPTURE:	
OS:	
Whole system:	
Multiple processor CPU	1.0
Locks/semaphore	0.8
Disk:	
df	0.7
I/O transfers per second	0.8
Number of I/Os	0.8
Page and swap	1.0
Context switches	0.6
System and user calls	0.8
Interrupts	0.7
Caching	0.7
By Process:	
Memory leak by process	0.4
CPU utilization	0.4
Locks/semaphore	0.5
Disk:	
I/O transfers per second	0.4
Number of I/Os	0.4

[‡] Weight = Extremely Critical:0.8-1.0; Desired:0.4-0.7; Wish List:0.1-0.3

Table 8-8   System Resource Management Functional Requirements (Continued)

Desirable Functional Requirement	Weight[‡]
Page and swap	0.4
System and user calls	0.4
Network:	
Collisions	1.0
Input packet errors	1.0
Message:	
Source/destination	0.8
Type	0.7
Volume	0.8
DATABASE:	
SYBASE:	
Hit ratio calculated from logical reads and physical reads	1.0
Physical I/O by table	0.8
Wait time associated with database blocks	0.8
Database usage	0.8
Temp table usage (tempdb)	0.8
Number of transactions	0.8
System statistics	
consistent gets	0.3
physical reads	0.7
disk sorts	0.3
row sorts	0.1
table fetch by rowid	0.3
table fetch continued row	0.8
table scan blocks gotten	0.3
table scan rows gotten	0.3
table scans	0.3
Oracle:	
Hit ratio calculated from logical reads and physical reads	1.0
Physical I/O by table	0.8

[‡] Weight = Extremely Critical:0.8-1.0; Desired:0.4-0.7; Wish List:0.1-0.3

Table 8-8   System Resource Management Functional Requirements (Continued)

Desirable Functional Requirement	Weight[‡]
Wait time associated with database blocks	0.8
Database usage	0.8
Temp table usage (tempdb)	0.8
Number of transactions	0.8
System statistics	
consistent gets	0.3
physical reads	0.7
disk sorts	0.3
row sorts	0.1
table fetch by rowid	0.3
table fetch continued row	0.8
table scan blocks gotten	0.3
table scan rows gotten	0.3
table scans	0.3
Progress:	
Hit ratio calculated from logical reads and physical reads	1.0
Physical I/O by table	0.8
Wait time associated with database blocks	0.8
Database usage	0.8
Temp table usage (tempdb)	0.8
Number of transactions	0.8
System statistics	
consistent gets	0.3
physical reads	0.7
disk sorts	0.3
row sorts	0.1
table fetch by rowid	0.3
table fetch continued row	0.8
table scan blocks gotten	0.3
table scan rows gotten	0.3

[‡] Weight = Extremely Critical:0.8-1.0; Desired:0.4-0.7; Wish List:0.1-0.3

Table 8-8   System Resource Management Functional Requirements (Continued)

Desirable Functional Requirement	Weight[‡]
table scans	0.3
REPORTING:	
Graphics	1.0
Trend reporting	1.0
Summary	1.0
ANALYSIS:	
Identify potential problem areas	0.7
What if Simulation	0.5
TOOL CONFIGURATION:	
On/Off control	1.0
Minimally intrusive	0.8
Captured data loaded into database or ASCII file	1.0
Minimal installation requirements	
Minimal hardware requirements	0.8
Minimal installation time	0.7

[‡] Weight = Extremely Critical:0.8-1.0; Desired:0.4-0.7; Wish List:0.1-0.3

System Administration in the Distributed Computing Environment 9 ☰

System Administration in the Distributed Computing Environment

We are often asked how Sun can justify the cost of a workstation on each employee's desktop. At Sun, Scott McNealy's key business indicator is revenue per employee. Since installing this environment over the last five years, the revenue per employee has more than doubled from almost $150K per employee per year to over $350K per employee per year. Scott has goaled the company to reach $500K per employee per year over the near-term future. How has the desktop environment supported this? We have empowered employees to perform critical functions for themselves using their desktop environment.

System administration was ugly at Sun during the early days. There were no controls in place; each business and sales office owned its own administration functions. This meant that there were disparate standards, and, in many cases, such as at sales offices, administration was handled by the local System Engineers (SEs). These SEs were highly skilled in UNIX because they were the ones providing technical support to the sales staff for Sun customers. They felt they could handle all of the local office needs (in terms of support) plus the customer support requirements. (The employee-to-system administrator ratio at that time was about 50:1). And, each SE thought he/she had the best approach to supporting the local desktop, server, and software needs. The end-users were getting by and were able to use the environment, but each day there could be a different configuration in place and the software could have changed. The SEs and local system administrators would sometimes make changes as often as every night. There was a lack of change control and also a loss in productivity when these changes were implemented without notification. End users weren't able to do their jobs effectively and there was lots of downtime. And, the SEs were spending an equivalent of one-half to a full headcount on local support issues, which took away from their real and most important function — supporting the customer!

Software for office automation (e.g., spreadsheet, desktop publishing, graphics) was usually licensed and purchased by each geographic sales area or business unit. Each site also ordered and installed its own workstations, servers, and local area networks and provided the connectivity to the wide-area network.

During the next several years, many changes were made to gain control, that is, to get the SEs back to doing the job they were paid to do and increase our employee-to-system administrator ratio to what it currently is, 125:1. These changes were difficult to implement because every site wanted to maintain its own control. *The first and most important change was to have the system administration function report to IT. Throughout our book, we emphasize centralized control for the infrastructure. The system administration function is one of the most important to have centralized. Having the system administrators as part of IT allows more cost-effective solutions, improved productivity, and the ability to support a fully distributed environment. Once this change happened, other improvements could take place.*

The next step was to develop and implement a common desktop tool environment. Desktop tools included several different products for each desktop function, but one standard set was supported centrally. For example, there were at least two different spreadsheets available (Lotus and Wingz) and different desktop publishing tools (Interleaf, FrameMaker, WordPerfect®). From a centralized control point of view, we tried to implement one kind of each tool; for example, we wanted to support just one desktop publishing tool, Interleaf. But the end-users rebelled; different people liked different tools (what a thought!). So we acquiesced and allowed different kinds of desktop publishing tools. Once this phase was complete and the development of the software distribution process was in place (i.e., SunDANS, which is discussed in Appendix A, "SunDANS"), we were able to put standard software sets at each location that were centrally controlled. Software now became more cost effective because of the ability to license the tools corporate-wide.

*Another difficult task was to take away security (**root** ownership) of software servers and desktops. Everyone wanted control of their own environments (especially the SEs). Once we provided better support and addressed the RAS issues, everyone was much more supportive of the changes. People came to work each day knowing that they had a productive environment; the desktop (which is critical for the job function at Sun) was on-line, available, and usable. Centralized control also gave equivalent headcount back to the sales offices because SEs could now spend their full time on customer support.*

This chapter focuses on the system administration function, a critical part of the infrastructure to support distributed computing environments.

— *Randy and Harris*

System Administration Requirements

System administration is one of the most important functions in the implementation and support of the distributed computing environment. There are two types of distributed computing environments that have separate system administration requirements: the end-user desktop and the production business system.

- The end-user desktop environment includes desktop hardware (that is, a workstation) and desktop software tools (that is, spreadsheets, graphics, desktop publishing, and email).

- The production business system is a client/server, peer-to-peer environment where the server is running the database engine (RDBMS) and application software, and the client is running graphical user interface (GUI) tools to access the server application.

We consider these two environments to be two separate functions that are supported differently even though a spreadsheet desktop tool, such as Lotus or Wingz, may be critical for the job function of the end-user.

Level of Service

Customers need to have a better understanding of the service they can expect from computer resources and how resources are being expanded. Additionally, UNIX System Administration support personnel need to understand what is and is not required of them. A well-documented service level agreement provides the foundation for this understanding, the basis for budgeting resource requirements, and reduces potential conflict between UNIX System Administration and customers over resource availability and utilization.

This service level agreement is primarily aimed at three groups:

- Business managers receiving IT services who need to ensure that the services delivered are in line with their business requirements at a cost they are prepared to meet

- IT staff delivering these services who need to fully understand the commitments that our customers require from us in order to provide quality service

- IT staff coordinating the delivery of these services to their respective business units to ensure maximum contribution to business effectiveness

---

Note – See Appendix H, "Service Level Agreement," for more information.

Employee-to-System Administrator Ratios

IT developed dozens of processes and tools to support end-user desktop and production business system requirements. For example, one of the more critical processes — developed to support regional system administration functions — automatically checks for "soft" hardware errors so that problems can be rectified before they become outages. Another tool allows the end-user to report problems or request service. These productivity tools have allowed IT to improve our employee:SA ratio to 125:1. We have found that the employee:SA ratio in heterogeneous environments is about 50:1. The more homogeneous and standard the environment, the higher the productivity and the employee:SA ratio.

There is currently a plan to increase this ratio over the next three years by implementing more processes and by using knowledge-based tools. This strategy is possible because our environment is very homogeneous. All employees have workstations on their desktops, and the number of PCs and MacIntoshes is minimal compared to the over 23,000 SPARC workstations and servers.

Some key bullets for our efforts to improve System Administration-to-user ratios are as follows:

- Attack high-leverage items that consume time to work towards increasing end-user:SA ratios.

- Install measuring capabilities

- Define and eliminate SA interrupts

- Empower users to help themselves through evangelizing the importance of training and through providing productivity tools

- Have one standard operating environment (i.e., Solaris 2)

- Leverage higher-performance servers to reduce amount of equipment required and thus reduce cost

- Enable workgroup computing to increase customer satisfaction

- Reduce turnaround time on work request completion to increase customer satisfaction

- Implement knowledge-based tools (AI) to empower customers to help themselves and to provide for proactive monitoring and repairing of systems and applications

- Integrate Assistance Center function for first line problem resolution

Dataless Client Environment

To better support the end-user desktop environment, we installed two key servers on every local area network. (On average, there are about 60 clients per local area network.) One server is a *file server* used for desktop data; the second server is identified as a *software server*. The term *dataless client* refers to an environment where an end-user has desktop disk space, but all data is stored on a server. At Sun, no data is stored on the desktop disk space, which is used exclusively for noncritical performance functions such as paging, swap, and root (security). See Figure 4-1 on page 36 for an example of this configuration.

Backup Support

Since many of our users are end-users and non-UNIX literate, the file server is automatically available to the end-user. The end-user deals exclusively with desktop tools; the file system automatically takes care of where the data is stored. IT provides an automated backup of the file server because that data is critical; our end-users do not back up their own disks. If the end-user has a problem, the SA can restore from the backup.

Tools Support

The software server contains all standard desktop tools supported by IT, such as spreadsheet software products and desktop publishing products. IT maintains centralized control of these software products. One software group in IT manages all software and licensing issues with vendors and provides standard version/release information of the supported software products list. Although there is only one supported list, it includes multiple kinds of products (for example, at least two spreadsheet products and two desktop publishing products). If an end-user wants to use an unsupported product, it must be installed on the file server by IT, but the end-user is responsible for the product's support. It is also possible for the local office (especially sales offices) to install local servers and install local software, again supported by local personnel.

When a new release of a supported standard product is installed, it undergoes internal quality assurance and testing standards, followed by an automated software distribution process that automatically updates releases on the software server attached to every local area network at Sun.

End-user Desktop Support

At Sun, the System Administrator (SA) is critical to supporting the end-user desktop environment. SAs are chartered to support desktop hardware, software, client or end-user servers, and local area networks. In the large campus environment, SAs are co-located with the end-users for easy access and to provide "one-stop shopping" solutions. In sales offices that are located around the world, SAs are placed in strategic regional locations.

SAs install only the Solaris operating environment on the desktop; they do not install any software product on the desktop. All other software products are installed on the software servers and "pulled down" to the desktop; that is, the end-user uses the mouse to point-and-click on the desired software product icon and the operating system automatically pulls the executable code from the software server. The software then runs on the desktop as another window process. The process remains on the desktop until the end user quits the process, needs a new release, or powers off the desktop workstation.

The recommended standard services provided by our System Administration staff are:

- System administration
- Disaster recovery
- System security
- Desktop applications support
- Hardware installation
- Hardware maintenance
- Software distribution support
- Telecommunications
- Local network services
- User training
- Software configuration
- Software installation
- Database administration
- System analysis
- Performance tuning

The recommended resources and equipment supported are:

- File servers
- Desktop software servers
- Network servers
- Disk usage
- Home directories
- Mail

Support Model

This section describes the support model for the end-user. (See Appendix D, "ServiceDesk," for additional information.)

Work Request Resolution Process

The work request resolution process is as follows:

1. User submits workstation work request through ServiceDesk.

2. Work request is automatically routed to appropriate System Administrator according to subnet assignment.

   If the System Administrator assigned to the subnet is out of the office, the request will be transferred to the backup System Administrator.

3. Each request must be acknowledged by the System Administrator within specified time frame or it will be escalated.

4. Each request must be closed within the specified time frame or it will be escalated.

5. After each ticket is closed, ServiceDesk automatically emails the feedback tool to the customer.
   - The feedback tool is the user's opportunity to report on the level of service
   - The System Administrators receive the daily feedback report, which allows them to monitor feedback results
   - The user will be contacted by the System Administrator if a feedback report of 3 (indicating poor support) is sent (2 indicates satisfactory and 1 indicates excellent support).

Trouble Ticket Resolution Process

The trouble ticket resolution process is as follows:

1. User submits workstation trouble ticket through ServiceDesk.

2. Trouble ticket is routed to a queue in the Assistance Center. This queue is the Assistance Center's main trouble ticket queue.

   a. Each request must be acknowledged within specified time frame or it will be escalated.

   b. Each request must be closed within specified time frame or it will be escalated.

   c. If the Assistance Center resolved the problem, the ticket is closed.

d. After ticket is closed, ServiceDesk automatically emails the feedback tool to the customer.
   • The feedback tool is the user's opportunity to report on the level of service.
   • The System Administrators receive the daily feedback report, which allows them to monitor feedback results.
   • The user will be contacted if a feedback report of 3 is sent.
   • We also recommend establishing a focal queue for trouble tickets that cannot be resolved by the Assistance Center.

3. If the unresolved trouble ticket is owned by the focal queue:

   a. Each request must be acknowledged within specified time frame or it will be escalated.

   b. Each request must be closed within specified time frame or it will be escalated.

   c. If that focal queue resolved the problem, the ticket is closed.

   d. After each ticket is closed, the focal queue communicates this to the user.

   e. After each ticket is closed, ServiceDesk automatically emails the feedback tool to the customer.
   • The feedback tool is the user's opportunity to report on the level of service.
   • The System Administrators receive the daily feedback report which allows them to monitor feedback results.
   • The user will be contacted if a feedback report of 3 is sent.

   f. If the focal queue is not able to resolve the problem, the ticket is sent to the System Administration responsible for the subnet.

4. Trouble ticket is now owned by the System Administrator.

   a. Each request must be acknowledged within a specified time frame or it will be escalated.

   b. Each request must be closed within a specified time or it will be escalated.

   c. If the System Administrator resolves the problem, the ticket is closed.

   d. After each ticket is closed, the System Administrator communicates this to the user.

   e. After each ticket is closed, ServiceDesk automatically emails the feedback tool to the customer.
   • The feedback tool is the user's opportunity to report on the level of service.
   • The System Administrators receive the daily feedback report, which allows them to monitor feedback results.
   • The user will be contacted if a feedback report of 3 is sent.

ServiceDesk Escalation

Table 9-1 and Table 9-2 show ServiceDesk escalation for regular workdays: 8 a.m. to 5 p.m., Monday through Friday.

Table 9-1 shows the escalation configuration for trouble tickets.

Table 9-1   Trouble Tickets Escalation Configuration

Service Group	Priority	Response Time	Close Time
System Administration	1	30 minutes	2 hours
	1	30 minutes	2 hours
	1	2 hours	8 hours
	2	4 hours	24 hours
	3	4 hours	24 hours

Table 9-2 shows the escalation configuration for work requests.

Table 9-2   Work Requests Escalation Configuration

Service Group	Priority	Response Time	Close Time
System Administration	4	24 hours	5 days

Supporting Mission Critical Applications

To support mission critical applications running around the world, the centralized "glasshouse" controls were extended around the Sun Wide Area Network (SWAN). Therefore, wherever the server is located, the data center infrastructure supports it. Database administrators support all databases; system programmers support the operating system as well as other third-party system management tools such as tape management and security. Each geographic area has an assigned central system programmer to support all production servers; however, in many cases, the local system administrator is relied on for support.

In this new production business environment, the SAs play a critical role. The SAs take care of backup tapes stored at the local site and also provide support to the data center for any hardware-related issues. For some mission critical applications, tape backups of the data are executed over the SWAN network to the data center; for other applications, the SA mounts the tape in the server, and the backup is then performed automatically by the processes developed by Sun.

The standard services provided by System Administration in support of the glasshouse (i.e., Data Center) support paradigm for *some* mission critical distributed systems are as follows:

- OS system administration
- Disaster recovery
- System security
- First-level applications support
- Hardware installation
- Hardware maintenance
- Software distribution support

These services are the same as provided by the central Data Center staff and can be contracted to regional system administration services. The Data Center still "runs" the processes and provides second-level support to the regional system administrator.

System Administration Utilities

The key to success in managing a decentralized network operation function includes effective productivity tools for systems administration such as:

- Automated software distribution for desktop and network software
- Automated file server disk backup processes
- Processes to monitor hardware/software for errors
- Automated disk restore processes

Table 9-3 describes some useful tools.

Table 9-3   Database Utilities

Tool	Description
dux	Reports on disk space usage within a single disk partition. Useful for identifying in which directories disk space has been consumed, especially when there are other partitions involved that you do not care about.
diskpatrol	Tracks end-user disk usage on servers (home directory and mail files).
prevent_maint	Tracks potential hardware problems on servers.
whatami	Gathers and summarizes various bits of system and user-related information. Useful for finding out about system hardware, system configuration, and network resource dependencies.
netcmon	Creates a histogram that charts the collision rate measured on all existing network interfaces over time. Useful for monitoring network load/performance.
nettstat	Measures network traffic distribution over a specified number of packets. Useful for identifying who is hogging network bandwidth.
dataless_backup	Backs up (tars) the files that make up the personality of the dataless clients. These files include /etc/fstab, /etc/aliases, /etc/rc[*], /var/spool/calendar/[*], and /var/spool/cron/[*], as well as others that define the system. The files are saved on the server.

Job Descriptions for System Administration Staff

The basic functions of system administrators are to provide quality system administration and local-area network support to Sun's end-user desktop environment and to progress toward higher levels of expertise in system administration. This section discusses the job descriptions for the system administrators who support the distributed computing environments.

System Administrator I

This function troubleshoots basic technical problems, modifies and maintains NIS maps, helps users with routine day-to-day problems, and provides basic system administration and network support of workstations, file servers, and printers. Table 9-4 describes specific duties and responsibilities, qualifications, and competencies requirements.

Table 9-4   Requirements for System Administrator I

Specific Duties and Responsibilities	• Brings up and upgrades servers and special purpose machines. • Performs and automates single machine backup and restore processes. • Coordinates and assist in small user group moves. • Troubleshoots regular NIS, network, hardware printer, and user problems. • Installs network routers and configures network software. • Develops, implements, and documents, midlevel system administration procedures. • Writes and troubleshoots shell scripts.
	• Provides general systems support to external user/customers. • Interacts with peers and manager regarding assignments.
	• Makes task-related decisions daily. • Makes recommendations regarding prioritization of own work.
Qualifications	Typically requires a B. S. degree in computer science or equivalent and 1-2 years UNIX experience (preferably Solaris) or an equivalent combination of training and experience.

Table 9-4   Requirements for System Administrator I (Continued)

Competencies	
	• Ability to use Solaris commands and to chain commands to accomplish tasks
	• Ability to troubleshoot and solve problems over the phone
	• Ability to act as liaison among project leads, managers, and the support group
	• Ability to lead and be effective in interorganizational groups and committees
	• Ability to handle constantly changing requirements or priorities
	• Ability to effectively convey ideas through oral and written communications
	• Ability to work effectively with users while providing a high standard of customer service
	• Ability to work efficiently in a group environment while promoting effective teamwork
	• Ability to write and debug shell scripts

System Administrator II

This function provides intermediate system administration and network support of workstations, file servers, and printers. This function also troubleshoots difficult technical problems, creates, maintains, and modifies NIS maps, resolves day-to-day problems for the user community, provides training assistance to less experienced staff, and automates repetitive task within the organization. Table 9-5 describes specific duties and responsibilities, qualifications, and competencies requirements.

Table 9-5   Requirements for System Administrator II

Specific Duties and Responsibilities	• Brings up gateways and new nets.
	• Installs, monitors, and troubleshoots backup and restore systems.
	• Coordinates medium-sized moves requiring installation of software and hardware. Sets up NIS maps and domains; troubleshoots difficult NIS problems
	• Troubleshoots a variety of common NIS, NFS, network and user problems; finds solutions to new problems.
	• Designs, implements and documents complex midlevel system administration projects.
	• Writes and troubleshoots large shell scripts and integrates them into system administration policies and procedures.
	• Provides general systems support to external user/customers.
	• Interacts with peers and manager regarding assignments.
	• Makes task-related decisions daily.
	• Makes recommendations regarding prioritization of own work.
Qualifications	Typically requires a B. S. degree in computer science or equivalent and 3-5 years UNIX experience (preferably Solaris) or an equivalent combination of training and experience.
Competencies	• Ability to use Solaris commands to manage, run and troubleshoot systems, problems and networks; basic understanding of C code
	• Ability to organize, lead, and be effective in inter-organization groups and committees; requires extending oneself to complete unassigned tasks and to occasionally take on tasks beyond job scope
	• Ability to work effectively with users while providing a high standard of customer service
	• Ability to work efficiently in a group environment while promoting effective teamwork; can provide feedback to manager on ways to increase customer/employee satisfaction
	• Ability to write and debug shell scripts

System Administrator III

This function provides advanced system administration and network support of workstations, file servers, and printers, troubleshoots the most difficult technical problems, creates, maintains and modifies NIS maps, provides training assistance to less experienced staff, automates repetitive task within the organization, and establishes new processes for improving department efficiency. Table 9-6 describes specific duties and responsibilities, qualifications, and competencies requirements.

Table 9-6   Requirements for System Administrator III

Specific Duties and Responsibilities	• Troubleshoots advanced technical problems using NIS expertise and all facets of Solaris.
	• Coordinates complex moves requiring installation of software and hardware.
	• Determines the big network picture and designs plans to anticipate and keep ahead of any changes to it.
	• Develops and implements network and user security policies and procedures.
	• Troubleshoots all types of NIS, network, and user problems; determines long-term solutions to new problems.
	• Designs and implements or directs others to design and implement system administration projects, policies, and procedures. Installs or directs others to install, monitor, and troubleshoot backup and restore systems.
	• Conducts training demonstrations.
	• Provides general systems support to external user/customers.
	• Interacts with peers and manager regarding assignments. Will interface with other internal groups.
	• Makes task-related decisions daily, recommends project and strategic direction, and participates in team decision making. Decisions directly impact project activities.
	• May act as the supervisor in absence of management.
Qualifications	Typically requires a B. S. degree in computer science or equivalent and 5-7 years UNIX experience (preferably Solaris) or an equivalent combination of training and experience.

Table 9-6   Requirements for System Administrator III (Continued)

Competencies	• Ability to modify C code
	• Ability to interact and handle complex issues with users
	• Ability to organize, lead and be effective in large interorganizational groups and committees
	• Ability to function as top technical resource for less senior staff members
	• Ability to work effectively with users while providing a high standard of customer service
	• Ability to work efficiently in a group environment while promoting effective teamwork
	• Can provide feedback to manager on ways to increase customer/employee satisfaction

Security 10 ≡

Network Security

In our customer presentations, we are always asked about network security, particularly regarding the distribution of mission critical applications across the network. At Sun, we took a very aggressive approach to implementing UNIX security on both our internal systems and our network.

Internal network security of the production application/server is discussed in the data center chapter, where we recommend that each production application/server contain security software that controls access to each application with the same security levels as provided in the mainframe environment.

Network security, however, is a function of the network operating system (i.e., Solaris). We tailored our security functions to target each network issue — desktop, engineering, and dial-in access — to ensure locktight safety. The network routers and gateways, security software, and other recommended processes were all top priorities to study.

The first-level access to the network comes from the desktop, and we had more than 20,000 network nodes to consider in developing our processes. The desktop operating system contained authentication of users and passwords. Guidelines were implemented on how often the password should be changed, the number of characters contained in a password and examples of commonly used passwords that should be avoided (because they could be easily broken). Automated processes were put in place to allow password changes every 30 days.

In the case of third-party access (Internet, third-party vendors, customers, etc.), we recommend that only one gateway be made available to each third party based on protocol (X.25, X.400, etc.). With this interconnectivity, we were able to implement some internally developed security processes (scripts and modified versions of FTP and Telnet) at each gateway to protect the local-area network. We called this process a firewall, because it allowed us to monitor each network packet and to detect any unauthorized access/entry or potential virus. We never had a problem with popular viruses entering the Sun network.

We also implemented security software at the building/local-area network level so that packets could be blocked in and out of a building or a local area network. Security gateways were placed between corporate-wide and engineering network backbones to limit access to the engineering network. In most cases, the only access available to the engineering backbone was for email traffic.

Dial-in access to the network was controlled through dial-in modem pools. A modem pool is a network server with up to 32 modems attached and a rotary of telephone access numbers. The security system on each modem pool required dial-back access to the employee. Once logged in, employee-users could access their own desktop machine. A separate modem pool was created for consultants and contractors working for Sun that gave them the ability to send/receive email only.

It is important to note that most commercial security products will not map one-for-one into the minds of mainframers as functional replacements for the security software to which they are accustomed on the mainframe. The UNIX environment was designed with an "open systems" view (now that has a familiar ring to it!), and UNIX security is also pretty "open." This chapter discusses the security products available today that we used to secure our network. In addition, we have enhanced several of these products to conform to certain requirements unique to our company.

Bottom line: Security controls should always be centrally located and controlled.

To paraphrase an old sage: There really is life after the mainframe....and, there really is security after the mainframe.

— Harris and Randy

Levels of Security

> *"Mainframe operating systems in general... tend to have less security problems than UNIX systems. Reasons include proprietary operating systems and no general access to the operating system source code. Security tends to be far more important to the mainframe customers, and therefore more of a marketing issue than has been typical in the UNIX marketplace. A security breach on a mainframe system providing service to a large corporation can have a severe monetary impact, either through fraud or the loss of trade secrets."*[1]

It is not uncommon for an organization planning a transition from the mainframe environment to the UNIX environment to be apprehensive that the transition will result in a less secure environment. The implication is, after all, that the UNIX environment is an "open system," and therefore is not secure.

At Sun, we took a very aggressive approach to the security of our internal systems and our network — and we have been successful in this effort.

Sun monitors five levels of security: desktop, LAN (building), security gateways, dial-in modem pools, and firewall. Responsibilities at each level are described in Table 10-1.

Table 10-1 Levels of Security

Level	Area Controlled	Description
1	Desktop	Determines whether user has authorized access
2	LAN / building	Blocks packets in and out
3	Security gateways	Limits access to engineering or other local area networks
4	Dial-in modem pools	Provides dial-back access to employees
5	Firewall	Controls access and packets between public networks (such as Internet)

---

1. Excerpted from "Dropping the Mainframe without Crushing the Users: Mainframe to Distributed UNIX in Nine Months" by Peter Van Epp and Bill Gaines, submitted to the LISA VI Conference at Long Beach, California (October 1992).

Security Staffing

Sun's security staff is known as Corporate Information Security (CIS). CIS provides a single point of contact for Sun computer and network security issues. Their responsibilities include:

- Coordinating policy and standards development
- Performing security audits
- Providing security consulting
- Developing, evaluating, and implementing new security technologies
- Investigating violations
- Providing internal security training

CIS has the primary responsibility for network intrusion and other electronic intrusion, as directed by the CIO. To support our Data Center, there is expertise in security software for both the mainframe and UNIX platforms.

Public Domain Security Products

There are three "public domain" software products (specifically written for the UNIX environment) that are favored by the CIS group:

- Crack — a password guesser
- COPS — Computer Oracle and Password System
- Kerberos — the *de facto* standard for open network systems authentication

These three freely available products, when combined, form a good UNIX security system.

Crack

Crack is designed to find UNIX eight-character DES-encrypted passwords by standard guessing techniques. It is flexible, configurable, and fast. It audits the system for weak passwords and uses source dictionary files (including any special dictionary files preferred by the customer).

COPS

COPS is a collection of more than a dozen programs that each take on a different problem area of UNIX security, including:

- File, directory, and device permissions/modes
- Poor passwords
- Content, format, and security of password and group files

- Programs and files running in /etc./rc* and cron(tab) files
- Root-SUID files (checks whether they are writeable, or whether they are shell scripts)
- Detects and reports any changes in important binaries or key files
- Users' home directories and startup files (checks whether they are writeable)
- Anonymous FTP setup
- Unrestricted FTP
- Decode alias in sendmail
- SUID uudecode problems
- Hidden shells inside inetd.conf, rexd running in inetd.conf
- Miscellaneous root checks

COPS can also generate a variety of analytical reports on system security.

Kerberos

Kerberos is a trusted third-party authentication service that performs the following services:

- Authenticates access throughout the network
- Uses timestamps, checksum, and encryption
- Authenticates by using master administration server, slave servers, and clients

Kerberos contains:

- An applications library
- An encryption library
- A database library
- Database administration programs
- An administration server
- An authentication server
- Database propagation software
- User programs
- Applications

Additional Security Products

There are now many commercially available security products similar to those already freely available. This market is driven by customer needs for improved security products. Many third-party software vendors such as Computer Associates and Legent either have already ported or are porting their product lines to UNIX. Some of the newest and most notable of these new products are described in Table 10-2.

Note – These new products are not exact functional replacements for the security software products available on the mainframe. The combination of the Crack, COPS, and Kerberos products (and their commercial versions) appears to provide the closest approximation to the security software system familiar to mainframes. In addition, the BoKS product, by encompassing the architecture of Kerberos with commercial versions of Crack and COPS, may be the most comfortable solution for mainframe managers.

Table 10-2 New Security Products

Product	Description
ASET	ASET (Automated Security Enhancement Tool) is part of SunSoft's SunSHIELD™ product line and is integrated into the Solaris OS. Its functionality is similar to COPS.
OpenV*GateKeeper	OpenV*GateKeeper from OpenVision implements system access controls across a distributed network. It specifies policies for logins, superuser access, and networking programs. It enforces comprehensive end-user password policy. OpenV*GateKeeper's functionality is a subset of the Kerberos authentication.
OpenV*Secure	OpenV*Secure from OpenVision is a commercial version of Kerberos (Version 5). It is supported by the Geer Zolot Consulting Group, which is staffed by people who were participants in the original design and implementation of Kerberos at MIT.
BoKS	BoKS from DynaSoft follows the Kerberos authentication architecture. BoKS includes a commercialized version of COPS (with a new GUI), a password cracker, and it supports single system, LAN, and WAN environments.

Data Center
Disaster Recovery Plan   11 ≡

Over the past several decades commercial businesses have invested heavily in mainframe disaster recovery programs. Based on our past mainframe experience, we have dedicated many person hours to documenting a plan and ensuring a successful off-site recovery in the event of a disaster of our "legacy systems.". Why? Our data center is located on top of an active earthquake fault...all data centers in California must be! A specialized team consisting of system programmers, operations analysts, and DBAs performs quarterly drills using a location provided by a disaster recovery vendor. The cost for using this third-party vendor was quite high, but it covered our risk. Much emphasis and effort had gone into implementing this successful mainframe security program. This same effort went into developing a UNIX disaster recovery plan.

For our UNIX environment, we have established a much more cost-effective method of performing disaster drills. We support two types of Production Server Rooms that are both connected to Sun's Wide-Area Network (SWAN): mission critical and non-mission critical server rooms. In our Disaster Recovery implementation plan, we designated several of these facilities around the world, called **Production Recovery Facilities** *(PRFs), that are to be used in the event of a disaster.*

Backup tapes of mission critical data are stored off-site. In case of an emergency, we would call our off-site tape storage vendor to deliver tapes to the PRFs. We are then able to restore mission critical systems to backup servers, non-mission critical production systems or development servers housed in a PRF, and, thereby, we can resume operations.

Based on our UNIX Production Acceptance Process (UPA), user-owners tell us up front whether their application is mission critical or not. If not, we document in the UPA that "in the event of a disaster, their non-mission critical servers could possibly be used to recover mission critical applications." If it is deemed mission critical, all disaster/recovery processes are put in place. The user-owners have become comfortable with this process, since the negotiations take place, up front, during implementation and testing.

Either internal or third-party disaster recovery plans can support an enterprise. Today, we are seeing more third-party vendors who are putting processes in place to support client/server disaster recovery. The capability is now there to install either a third-party or an internal disaster recovery plan based on your company's specific business requirements.

— Harris and Randy

What Do You Do When an Emergency Occurs?

Sun has documented and implemented a disaster recovery plan for its UNIX environment. Several server rooms, called Production Recovery Facilities (PRF), throughout the global network are designated to be used in the event of an emergency. Backup tapes of critical data are stored off-site. In the event of an emergency, the off-site tape storage vendor will be instructed to deliver tapes to the PRF. Critical systems will be restored to any noncritical production systems or development servers housed in the PRF, and operations can then be resumed.

The data center disaster recovery plan is based on the concept of a Production Recovery Facility (PRF), which is a standard data center environment containing all the hardware and network connections needed to act as a data center. In essence, the PRF will become a data center in the event of the loss of the real data center. The plan assumes the following:

- Regular tape backups of the UNIX filesystems and databases on the critical production servers are being made, using a Tape Management System that allows the backup tapes to be managed and controlled.

- Backup tapes are being stored at an off-site storage facility. These tapes are available and undamaged.

- A procedure is in place to get the backup tapes from the off-site storage facility to the recovery center.

- Required personnel and transportation are available to staff the recovery center.

Note – The plan does *not* provide for recovery of workstations, software servers, and data servers. These services are outside the scope of the data center infrastructure.

This chapter details the Data Center disaster recovery plan. The purpose of this plan is to provide for recovery of the mission critical business processing performed on the UNIX production servers in the Data Center in case of loss of the Data Center's processing capability due to an unforeseen incident. The recovery goal is to recover the mission critical UNIX processing capability within 24 hours from the time a disaster is declared.

Figure 11-1 shows the infrastructure to support both production environments. In the event of a disaster, some of our 12x5 server rooms have been classified as Production Recovery Facilities (PRFs) where we house servers dedicated for disaster-recovery testing. The server user-owners tell us up front whether their application is mission critical or not. If not, the UPA process states that their non-mission critical servers could possibly be used to recover mission critical applications. If it is deemed mission critical, all disaster/recovery processes are put in place. The user-owners have become comfortable with this process since the negotiations take place, up front, during the implementation and testing phases.

Backup tapes of mission critical data are stored off site. In the event of an emergency, the off site tape storage vendor would deliver tapes to the PRFs. We would then restore mission critical systems to backup servers, non-mission critical production systems, and development servers housed in the PRF. Operations could then resume.

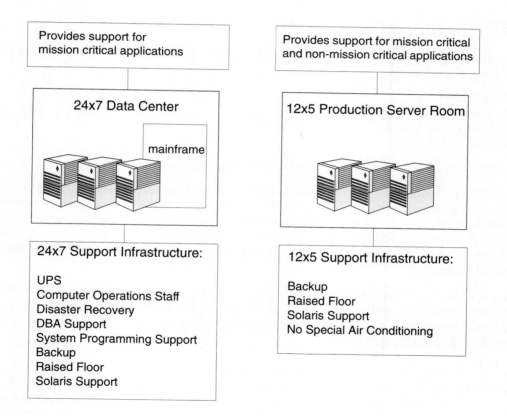

Figure 11-1   Disaster Recovery of UNIX Applications

11

PRF Location

Because this is a distributed solution, the PRF can be located anywhere. The only requirements are:

- The PRF must be connected via communication link to the wide area network
- The PRF must be a part of the same DNS domain as the data center it backs up

There can be as many PRFs as needed to provide the necessary level of disaster recovery protection for the corporation. Because the physical location of the PRF is independent of the data center it backs up, PRF locations can be chosen for convenience, cost, or any other criteria and may also be provided by a third-party vendor.

PRF Configuration

Because it will become a data center in the event of a disaster, the PRF should meet the following requirements:

- Backup servers
- Non-mission critical servers
- Development servers
- Appropriate security

The PRF user-owner approves its use for restoring mission critical applications.

The PRF will contain a replica server (called the *backup*) for each mission critical server (called the *primary*) in the data center to be backed up, in addition to any other servers that will be needed for the network connection (such as gateways, routers, or security relays). It will also contain special-purpose recovery servers that keep a real-time, up-to-date record of the backup tapes and the system configurations of the servers that can be restored in this PRF.

There will be a network connection from the PRF to the wide-area network. The network connection will have sufficient bandwidth to support the traffic in recovery mode; additional bandwidth may be needed to support backup dumps over the network if that capability is implemented.

Recovery Process

At recovery time, the designated servers in the PRF will be booted and restored from the backup tapes of the primary servers. The goal is to have the backup server come up and appear to the rest of the network as if the primary server had just been booted, with no changes needed to any client machine anywhere on the network.

As part of the process of restoring the primary servers, the names of the backup servers will be changed to the names of the primary servers. However, the IP addresses of the backup servers will *not* be changed (that is, the backup servers will keep their original IP addresses).

As part of the recovery process, the Domain Name Service (DNS) and Network Information Service (NIS) tables must be updated to reflect the new mapping between machine names and IP addresses.

Recovery Activities

Once formal declaration of a disaster has been made, the following activities will begin.

- Restore the business-processing environment
  The off-site data storage vendor will be notified to ship the backup tapes to the PRF. As soon as the tapes arrive, restoration of the operating environment will begin.

- Run production from the PRF
  Once the business-processing environment has been restored, production operation will begin. Full production processing will be available, but development activity may be restricted.

- Prepare for leaving the PRF
  Depending on the extent of damage to the main data center, there will be two options available:

  a. Repair and reoccupy the data center

  b. Obtain a replacement facility

  c. Change the PRF to a data center

As soon as the operating environment is restored in the PRF and production is under way, a team will be selected and work will begin to implement one of these options.

Recovery Implementation

The purpose of the recovery plan is to provide recovery capability for a mission critical application in case of a disaster that affects the main data center. This implementation is also intended to prove the validity and viability of the conceptual design.

Backup Schedule

Backups are initiated by batch jobs on the machine being backed up. Tape backups are taken according to the following schedule:

Saturday A.M.	full backup
Monday P.M.	incremental Level 1 backup
Tuesday P.M.	incremental Level 1 backup
Wednesday P.M.	incremental Level 1 backup
Thursday P.M.	incremental Level 1 backup

Backup Content

Prior to the start of the tape backup, the raw partition databases are dumped to a UNIX file, which is then backed up to tape like all the other files. Unlike the other files, the root (/) and /usr file systems are dumped in full every day so that the machine can be booted once those two file systems are restored from the latest tape.

Backup Tape Retention

Backup tapes are rotated off-site the day after they are created. Daily incremental tapes stay off-site for six days, and are returned on the seventh day, to be reused that night. Weekly full backup tapes remain off-site for four weeks, and are returned on the Friday on which they are to be re-used.

Any full backup taken on a Friday that is a fiscal month-end becomes a monthly backup and is kept off-site for 13 months.

Any full backup taken on a Friday that is a fiscal year-end becomes a yearly backup and is kept off-site for seven years.

Backup Tape Labeling and Control

There is a set of backup tapes for every production machine. The Data Center tape library is responsible for labeling and controlling backup tapes and for coordinating with the offsite storage vendor. Each day, the tape librarian prepares a list of tapes to be picked up by our vendor and the date when each tape is to be returned.

Each backup tape contains an internal electronic label (and a corresponding external physical label) consisting of a 9-digit identifier, in the following format:

SSS:nnnnn

where *SSS* indicates which machine's backup is on this tape and *nnnnn* indicates frequency and volume sequence number of this tape. The Data Center Operations group maintains tables that associate each machine with its *SSS* code and allow the *nnnnn* code to be interpreted.

Disaster Recovery Personnel

The disaster recovery team personnel and their respective responsibilities are outlined in Table 11-1.

Table 11-1 Disaster Recovery Team Personnel

Job Title	Responsibility
Project Lead	The ranking data center manager available at the time of the disaster. Responsibilities include: • Direct the activities of the Recovery Team • Adjust and modify responsibilities and assignments as necessary • Communicate status of the recovery effort to corporate management and to Public Relations department as required • Keep the Help Desk informed of the status of the recovery effort Works closely with the Facilities Department. Responsibilities include: • Determine extent of damage to data center and estimate time to repair • If repair of damaged data center is possible, begin planning for repair and reoccupancy • If repair of damaged data center is not possible, begin planning for move to cold site or replacement data center, as determined by management
Disaster Recovery Team	Consists of representatives from Computer Operations, Production Control, System Programming, and DBA. The team's responsibilities include: • Recover backup tapes from off-site storage and organize for restore • Restore full processing capability at the PRF by executing the restore script
Network Team	Consists of representatives from the Network Department. The team's responsibilities are to provide network support as needed. Responsible for DNS and NIS changes that support this move of mission critical applications.

Recommended Restore Script for Disaster Recovery

This section contains step-by-step procedures for restoring machines in the PRF.

Recall Backup Tapes from Off-site Storage

1. Using the Online: Backup database, determine the serial numbers of the latest incremental and full backup tapes for all servers to be restored.

```
#/usr/local/get_tapes

(this script executes the Online: Backup dumpdm command to list all dumps
in the database; the format is:
    #/usr/etc/dumpdm -s drcentral -v tapelist)
```

2. Call the off-site storage vendor and have the tapes delivered to the PRF.

Prepare for Recovery

1. From a console on the backup machine, halt all backup machines that are to be restored, in preparation for restoring.

2. Update the DNS and NIS tables with the new IP addresses for the servers and push out the updates. Rebuild ypmaps on all ypmasters in domain. This procedure is done by the Network Administration group.

   To get the IP addresses, list the IP addresses of the backup machines:

```
#ypcat hosts | grep BackupMachine_IP_address
```

The *BackupMachine* has been a ypslave in the ops domain; however, assuming that the normal production ypmaster is no longer operational, we will now convert the *BackupMachine* to a ypmaster for the ops domain.

1. Get the latest hosts ypmap on *BackupMachine*. This ypmap should reflect the changes made to the domain.

```
#mv /etc/hosts /etc/hosts-
#cp /etc/swan.hosts/domain_name /etc/hosts
```

2. Kill ypbind, rebuild the ypmaps, and start the *BackupMachine* as a ypmaster.

```
#ps ax | grep ypbind
#kill <processid>
#/usr/etc/yp/ypinit -m
#/usr/etc/ypserv
#/usr/etc/ypxfrd
#/usr/etc/ypbind
```

1. Modify the Online: Backup database to reflect the new IP addresses of the recovery servers.

```
#cd /home/BKcopilot1.0
#mv drtsellery.IP_address_old drtsellery.IP_address_new
#mv drtschan.IP_address_old drtschan.IP_address_.9
#mv drtssamspade.IP_address_old drtssamspade.y.IP_address_
#mv drtsrockford.IP_address_old drtsrockford.y.IP_address_
#mv drtscolumbo.129.150.193.9 drtscolumbo.y.IP_address_
#/usr/etc/dumpdm tapefile_rebuild
```

Obtain Setup Information

1. Print out the system configuration maps for the servers to be restored. These are available on the *BackupMachine* in:

/home/autosysconfig/<*servername*>.<*dayofweek*>

2. Make sure you know the root, operator, and Sybase SA passwords for the servers to be restored.

Restore / and /usr File Systems

1. Boot MUNIX from CD-ROM.

```
for Sun4 kernel architecture:
>b sd(,30,1)

for desktop SPARCsystems (except SPARCstation 2):
            ok boot sd(,6,2)
                or
            >b sd(,6,2)

for SPARCstation 2:
            ok boot cdrom
                or
            >b cdrom
```

2. The load process will prompt you to enter the format program. Format, partition, and label the system disk. Choose the system diskID and partitioning information as specified in the setup information.

 Caution – Remember to label the disk before you exit the format program.

3. Reboot using the just-installed miniroot.

4. Make filesystems on the system disk for restoring the / and /usr file systems.

Note – If the disk you are restoring to is a SCSI disk rather than an IPI, the device name will be dev/rsdXX rather than /dev/ridXX.

The following commands assume that the root file system is on partition *a* and the usr file system is on partition *g*. If this is not the case, modify the commands accordingly.

```
#newfs /dev/rid000a
#newfs /dev/rid000g
#fsck /dev/rid000a
#fsck /dev/rid000g
```

5. Create a temporary directory to use in restoring from tape; mount the file system to be restored on the new directory, and cd to the new directory.

```
#mkdir /mnt
#/etc/mount /dev/id000a /mnt
#cd /mnt
```

6. Insert the latest backup tape in the tape drive and rewind the tape. All backup tapes, both full and incremental, contain a full dump of / and /usr, so use the latest tape, whether it is full or incremental.

```
#mt -f /dev/rst0 rew
```

7. Restore the root file system. It should be the first dump on the tape. Confirm this by referring to the dump list.

```
#/etc/restore rvf /dev/nrst0
```

8. Remove the restoresymtable file that restore creates in the working directory during its operation.

```
#rm /mnt/restoresymtable
```

9. Install a new bootblock. This is required after restoring the root partition.

```
#cd /usr/mdec
#installboot /mnt/boot bootid /dev/rid000a
```

10. Unmount the newly restored file system and check it again.

```
#cd /
#/etc/umount /dev/rid000a
#/etc/fsck /dev/rid000a
```

11. Forward space the tape to the next dump, which should be the /usr file system. Confirm this by referring to the dump list.

```
#mt -f /dev/nrst0 fsf 1
```

12. Mount the file system to be restored.

```
#/etc/mount /dev/id000g /mnt
```

13. Change directory and restore /usr.

```
#cd /mnt
#/etc/restore rvf /dev/nrst0
```

14. Remove the restoresymtable file that restore creates in the working directory during its operation.

```
#rm /mnt/restoresymtable
```

15. Unmount the newly restored file system and check it again.

```
#cd /
#/etc/umount /dev/rid000g
#/etc/fsck /dev/rid000g
```

16. Mount the root file system and go to the /etc directory.

```
#/etc/mount /dev/id000a /mnt
#/etc/mount /dev/id000g /mnt/usr
# cd /mnt/etc
```

The / and /usr file systems have now been restored, but the machine is still running miniroot. Before booting from the newly restored OS, some changes must be made to reflect the recovery environment.

If you need to use vi at any time prior to booting from the full OS, you must set up the environment properly for vi. Enter the following commands to do so.

```
%sh              (start a Bourne shell if not already in one)
#TERM=tvi925     (if you are using a Wyse terminal)
#TERM=sun-cmd    (if you are using a Sun terminal)
#export TERM
#LD_LIBRARY_PATH="/mnt/usr/lib"
#export LD_LIBRARY_PATH
#PATH="$PATH:/mnt/usr/ucb"
#export PATH
```

17. Temporarily remove from fstab all entries other than / and /usr.

```
#cp fstab fstab-
#<use vi or ed to remove entries other than / and /usr>
```

Caution – Perform the following step *only if* /var/spool/cron/crontabs exists on the system disk.

18. Move all files and directories in /var/spool/cron/crontabs to a temporary directory.

```
#mkdir /mnt/var/spool/cron/crontabs.temp
# mv /mnt/var/spool/cron/crontabs/* /mnt/var/spool/cron/crontabs.temp
```

19. Make a backup copy of rc.local and change rc.local as needed; the comments in the file will tell you what changes are needed. The purpose of this is to ensure that only the processes needed for the restore are started until the restore is complete.

```
#cp /mnt/etc/rc.local /mnt/rc.local-
# <use vi or ed to edit the file>
```

20. Change the IP address in the restored /etc/hosts file to the correct address.

```
#<use vi or ed to edit the file>
```

21. Reboot the machine in single-user mode.

Restore Other UNIX File Systems

22. Partition the rest of the disks using the predefined partition maps.

```
#format -x /etc/partition.dat
from the PARTITION MENU, choose "select" to select a predefined table; then
from the table choose the entry number which corresponds to the disk being
formatted.
Label the disk before you exit.
```

Code Example 11-1 on the next page is an example of this.

23. Restore the fstab file.

```
#cp /etc/fstab- /etc/fstab
```

24. Make new file systems for all file system names listed in fstab (except / and /usr, which have already been restored). Use newfs and fsck.

25. Use Online: Backup to restore all remaining filesystems from the backup tapes. Refer to the list for the file systems to be restored. Perform the following commands for each file system to be restored:

```
#mount <filesystemname>
#cd <filesystemname>
#recover -s drcentral
=> fastrecover <filesystemname>
=> rrestore
```

26. Reboot multiuser and login as operator or any valid user.

Code Example 11-1   Partition Disks Using Predefined Partition Maps

```
drrockford# format -x /etc/partition.dat
Searching for disks...done
AVAILABLE DISK SELECTIONS:
        0. id000 at idc0 slave 0
           id000: <CDC IPI 9720 cyl 1631 alt 1 hd 15 sec 82>
        1. id001 at idc0 slave 1
           id001: <CDC IPI 9720 cyl 1631 alt 1 hd 15 sec 82>
        2. id010 at idc1 slave 0
           id010: <CDC IPI 9720 cyl 1631 alt 1 hd 15 sec 82>
        3. id011 at idc1 slave 1
           id011: <CDC IPI 9720 cyl 1631 alt 1 hd 15 sec 82>
Specify disk (enter its number): 3
selecting id011: <CDC IPI 9720>
ISP-80 working list found
[disk formatted, defect list found]
FORMAT MENU:
        disk       - select a disk
        type       - select (define) a disk type
        partition  - select (define) a partition table
        current    - describe the current disk
        format     - format and analyze the disk
        repair     - repair a defective sector
        show       - translate a disk address
        label      - write label to the disk
        analyze    - surface analysis
        defect     - defect list management
        backup     - search for backup labels
        quit
```

Code Example 11-1   Partition Disks Using Predefined Partition Maps (Continued)

```
format> pa
PARTITION MENU:
        a      - change `a' partition
        b      - change `b' partition
        c      - change `c' partition
        d      - change `d' partition
        e      - change `e' partition
        f      - change `f' partition
        g      - change `g' partition
        h      - change `h' partition
        select - select a predefined table
        name   - name the current table
        print  - display the current table
        label  - write partition map and label to the disk
        quit
partition> se
        0. CDC IPI 9720
        1. id000
        2. id001
        3. id010
        4. id011
Specify table (enter its number) [4]: 4
partition> print
Current partition table (id011):
    partition a - starting cyl     0, # blocks    1230 (1/0/0)
    partition b - starting cyl     0, # blocks       0 (0/0/0)
    partition c - starting cyl     0, # blocks  200613 (1631/0/0)
    partition d - starting cyl     1, # blocks  226320 (184/0/0)
    partition e - starting cyl     0, # blocks       0 (0/0/0)
    partition f - starting cyl     0, # blocks       0 (0/0/0)
    partition g - starting cyl   185, # blocks  901590 (733/0/0)
    partition h - starting cyl   918, # blocks  875760 (712/0/0)

partition> quit
```

Restore the Databases

Note – This example is for the Sybase database.

27. Change to user id `sybase` and go to install directory.

```
#su sybase
%cd SYBASE/install
```

28. Save the RUN_*<dbservername>* and errorlog_*<dbservername>* files. Note that there may be multiple dbservers on each machine; this entire section must be performed for each dbserver.

```
%mv RUN_<dbservername> RUN_<dbservername>-
%mv errorlog_<dbservername> errorlog_<dbservername>-
```

29. Use vi to remove the *<dbservername>* entry from the interfaces file in `$SYBASE`.

```
%vi $SYBASE/interfaces
```

To finish the restore, you will need some database information for sybconfig and the database reload. That information is in `$SYBASE/install/`*<dbservername>*`.info`. It can be printed out from the *BackupMachine*. Print it now.

30. Run sybconfig.

```
%sybconfig
```

sybconfig will ask you to select some options. Select the following:

```
select 1 - install SQL server
select 2 - install new SQL server
select 1 - raw disk partition for master device
```

Now sybconfig will ask for some information. The source of this information is $SYBASE/install/*<dbservername>*.info.

```
enter the full pathname of the master device raw partition
enter the size of the raw partition
enter the dbservername
enter the Sybase query port
press Return to select the default character set
select option 1 - binary sort order (this is the default)
enter c to continue - bypass additional character sets
```

Now you will get lots of Sybase messages; at the end, enter x to exit. At this point, the SQL dbserver has been installed.

31. Start an SQL session and create the master dump device.

```
%isql -Usa -S <dbservername>
passwd: <return>
```

First, we have to initialize any other diskthat contains a master database; skip this step if the master database is on a single disk. The parameters enclosed by < > should be obtained from the .info file printed earlier.

```
1> disk init name="<masterdevicename>",
physname="<masterdevicephysname>",vdevno=<virtualdevnum>,
2> size=<devicesize>
3> go
```

Now create the master dump device.

```
1> sp_addumpdevice "disk", masterdump, "<pathnameofdump file>",2
2> go
```

32. Shut down the dbserver and terminate the SQL session.

```
1> shutdown with nowait
2> go
```

33. Update the RUN_*<dbservername>* file to add -m option to the dataserver command and run RUN_*<dbservername>*.

```
%vi RUN_<dbservername>
%RUN_<dbservername> &
```

34. Start an SQL session and load the master database.

```
%isql -Usa -S <dbservername>
passwd:<enter>
1> load database master from masterdump
2> go
```

At this point the SQL dbserver will shut down automatically.

35. Change the sort order and character set parameters as specified in .inf.

```
%buildmaster -d /dev/rid001d -y cdflt_sortord=<cdflt_sortord>
%buildmaster -d /dev/rid001d -y cdflt_charset=<cdflt_charset>
%buildmaster -d /dev/rid001d -y cold_dflt_sortord=
<cold_dflt_sortord>
%buildmaster -d /dev/rid001d -y cold_dflt_charset=
<cold_dflt_charset>
```

36. Update the RUN_*<dbservername>* file to delete -m option from the dataserver command and run RUN_*<dbservername>* in background.

```
%vi RUN_<dbservername>
%RUN_<dbservername> &
```

37. Reconfigure the dbserver to allow updates.

```
%isql -Usa -S <dbservername>
passwd: <enter sa password>
1> sp_configure allow_updates, 1
2> go
1> reconfigure with override
2> go
1> begin tran
2> go
```

38. Update the status of all databases, one at a time.

```
1> update sysdatabases set status = 256 where name=<databasename>
2> go
...(repeat for each database)
1> commit tran
2> go
```

39. Shut down and restart the dbserver and the SQL session.

```
1> shutdown with nowait
2> go
%RUN_<dbservername> &
%isql -Usa -S <dbservername>
passwd: <enter sa password>
```

40. Drop all the databases, one at a time.

```
1> dbcc dbrepair(<databasename>, dropdb)
2> go
... (repeat for each database)
1> sp_configure allow_updates, 0
2> go
1> reconfigure with override
2> go
1> shutdown with nowait
2> go
```

41. Restart the dbserver and the SQL session.

```
%RUN_<dbservername> &
%isql -Usa -S <dbservername>
passwd: <enter sa password>
```

42. Create the databases. The log on command is needed only if the log is on a separate device. The alter command is needed only if the database is in multiple extents.

```
1> create database <databasename> on <devicename>=<size>
2> log on <devicename>=<size>
3> go
1> alter database <databasename> on <devicename>=<size>
2> go
... (repeat for each database)
```

43. Load the databases.

```
1> load database <databasename> from <databasedumpdevice>
2> go
```

44. Check the loaded databases.

```
1> dbcc checkdb
2> go
1> dbcc checkalloc
2> go
```

45. Terminate the SQL session.

```
1> quit
2> go
```

☰ 11

Final Cleanup and Reboot for Production

1. Restore crontabs file if necessary.

```
%su
#mv /var/spool/cron/crontabs.temp/* /var/spool/cron/crontabs
#rmdir /var/spool/cron/crontabs/temp
```

2. Restore rc.local.

```
#mv /etc/rc.local- /etc/rc.local
```

3. Reboot.

```
#reboot
```

The system is now ready for production.

Some Things to Consider
When Rightsizing   12 ≡

During our worldwide travel and discussions with thousands of customers, we are constantly asked about the cost and benefits of client/server distributed systems versus the centralized mainframe approach. There have been many articles and books written on client/server environments that suggest that costs will increase when implementing this new environment. We still don't see how they can write about it until they have actually implemented it! They say "support costs will increase because it requires staff at all remote distributed locations.. Not true! It depends on how you implement the new distributed environment. We have found that support costs can actually decrease by implementing the centralized control model. Using this model can lower not only the support (i.e., labor) costs, but it can also reduce other costs like software licensing, software maintenance (i.e., version/release control), and time to market (i.e., implementing new business solutions). In addition, the hardware and hardware maintenance costs are less. This chapter addresses these issues in more detail.

We have also been approached on the "total cost of ownership" model. This model tends to indicate that the overall total cost of implementation and ownership (to the corporation) will increase. Our answer is twofold: first, we discuss some of the real cost issues stated above (additional details in this chapter), and, second, we talk about the most important aspect of client/server distributed computing — business productivity improvements. If we can implement new systems and processes that reduce the quote-to-collect-time (i.e., the time from a valid sales quote to the time the customer pays the bill) by 150%, then why not implement these systems? This process alone has put millions of dollars cash in the bank at Sun. If we can provide systems that give the business a competitive advantage, then why not implement them? Sun has become one of the top-managed Fortune 100 companies because of its IT processes. These are the appropriate views to take when considering the implementation of this new paradigm. If we can more than double the revenue-per-employee ($150K/employee/year to over $350K/employee/year), then why not?

These cost/benefit challenges today face all IT directors, managers, and CIOs. Those who take a proactive approach to gain control of the infrastructure and implement systems for competitive advantage will win. Thosewho don't will just become a "shelf-life" statistic.

— Randy and Harris

Cost Analysis

Moving to client/server and distributed systems requires some investment, including initial costs for:

- Hardware and software
- Training

Hardware and Software

For the purposes of funding, the initial cost of hardware and software to implement a distributed system can be viewed in two ways:

1. As a development project
   This model assumes that funding is part of the research and development budget.

2. As cost avoidance
   This model frees mainframe MIPS or avoids mainframe upgrades. Costs are avoided that can reduce your overall IT budget. For example, Sun's early rightsizing efforts saved an estimated US$8 million (list price) in mainframe upgrade costs. We recommend using this model.

To minimize initial investment, begin with a pilot project that can provide immediate benefits. For example, a good pilot project is to move a non-mission critical system, such as SAS processing from the mainframe to the UNIX environment. Moving SAS processing to the UNIX environment frees mainframe MIPS for other critical functions as well as delays (and possibly eliminates) the cost of mainframe upgrades. It also delivers SAS to the end-user at a lesser cost.

Training

Training the existing staff to support the new technologies is important. We recommend the following classes as a minimum for training:

- System Administration Essentials
- System Administration for Solaris
- Shell Programming

The estimated cost for these three classes is approximately US$2,500 to US$3,000 per employee for external (off-site) training. Internal (on-site) training at your company by a third-party vendor could reduce these costs by as much as US$1,000 to US$1,500 per employee (plus travel expenses).

If you need to choose among the three classes, we recommend the shell programming class, as system administration can be learned from books. You can also use the "train the trainer" philosophy; that is, train one senior person, who would then teach the other staff members.

Senior technical personnel (Database Administrators and System Programmers) could require an additional five (advanced) courses with approximate costs of US$1,200 to US$1,500 per class.

Table 12-1 is an example of total training costs (off-site training excluding travel expense) for a computer operator/production control person (*Employee A*) and a senior system programmer/database administrator who is also taking the advanced courses (*Employee B*).

Table 12-1 Example of Training Costs

	Employee A	**Employee B**
Initial 3 classes	US$2,500 to US$3,000	US$2,500 to US$3,000
Advanced Training (5 classes)	0	US$6,000 to US$7,500
Total Training Cost/Person	US$2,500 to US$3,000	US$8,500 to US$10,500

Another point to consider in regard to training is that we, as data center managers, usually maintained a small budget for continuous training of our staffs. Each time a new mainframe operating system or networking software release was issued, we sent our staff to training (usually off-site) for that product. We also budgeted for user group fees and attendance (for example, GUIDE and SHARE). These same budgets could also be used for UNIX training. Using this approach lessens the training burden and may not require additional investment. In other words, you can use existing budgets for UNIX training. The fallacy of "huge training investment" does not hold true with this approach.

Note – If attrition does occur, we recommend hiring experienced personnel in the new disciplines.

12

Benefits Analysis

Moving to client/server and distributed systems has many benefits, including:

- Operating expense reduction
- Increased software development productivity
- Improved business productivity

We like to refer to this as the four R's:

- The *right* information
- To the *right* people
- At the *right* time
- At the *right* price

Operating Expense Reduction

Areas of operating expense reduction include the reduction in costs for hardware, software, and labor. We estimate that overall operating costs will be reduced by a minimum of 30% to 40% once the migration off the mainframe is complete. If your company has a requirement to keep the mainframe, the cost reduction would be in terms of cost avoidance. You can also look at cost comparison for a new application. Determine the total mainframe costs versus a client/server solution. Normally the client/server solution is less.

Reducing Hardware Costs

An example of cost reduction in hardware is a comparison of cost per MIP on the mainframe versus a UNIX server (for example, a SPARCcenter™ 2000). Our internal data center's cost per mainframe MIP was approximately US$1200 per MIP per month. Based on a three-year depreciation after the purchase of the server, the data center's cost per server MIP was approximately US$25 per MIP per month — the cost after the third year will be for upgrades and maintenance only.

Reducing Software Costs

There are two areas in which to compare software costs:

1. The operating system
   The license cost for MVS and VM operating system was approximately US$500,000 per year (including all IBM products); the license cost for the Solaris operating environment is approximately US$1,200 per year for an unlimited number of licenses.

2. Third-party software products

For example, the cost of change/migration software for UNIX is approximately 1/3 of the mainframe cost for equivalent functionality.

Reducing Labor Costs

Additional cost reduction can be provided in terms of direct labor. For example, after we implemented the functionality to support a "lights-out" data center and eliminated mainframe processing, we found that eventually a computer operations staff would no longer be required. The computer operations staff has been reduced from 24 to 10 (that is, reduced by a total of 14). Both of the system programming staffs were reduced by 2 persons each (that is, a total of 4 people). These solutions occurred as part of our mainframe out-sourcing effort where the remaining mainframe applications are supported by a third-party vendor. By automating processes and implementing the UPA process, any new client/server system can be implemented and supported by this same staff.

Note – As the Computer Operations staff was reduced, some were retrained for either System Administration or Production Control Analyst positions.

Increased Software Development Productivity

Moving to a UNIX client/server environment can also provide productivity improvements in the areas of internal software development. For example, internal development cycles can be reduced by 30% to 40% with approximately 20% less labor.

Note – Our application development staff was retrained to program in UNIX and the C++ language instead of the COBOL language.

Business Productivity Improvements

Two key business indicators at Sun that improved greatly by implementing distributed computing solutions were the quote-to-collect time (by 150%) and the inventory cycle turns (by double).

Issues to Resolve

There are a number of issues that need to be addressed and resolved, including:

- Organizational issues
- Human Resources issues
- Process issues
- Investment in rightsizing tools
- Server room standards and auditing
- Chargebacks

Organizational Issues

You may encounter organizational issues early in your rightsizing effort.

For example, Sun's Data Center acquired an organization in 1992 that was chartered to support only one business unit. The acquired organization consisted of a DBA, System Programmer, two Operations Analysts, and a manager; they felt they were properly structured to support a client/server distributed model. They resided in the business unit that they were supporting. This self-contained organization did not want to be part of the old mainframe data center infrastructure which we kept intact. This group was allowed to remain "as is" and support only distributed systems for nearly a year to evaluate which support paradigm (centralized or decentralized) would work best in a distributed environment. Well, we quickly found out as the following issues arose:

- Changes were made without notification
- System uptime availability was maintained at less than 85%
- No career advancement took place within the self-contained organization
- No backup personnel support existed

Once we placed both mainframe and distributed systems support under the same structure and control, changes were controlled, the same RAS was provided regardless of the platform, better career opportunities were provided, and personnel were available to provide backup support for all environments.

Human Resource Issues

You may encounter human resource issues, such as salary discrepancies between UNIX and mainframe staff, when transitioning your staff.

In our experience, salaries for mainframe technical staff members were (on the average) 30% to 40% higher than those of the UNIX staff members doing the same job function. However, we were able to eliminate the morale issues caused by the pay discrepancies by early and frequent communications with the staff. We have been able to use our yearly review process (which we call *focals*) as a means to balance the pay discrepancies. Our mainframe staff, although understanding, was not overjoyed knowing that they would not receive significant salary increases until the discrepancies were balanced out. For example, if our average increase was 4%, the mainframers would probably get a 1% increase while our UNIX people would receive a 7, 8, or 9% increase. This took place every year until we balanced it out. However, they do realize that our training programs have increased their marketable skills by at least twofold.

Process Issues

You may encounter resistance to processes.

For example, the UPA process was resisted by UNIX developers around the Sun world who wanted no part of mainframe disciplines. When the UPA process was developed, many roadblocks were encountered: The UNIX side did not want controls placed on their environment such as the ones placed on critical mainframe applications. The UPA process was considered a waste of time by UNIX personnel, who made numerous comments such as:

> *It is too cumbersome.*
> *UNIX is more wide open.*
> *It will never work in a distributed environment.*

However, we did not back down from our position but, instead, worked closely with them to negotiate the issues. We streamlined the UPA process and took advantage of both UNIX and mainframe experiences. Eventually, the business units that had been allowed to support their own applications — rather than go through our process — found they could not maintain the required level of RAS and, in time, made the change. In addition, they were working full-time on maintenance and support instead of working on their chartered (i.e., development) responsibilities.

Investing in Rightsizing Tools

You may encounter the issue of how much to invest in rightsizing tools. It is necessary to understand integration issues and the importance of integrating technology. Automated software tools that allow interoperability between heterogeneous environments are required in order to start the process of integrating distributed applications with mainframe applications.

For example, when Sun implemented its Product Distribution Center (PDC) in Europe, we used SunRAI to support interaction between third-party RDBMS systems and our mainframe.

Since many of these integration tools are now commercially available, the issue now becomes finding the right tools to fit the business rather than investing heavily to internally develop them.

Implementing Server Room Standards

You may encounter issues relating to server room standards.

For example, the UPA process allowed the user/owner to decide where to house a production server in *any* location around the world. This ability created new challenges in server room standards, such as environmental issues, cabling and connectivity issues, security, and the lack of tools to administer these server rooms. A new set of standards related to remote production server rooms needed to be defined. To accomplish this, an audit procedure was developed to ensure that the server rooms were in compliance and could support critical applications. Quarterly audits are performed to ensure compliance; the local system administration function is responsible for correcting any deficiencies found.

Audit Process

The section contains an explanation of the audit process, frequency, and how the CAR (Corrective Action Request) process is applied to the physical audits of the fileserver rooms. Table 12-2 on page 181 shows the CAR checklist used by the auditors. The auditors are usually senior members of the Data Center staff.

The auditor records the date, server room, and owner of the fileserver room. *CAR Due* refers to the date when the fileserver room owner must comply with all cited violations. Typically the time frame will be 30 calendar days. *CAR Completed* refers to the fact that a compliance audit has taken place and the violations previously cited have been corrected on the date specified.

Frequency

• Each fileserver room will have a physical audit performed once per quarter.

• Audits will be not be announced in advance.

Table 12-2 Server Room Physical Audit Checklist

Date:		Server Room:		Auditor:
Car Due:		Owner:		Car Completed:

	Yes	No	Checklist item
SAFETY			Is there a fire extinguisher in the room?
			Is there emergency lighting in the room?
OPERATIONAL			Is proper clearance access available to all equipment?
			Are all power cables properly labeled?
APPEARANCE			Is the room free of unused equipment, packing material, parts, carts, and anything else not needed for daily operation?
			Are the servers and other equipment on the raised floor arranged such that floor space is used efficiently?
			Is equipment placed such that an orderly, professional-looking appearance is achieved?
			Is the area under the raised floor clean and free of debris and foreign objects?
			Are the floor tile cutouts properly finished with protective material so that no rough edges are exposed?
			Are all cables and wires under the floor?
			Are all floor tiles level and solidly seated?
			Are all servers labeled with the standard AIS server label?
			Is the under-floor wiring neat and orderly?
			Have all unused cables been removed from under the floor?
			Are all equipment doors and access panels in place and properly fastened?
COMMENTS:			

Responsibility

♦ **Auditor Responsibilities**

- Performs audit.

- Auditor must be specific as to the violation, offering such information as location within the fileserver room, names of servers, equipment, cables, muxes, and so forth.

- The auditor's results will be sent to the fileserver room owner via email. A care copy will go to owner's supervisor and a second copy to the Administrator.

- At the request of the fileserver room owner, the auditor is available for a walk-through to explain cited violations.

- A secondary, unannounced compliance audit will be performed within one week of the original 30 calendar days. This audit will seek to confirm that the violation cited for a fileserver room has been corrected.

- The results of the compliance audit will be published to the fileserver room owner, his/her supervisor, with a copy to the administrator.

- Compliance audits older than 35 calendar days will be forwarded to the next level of management if appropriate corrective action has not been taken.

♦ **Fileserver Room Owner Responsibilities**

- Understand what the scope and the impact of the physical audit process means to an owner of a fileserver room.

- Communicate the physical audit requirements to employees having access to the fileserver room. Obtain buy-off from those employees that they understand their responsibilities within the fileserver room based on the attached audit form.

- It is the responsibility of the owner of the fileserver room and his/her supervisor to take any corrective action deemed by the physical audit as noncompliant.

- The owner and supervisor have 30 calendar days to correct any violations.

- If there are still outstanding violations after 30 calendar days, it will be required by the owner/supervisor to submit a written explanation of the delay and a written plan of action specifying a date of compliance/completion to the auditor, his/her supervisor, and the next level of management, as well as the administrator.

- A final compliance audit will take place to close the past-due compliance audit. Results will be forwarded to appropriate personnel.

Chargeback Issues

You may encounter the issue of chargebacks. It is most effective to keep the chargeback mechanism simple. Table 12-3 is an example of how IT services are automatically tracked.

Table 12-3 Keeping Track of IT Services

IT Service	Chargeback
Network services	Connection to wide area network, email, voice communications, internet services, various forms of remote connectivity for customers, vendors and employees.
Telecommunications services	Standard telecom services included 5-digit dialing around the world, transferring, conference, programmable features, structured coverage paths, and voice mail. Additional services include telephone maintenance on the failing equipment, external direct-dial interfaces to the central office, and setup and administration of operational databases.
Software services	Standard desktop software (such as spreadsheets and desktop publishing) and licensing provided to all employees. Includes support for standard databases as well as software distribution.
Help Desk	Includes 24-hour, 7-day support.
Desktop services	Includes client and server hardware maintenance, operating system installation and support for clients and servers. Other services include performance and tuning, capacity planning, backup services, and local area network support.
Production server Room services	Services for application servers connected to the wide-area network, including hardware maintenance, operating system installation and support, performance and capacity planning, DBA support, backup services, and local-area network support for a 24 x 7. These services operate 365 days a year.
Moves, adds, and changes	A flat rate is assessed for workstation moves and another rate for telephone moves.
Consulting services	Provides consulting for programming and other technical tasks as desired and available.
Assistance Center	Provides software and systems support 24 hours a day, Monday through Friday; 8 hours a day, weekends and holidays.
	A standard price is assessed for each service per month per employee. A monthly service charge is billed to each customer (that is, the department or division).

SunDANS

Note – This tool is available through SunIntegration Services.

SunDANS™ (Sun's Distribution Administration of Network Services) is a set of standards, mechanisms, and systems administration practices. The result is a subscription service operating through a layered distribution network, delivering standard, access-enhanced, administration-optimized versions of software packages to local servers.

The other key function of SunDANS is usage license management for those software products that are usage licensed; for example, desktop tools such as Interleaf and FrameMaker. SunDANS monitors the usage of licenses and notifies when problems occur, allowing the environment to be proactively managed.

Table A-1 describes several features of the SunDANS environment.

Table A-1   Features of the SunDANS Environment

Feature	Description
Standard server structure	The SunDANS software filesystem layout is consistent from server to server. This filesystem, which may span disks, has two conceptual "halves": one half originates from the master SunDANS server, the other half is for the introduction of local packages and for custom configuration data.
Enhanced delivery	Packages that originate from the master are cloned faithfully to client sites. While a small core of operating software is required for participation, the majority of packages are acquired by a subscription process. These subscription requests are submitted by the systems administrator through the *distribution-management mechanism* (distmgr). The distmgr is also used to set up (rdist-based) package deliveries to client sites through a limited-privilege account.
Standard user connections	User connections required to access software from a SunDANS server are consistent and minimal. All users mount the software server in the same manner, regardless of architecture. All users use the same software-access path (i.e., a path that requires no updates for new SunDANS software).

Table A-1   Features of the SunDANS Environment (Continued)

Feature	Description
easy-access mechanisms	Most software commands are accessed through a single directory on the software server. When new software is added, the commands appear in this directory and are available to the user without updating the user's environment. Wrappers (i.e., intelligent front-end routines) for each package navigate and set up at runtime. Other SunDANS mechanisms allow command-line access to available down-rev versions and access to a variety of product information.

How Does SunDANS Work?

Figure A-1 illustrates how the SunDANS distribution tool works.

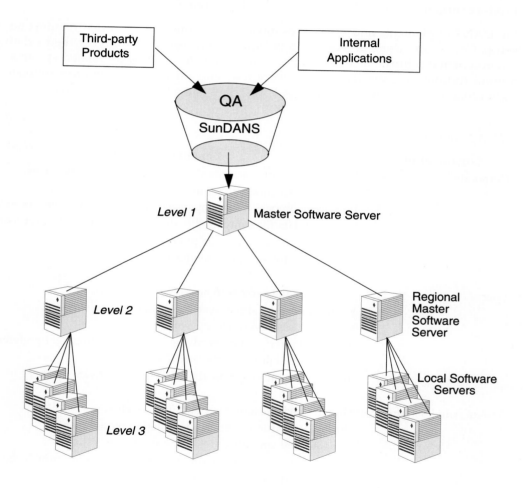

Figure A-1   Software Distribution (SunDANS)

The software change is quality assured and tested, then 'migrated' to the level 1 and 2 servers. The system administrators group is responsible for moving the changes to the level 43 or local software servers.

Benefits of SunDANS

SunDANS delivers a wide spectrum of benefits to users, to systems administrators, to product support personnel, and to Help Desk personnel.

SunDANS implements and distributes most applications in a form that requires no user setup. Converting users to SunDANS is mainly a process of simplifying their existing environmental setups. Once this conversion is done, local software-related systems administration is drastically reduced. Very few return trips are needed to administer individual user environments. Table A-2 describes some SunDANS benefits.

Table A-2   Benefits of SunDANS

Organization	Benefits Realized
Corporate	Increased user productivity due to immediate variety access.
	Increased user productivity due to high availability access.
	Less access impact when employees move to different nets or groups.
	Increased data file compatibility due to consistent software versions.
	Ability to track and manage product usage.
	Lower costs for software maintenance.
User	More immediate access to new software choices.
	Reduced need for direct systems administrative support.
	Reduced loss of productivity from moves.
	Simplified interface for specifying software environment preferences.
	Increased visibility of software choices.
	Improved communication about changing software choices.
System Administrator	More immediate access to new software choices.
	Drastically reduced software installation requirements.
	Standard and simplified delivery mechanism.
	Consistency of software in different areas to simplify troubleshooting.
	Standardized filesystem locations.
	Standardized (and minimal) user connections to software servers.
	Reduced need to adjust user environment setups.

Table A-2 Benefits of SunDANS (Continued)

Organization	Benefits Realized
	Increased visibility of software choices.
	Improved communication about changing software choices.
Product Support	A more consistent environment greatly simplifies delivery issues.
	Ability to deliver widely with one central submission process.
	Improved visibility into the "where" of delivery.
	Ability to implement sensible default operation for users.
	Reduced need to publish access and installation instructions.
	Possibility of "narrow-casting" info to users via wrappers.
	Possibility of "usage tracking" via wrappers for user lists and stats.
	Ability to control and tailor the version migration process.
	Expectation that most users are seeing an identical installation.
	Expectation that most users have the identical setup for a product.
Trouble Desk	Higher reliability produces fewer trouble calls.
	Expectation that most users can "self start" new software.
	Reduced need to track and interpret access/installation instructions.
	Expectation that most users are seeing an identical installation.
	Expectation that most users have the identical setup for a product.

SunRAI B

Note – This tool is available through SunIntegration Services.

SunRAI (Sun's Remote Application Interface), developed and supported by Sun's IT organization, is a connectivity tool that enables UNIX-based applications to communicate with other UNIX applications and mainframe applications. SunRAI is designed with a set of front-end (client) and a set of remote (server) application components. Each SunRAI installation handles multiple client applications, multiple remote applications, as well as simultaneous multiple messages from each client.

The most significant feature of SunRAI is its ability to connect applications rather than servers. As a result, both users and programmers are shielded from complex mainframe and UNIX interfaces and processes. SunRAI is implemented at the programming level and administered by a system programmer. SunRAI reduces the programming effort currently required to send synchronous and asynchronous messages across networks.

This tool can handle the heterogeneous transaction processing needs for most commercial accounts. It is based on TCP/IP and can transmit high volume transactions independent of distance. It sends both asynchronous and synchronous messages. Asynchronous messages can be sent in interactive or batch mode.

SunRAI messages contain object/method descriptions of application interactions. SunRAI objects are collections of data that are linked to real world entities, such as a customer order or a part number. Objects share a common structure and a common behavior between the client and the server applications. The tool guarantees that messages are transmitted in a secure, prioritized, and properly sequenced order. It provides complete recovery facilities against network or component failure as well as a complete log of messages for investigating problems. All existing application security is maintained, and no new security is added.

SunRAI is easy to administer and maintain. Its System Administration Tool (SAT) has an OpenWindows-based interface and contains highly functional, yet easy-to-use, performance monitoring, tuning, recovery, and analysis functions. SAT serves both the client and remote components.

Table B-1 is a summary of SunRAI features and benefits.

Table B-1 SunRAI Features and Benefits

Features	Benefits
Application transparency	Transparency for programers and end-users reduces implementation and training requirements.
Synchronous and asynchronous transaction support	Batch and real-time data transfer is possible.
Message sequencing	Guarantees message order for sequence-dependent messages.
Network error recovery	Complete recovery facilities save messages even if a network or component fails.
Message audit trail	Complete logging of messages for problem investigation.
Security	All existing application security maintained. No new security added.
System Administration Tool (SAT)	OpenWindows administration tool for performance analysis and system monitoring.

Object-based Methodology

SunRAI employs a unique object-based methodology. SunRAI objects are collections of data that are linked to real-world entities, such as a customer order or a part number. Objects share a common structure and a common behavior between the client and the server applications; methods are operations used to change the state of SunRAI objects. Object/methods are easier to extend and maintain than standard transactions and procedures.

SunRAI object/methods are abstractions for managing application-specific transactions and procedures. SunRAI object/methods can map to one or more transactions on the server application's database, create or destroy object instances, and query the state or update one or more attributes.

Note – SunRAI object/methods do not incorporate the concept of inheritance that is a characteristic of many object-based methodologies.

SunRAI Architecture

SunRAI contains a set of front-end (client) and a set of remote (server) application components. The client components include the Front-end Application Programming Interface Library (FAPL), an Object Resolution Table (ORT), and the Client Message Handler (CMH). The remote components include the Remote Application Programming Interface Library (RAPL), an ORT, the Server Message Handler (SMH), and the Application Server (AS).

Note – The Application Server is not part of SunRAI; an Application Server must be written for each remote application.

SunRAI integrates the client application and the server application; however, it is *not* part of either application. Figure B-1 illustrates the SunRAI architecture.

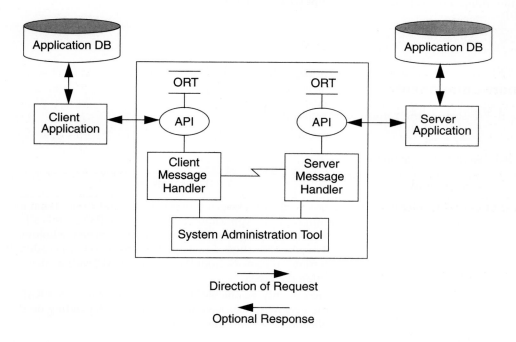

Figure B-1   SunRAI Architecture

Client Components

Table B-2 describes the client components.

Table B-2   SunRAI Client Components

Component	Description
Client Message Handler (CMH)	Transmits messages from the client to a designated server application. It ensures that all messages are sequenced and logged. Each CMH handles messages from single or multiple clients. The CMH also monitors message traffic and collects useful data for tuning SunRAI. There can only be one CMH in a node; however, a SunRAI implementation may have multiple nodes, depending on the application load and the message volume.
Front-end Application Programming Interface Library (FAPI)	A set of function calls that the client application uses to communicate with the CMH.

Remote Components

Table B-3 describes the remote components.

Table B-3   SunRAI Remote Components

Component	Description
Server Message Handler (SMH)	Receives client messages from the CMH and routes them to the appropriate Application Server (AS). SMH controls all AS processes. A background process monitors message volume and increases or shuts down applications servers as needed. It also routes responses from the AS to the originating client through the CMH. There can only be one SMH in a node; however, a SunRAI implementation may have multiple nodes, depending on the application load and the message volume.
Remote Application Programming Interface Library (RAPI)	A set of function calls used by the AS to translate messages to send to the application server. The AS uses the RAPI to communicate with the SMH.

Table B-3   SunRAI Remote Components (Continued)

Component	Description
Object Resolution Table (ORT)	Performs client and server functions. Each server application has a separate ORT. Each ORT maps object/methods to specific transactions. RAPI uses the ORT to translate a client's object/method messages into server specific transactions.
	A copy of the ORT resides on the CMH to enable the CMH to construct message keys. Message keys contain data required to sequence dependent transactions.
Application Server (AS)	SunRAI requires an application server to exchange messages between a client and a remote application. When a client sends a SunRAI message, the message must be translated by the RAPI into a valid server transaction. The AS executes this valid transaction and returns a response to the client.

B

The Sun Paperless Reporter C ≣

Note – This tool is available through SunIntegration Services.

The Sun Paperless Reporter provides a generalized data distribution mechanism and an on-line report viewing tool. It supports and distributes reports generated on mainframes, HP3000s and UNIX production servers to users throughout the world. The Sun Paperless Reporter supplements or replaces printing technology with a display-oriented solution providing on-line viewing of "printed" output. In addition, the tool encourages the use of the display device as the standard output media, thus encouraging the movement toward a paperless office.

The tool can also be used to distribute data downloaded from the mainframe to UNIX systems using standard UNIX commands. Once on the server, the download can be loaded into other products such as Sybase or Lotus for further processing. This tool has the same functionality and security as defined by some mainframe products; in addition, it also meets Sun's requirement to archive data to tape for off-site retention.

Figure C-1 shows a pictorial view of the Sun Paperless Reporter.

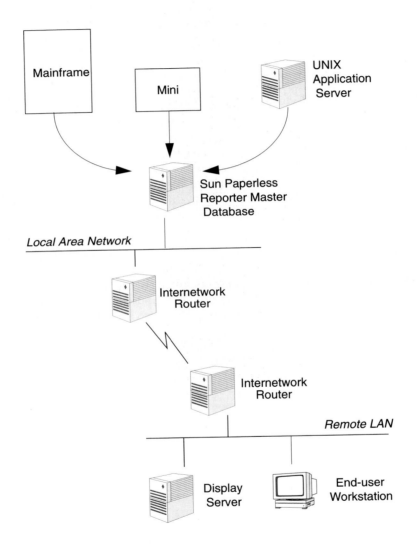

Figure C-1   Distributed Viewing (Sun Paperless Reporter)

Features of the Sun Paperless Reporter

Table C-1 describes some of the features of the Sun Paperless Reporter.

Table C-1   Features of the Sun Paperless Reporter

Feature	Description
On-line report viewing	Provides on-line viewing of IT-generated reports to reduce the physical number of printed report pages and the associated distribution problems.
Data distribution	Provides an automated data distribution function that distributes both IT-controlled and user-controlled reports. Reports are distributed to users by copying the report out to the Sun Paperless Reporter servers local to the users. Once on the server, the reports appear to the user as standard UNIX files and can also be directly accessed by other processes.
Application execution	Supports execution of applications under its Viewing Tool, allowing users to select an application which the Viewing Tool then executes. Executing applications under the Viewing Tool provides a secure and consistent platform because initiation of the Viewing Tool requires the user to enter a password.
Security	Provides a secure environment where data access and integrity is controlled. Only authorized users can access a given report, and access is limited to read-only requests to ensure the integrity of the data. The access information is maintained in a database with a restricted set of update authorized users.

Distributing Reports

The Sun Paperless Reporter can receive distribution requests from several sources. Each separate source uses a separate mechanism, which creates a standardized Sun Paperless Reporter distribution request. This standardization is essential to providing the user with a consistent view of the data. Regardless of source, the report is copied to the appropriate Sun Paperless Reporter servers, and authorized users are given access.

Since the Sun Paperless Reporter distribution is automatic, it can be made very reliable. Reports generated by the mainframe and by Sun workstations can be created, loaded into the Sun Paperless Reporter, and distributed without human intervention to standard UNIX file systems on local file servers.

C

Reports are loaded into the Sun Paperless Reporter from several sources, each via a different mechanism. Although different, each mechanism provides the report, the report name, and information about the source. The tool derives a list of receiving servers and users for this report from the report name and converts the distribution information and report into an internal distribution request. Table C-2 describes the sources of reports.

Table C-2   Sources for Reports

Source	Description
Mainframe	Mainframe reports are loaded using the Sun product SunLink Data Exchange Feature. A Sun workstation is channel-attached to the mainframe and emulates a mainframe NJE node. The Sun Paperless Reporter automatically receives reports as they arrive on this Sun NJE node.
Sun	Reports can be loaded into and distributed from an arbitrary source on the Sun network.
HP	HP reports are loaded using a tape.

Both mainframe and Sun workstation distribution requests are completely automated. Using standard mainframe tools, mainframe generated reports automatically can be created, loaded into the Sun Paperless Reporter, and distributed to the users without any human intervention.

The Sun Paperless Reporter distributes reports by copying them to the appropriate Sun Paperless Reporter servers into a shared directory. Users provide a pointer to their own directory in order to access the reports they are authorized to view. In this manner, several users on a given Sun Paperless Reporter server have access to the same report, and the disk storage is shared among users on the server (not on their local workstations).

Viewing Reports

The definition of who views the reports, the servers that store the user's reports, and which users are authorized to view reports are all maintained in a Sybase database. This database is also used to maintain distribution request queues.

Individual directories on a Sun Paperless Reporter server contain the reports each user is authorized to view. Users can either view these reports (in compressed ASCII format) using the Viewing tool or access them via standard UNIX commands. Users view the reports from their workstation and print only the sections of the report they require to their local desktop printer. Reports generated on the mainframe (for example, Cullinet™), Sun (for example, FrameMaker, and InterLeaf) or HP (for example, General Ledger™) are all accessible from the same user directory using the same Viewing Tool.

The distribution features allow users to share user-generated reports (such as status reports, organization charts, and design documents) with other users supported on the worldwide network.

Users can also request the Sun Paperless Reporter to distribute arbitrary data as a report and then use this report as input data to another process. For example, customized mainframe data extracts could be distributed as Sun Paperless Reporter "reports." Each time a new "report" arrives, a user-supplied script can be initiated which processes the data further.

Maintaining Report Access and Distribution Information

A Sybase database is used to maintain the report access and distribution information. All reports, users, and servers are defined in this database, along with the definition of which users can view which reports. For each new distribution request, the Sun Paperless Reporter queries this database to determine which servers need a copy, and on that server, which users need access. Reports are distributed based on information maintained in this database.

A database maintenance application is also provided. This application supports updates, additions, queries, and reporting on the tables in the Sun Paperless Reporter database.

Benefits of the Sun Paperless Reporter

Reports are available to the users as soon as they are loaded into the Sun Paperless Reporter. Distribution starts as soon as the report is loaded, an advantage over centralized report printing where the distribution is provided by couriers.

C

ServiceDesk

ServiceDesk is an integrated suite of tools that enables users to quickly and easily submit work requests and trouble tickets—on-line. It automatically routes requests to the responsible technician and enables that technician to immediately act on the user's specified desktop needs. In addition, ServiceDesk provides users with real-time status updates and task progress notification. It is intended for all personnel working on a desktop and for technicians responsible for maintaining desktop computing environments.

▼ If you are a user in need, ServiceDesk helps you by doing the following:

- Reduces the time and paperwork required to submit a work request
- Enables you to enter and track requests electronically
- Automatically provides—via email and in real time—the status of each item of your request
- Provides a communication link between you and the technician performing the work
- Allows others to submit work requests for you
- Provides you with a mechanism to rate the quality and timeliness of service performed

▼ If you are an SA, ServiceDesk helps you by doing the following:

- Streamlines the process of moving personnel and departments
- Automatically updates the POSS database
- Improves coordination between you and other support groups working on related tasks
- Alerts you to aged work requests and trouble tickets
- Automatically routes service tasks to the appropriate technician

▼ If you are a service manager, ServiceDesk helps you by doing the following:

- Enables you to track the hours spent per technician, per task, and so forth
- Provides a single tool to gather statistics on all provided services
- Improves coordination among service groups

- Enables you to set up scheduled reporting and automatic execution of report program runs on a monthly, weekly, or daily basis

This appendix provides an overview of ServiceDesk, including:

- Relationship to the Information Technology (IT) service model
- Functions, features, and objectives
- Interface to the Point of Sevice System (POSS) database
- Integrated tools — DeskTop, Technician, and Feedback
- Information flow between the three tools
- Reporting capabilities

ServiceDesk Introduction

This section provides an introduction to the ServiceDesk suite of graphical tools and explains the IT service model from which this application was built.

ServiceDesk, an integrated suite of customer service tools, clearly demonstrates Sun's commitment to customer satisfaction. In a nutshell, ServiceDesk enables all users to quickly and easily submit and track work requests and trouble tickets—on-line.

The ServiceDesk application comprises three graphical tools:

1. ServiceDesk's DeskTop Tool automatically routes a work request or trouble ticket from the user's desktop to his/her System Administrator (SA). It also provides users with the status of work requests, and notifies users once every task is completed.

2. ServiceDesk's Technician Tool enables the SA and/or technician to immediately act on the user's specified desktop needs.

3. ServiceDesk's Feedback Tool ensures the highest level of customer satisfaction. Users rate the quality and timeliness of the service performed and are assured serious consideration of all comments submitted.

To truly understand the intent and function of ServiceDesk, it is important to understand the service philosophy and how it benefits the entire user community at Sun.

Service Philosophy

Sun's overriding goal is to consistently provide users with personalized, timely, and high-quality service. In order to attain that goal, IT realized the need for a new service model—one that could dramatically and cost-effectively improve existing service practices and procedures. This service model centers around the concept of the *desktop* and a System Administrator for each user.

"Desktop" Defined

In terms of this new service model, a desktop consists of a user's

- Workstation hardware
- Telephone and associated voice service options (e.g., audix)
- Operating system and application software
- Network connectivity

While each user is responsible for requesting service, the actual installation, maintenance, software support, and service of this desktop is the ultimate responsibility of the user's System Administrator.

Desktop System Administrator

Each user now has his/her own System Administrator (SA). While the SA must handle the service needs of multiple users, each user has a single, consistent point-of-contact for all the user's desktop service needs. All services are provided at the lowest possible cost. The SA is accountable not only for receiving service requests, but for managing (and in many cases performing) the work required in the fastest, most professional, and most personalized manner. The SA is also responsible for keeping each assigned user apprised of work status.

The SA may not actually perform all desktop-related service tasks, but he/she is responsible for monitoring the user's satisfaction with all submitted requests. The SA is aware of all requests submitted by the assigned user and is responsible for making sure that the entire service process runs smoothly. The SA may have to coordinate the activities of several technicians to solve complex problems, but, ultimately, the SA is responsible for the work performed and for the level of customer satisfaction.

SAs use ServiceDesk to monitor any work taking place on behalf of their users. In this way, ServiceDesk is used as the communication link between the end-user, the SA, and the technician(s) involved.

Commitment to Customer Satisfaction

Customer satisfaction is ServiceDesk's highest priority. The tools are easy to use, and require minimal data entry. For example, if the user doesn't want to enter any data, the SA or technician is responsible for calling the user and obtaining the necessary information.

ServiceDesk's Feedback Tool also emphasizes the commitment to customer satisfaction. ServiceDesk wants feedback on every request—not just once a year from an annual survey. If the work is not performed adequately, there will be follow-up to determine the reason.

D

ServiceDesk Overview

This section lists ServiceDesk objectives, describes its interface to POSS, and explains its numerous functions, features, and requirements.

ServiceDesk Objectives

ServiceDesk was conceived out of the desire and commitment to improve customer service within Sun. In conjunction with the improved service model (described earlier under "ServiceDesk Introduction"), ServiceDesk is designed to:

- Improve service responsiveness
- Eliminate the paperwork previously required to submit a work request
- Eliminate the potential for "lost" paperwork
- Reduce the time required to submit work requests
- Enable users to electronically submit and track their work requests
- Automatically route on-line requests to the appropriate technician(s)
- Update the Point of Service System (POSS) database with information related to work performed on computing assets
- Improve the coordination of efforts between support groups working on related requests
- Provide a feedback mechanism by which to evaluate and measure customer satisfaction, as well as technician performance
- Improve report processing and generation
- Streamline the process of requesting and tracking services, for both end-users and technicians
- Streamline the process for moving people and departments

A later section, entitled "ServiceDesk Tools," explains the three integrated ServiceDesk tools and how they work together to accomplish the above objectives.

Interface To POSS

ServiceDesk interfaces to POSS, the database that tracks the following computing assets within Sun:

- Workstations

- Telephones
- Network devices
- Software

To be an effective system, POSS must reflect all changes to computing assets (e.g., memory added to a workstation). The ServiceDesk interface to POSS, then, enables the technician/user to request the change (e.g., add memory) via ServiceDesk. When the technician completes the task, an automatic update is sent to POSS so that the integrity of the hardware inventory data remains intact. This interface is of particular benefit to technicians, in that it precludes them from having to access POSS to update this database.

ServiceDesk also uses POSS as a data source. Employee, location, telephone, and hardware information displayed in ServiceDesk windows is all derived from POSS.

Task Authorization

ServiceDesk DeskTop and Technician tools enable users and technicians to request certain tasks on-line. Some tasks, due to their expense and severity, require authorization by the user's manager before they can be processed. The authorization process is automatically activated when the user requests a task requiring authorization. The manager is notified via email as soon as the request is submitted, and the request stays on hold until an authorization has been issued.

Documentation and Training

Because the DeskTop and Feedback tools are intuitive, graphical, and easy to use, there is no written documentation required. There is, however, on-line help for each of these tools. Users of the DeskTop tool can also watch a brief, on-line video demonstration of the tool's functions and procedures.

ServiceDesk Tools

This section provides a detailed description of each ServiceDesk tool and explains the flow of data into and out of the ServiceDesk application.

DeskTop Tool

The DeskTop Tool is available to every workstation that meets the ServiceDesk requirements. In order to streamline the process of submitting work requests, the DeskTop Tool:

- Reduces the time and paperwork required to submit a work request

- Enables users to enter and track requests electronically

- Provides a means to submit requests on behalf of other users

- Automatically provides status (via email) and real-time status (via the Status Inquiry button) of each item of a work request

- Automatically notifies the user when each task has been completed

The DeskTop Tool is extremely easy to use and is essentially a simplified, electronic version of the previously used paper work requests. The user enters only as much information as he/she has, or wishes, to enter; the user's SA is responsible for contacting the user to obtain any necessary information that was not provided on-line.

The base window, illustrated in Figure D-1, enables the user to specify the type of request to be submitted (i.e., telephone, workstation, network, or software service/support).

The Demo button allows a user to run a short instructional presentation on the use and operation of the DeskTop Tool.

Figure D-1   DeskTop Tool Base Window

Once the type of request has been selected, a window prompts for the necessary information. For example, Figure D-2 illustrates a typical ServiceDesk Telephone Service work request window.

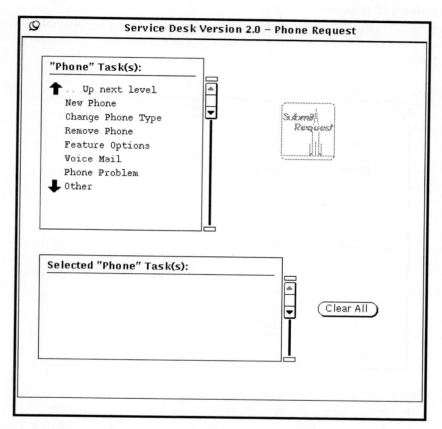

Figure D-2   DeskTop Tool Telephone Service Window

Users of the Desktop Tool can request service for their workstation, network connection, software applications, and their telephone. The request submission process (in this case for telephone service) is as follows:

1. The user selects the appropriate task from the Phone Request window, and one or two of the following pop-up windows typically appears:

- One pop-up window displays existing information (provided by POSS) about the service/equipment (this window does not open if the user is requesting a new equipment).
- The other pop-up window (termed the *data collection* window) prompts for information still required.
- If the user selects the "Problem" option (e.g., Phone Problem), a special *data collection* window (as shown in Figure D-3) displaying a selectable list of common problems will open.

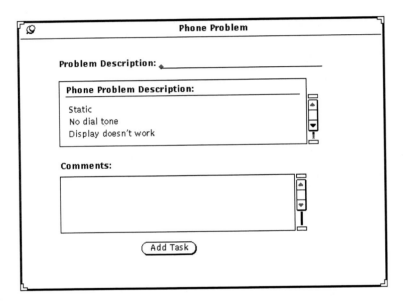

Figure D-3   Example of a "Problem" Window

2. The user completes or fills out as much of the data collection window as desired.

3. The user clicks SELECT on the Add Task button (situated in the Data-Collection window). This action adds the task to the Selected Phone Item(s) pane.

4. Steps 1 through 3 should be repeated for each additional task requested. When all tasks have been added to the Selected Phone Item(s) pane, the user clicks SELECT on the Submit Request icon.

Note – Users must submit separate service requests for distinct job types. For example, workstation tasks and phone tasks cannot be submitted on the same service request.

5. The user may also modify or delete a task by highlighting the task and then changing the information in the data collection window. The Clear All button enables the user to clear all information entered and start again (provided the user has not clicked SELECT on the Submit Request icon).

6. The user may check on the status of the request at any time, simply by clicking SELECT on the Status Inquiry button in the Desktop Tool base window.

Technician Tool

The Technician Tool is used by SAs to perform daily job functions. It enables support staff to:

- Receive on-line work requests

- Take action on submitted requests

- Document service activity performed

- Streamline the process of moving personnel and departments

- Improve coordination among support groups working on related tasks

- Provide status information to the end-user

- Notify the user when each task is completed

- Request the user's feedback on the quality of service performed

- Update the POSS database with changes in telephone, hardware configuration, and/or other asset data

- Generate and schedule production of reports relating to services performed

- Analyze hours spent per desktop, per technician, and so forth, based on data collected by the tool

Figure D-4 illustrates the base Work Queue window, which automatically opens after the technician logs in to the Technician Tool. From this window, the technician takes action on a particular task.

Task_Id	Owner	Status	F	Last_Name	Submit_Time	Task_Full_Name	Pr
654-A	cwrs	Submitted	e	cagle	01/07/93 13:16	Phone/Voice Mail	0
653-A	cwrs	Submitted	e	cagle	01/07/93 13:15	Phone/Voice Mail	0
652-A	cwrs	Submitted	d	coburn	01/07/93 10:08	Phone/New Phone	0

Work Queue — Find ▽, Request... ▽, Print ▽, Reports ▽, System Maint ▽

No new tasks received — 42 Record(s) Returned

Figure D-4   ServiceDesk Technician Tool Base Window

Feedback Tool

ServiceDesk includes a built-in feedback mechanism called the Feedback Tool. Once a work request has been completed, the Technician Tool automatically emails the requestor and includes an attachment to the message. The user simply double-clicks on the attachment icon to display the Feedback Tool window, illustrated in Figure D-5.

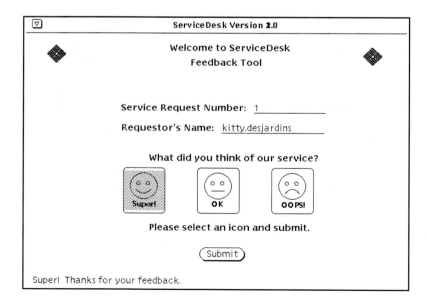

Figure D-5   Feedback Tool Window

Once the user responds to the on-line survey, he/she clicks the Submit button to route the information back to the ServiceDesk database. The response is then brought to the attention of the SA, who responds appropriately.

The Feedback Tool emphasizes ServiceDesk's commitment to quality and its interest in serving its users. It goes far beyond the "annual survey" approach to service feedback and solicits user comments on how each and every service request was handled. The on-line feedback provided is collected and analyzed continually. If a service request is not resolved adequately, properly, and/or in a timely manner, the situation is addressed and the reason is discovered. Such service problems will be rectified and corrected, and the service level improved in the future.

Information Flow

Information flows into and out of the ServiceDesk application as follows:

1. The user submits an on-line work request using ServiceDesk's DeskTop Tool.

2. The user's request is received into the ServiceDesk Sybase database, and is then routed to ServiceDesk's Technician Tool for service dispatch.

3. The technician updates the ServiceDesk database with status information on work performed.

4. Using the Technician Tool, the technician emails the user to provide service status information.

5. Once the job is completed, the SA notifies the user (via email) of work completed. An attachment, ServiceDesk's Feedback Tool, accompanies the notification.

6. The user rates the timeliness and quality of service performed and returns any feedback (via email) to the ServiceDesk database.

Figure D-6 is an actual example of a monthly report generated by the feedback received.

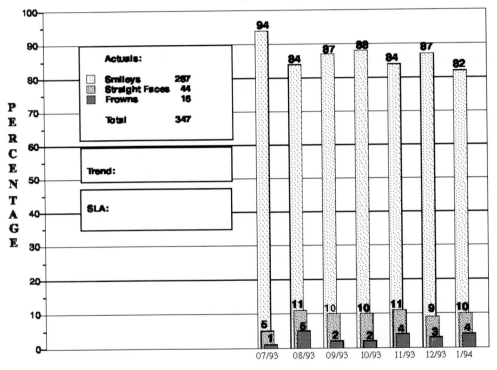

Figure D-6   Example of ServiceDesk Rating Report

An Example Morning Report

Note – This tool is available through SunIntegration Services.

The example in this appendix was taken from an actual morning report. See Chapter 8, "System Management Tools," for a detailed description of the tool that provides this report.

```
                        DATA CENTER MORNING REPORT
  Wednesday                                                  May 11, 1994


     -----------------------------------------------------------------
  |           Availability in 24-hour Period (07:00 through 07:00)        |
     -----------------------------------------------------------------
  |                                                                       |
  |          ************ Unix Production Systems **************          |
  |                                                                       |
  |Day/Hi      System       Application     Uptime   Mins   Percent   Outages |
  |=======     ======       ===========     ======   ====   =======   ======= |
  |328/328     casdata      score           24-hrs   1440   100.0%        |
  |121/202     costlog      costlog         00-20    1200   100.0%        |
  |345/345     dividends    dividends       8-18     600    100.0%        |
  |508/508                  futures         8-19     660    100.0%        |
  |177/177     falcon       fixed/assets    24       1440   100.0%        |
  |131/155     forecast     costmgt         00-21    1260   100.0%        |
  |168/168     forecast1    costmgt         00-21    1260   100.0%        |
  |111/202     hrisun1      caps            06-18    720    100.0%        |
  |512/512     hrisun2      WWHR-rollup     06-18    720    100.0%        |
  |172/262     hrisun3      caps            06-18    720    100.0%        |
  |283/283     journal      thejournal      8-18     600    100.0%        |
  |168/264     inqcas       inqcas          07-18    600    100.0%        |
  |252/252     iropux1                      24-hrs   1440   100.0%        |
  |398/398                  netadmin        03-23    1200   100.0%        |
  |398/398                  wwinv           24-hrs   1440   100.0%        |
```

```
|398/398                     mtbf           24-hrs   1440   100.0%          |
|336/336                     sunirs         24-hrs   1440   100.0%          |
|313/313    iropux3                         24-hrs   1440   100.0%          |
|336/336                     autoload       6-21      900   100.0%          |
|380/380                     bbb-email      6-21      900   100.0%          |
|336/336                     EDI            24-hrs   1440   100.0%          |
|380/380                     scc-email      6-21      900   100.0%          |
|243/243    midway           midway         23-20    1260   100.0%          |
|166/264    opsybase         opsybase       24-hrs   1440   100.0%          |
| 82/173    portfolio        portfolio      24-hrs   1440   100.0%          |
|268/268    sgclubhouse      sunglobe       24-hrs   1440   100.0%          |
| 13/171    sggolfbag        sunglobe       24-hrs   1440   100.0%          |
| 77/171    sggolfclub       sunglobe       24-hrs   1440   100.0%          |
|432/432    sggolfcart       sunglobe       24-hrs   1440   100.0%          |
|122/165    sggolfball       sunglobe       24-hrs   1440   100.0%          |
|110/177    sgwatertrap      sunglobe       24-hrs   1440   100.0%          |
|197/197    sgsandtrap       sunglobe       24-hrs   1440   100.0%          |
|144/274    sgscorecard      sunglobe       24-hrs   1440   100.0%          |
|108/108    sgteedoff        suncap         24-hrs   1440   100.0%          |
|512/512    srprod1          sunrai         24-hrs   1440   100.0%          |
|511/511    srprod2          sunrai         24-hrs   1440   100.0%          |
| 93/133    sunbias          sunbias        04-00    1200   100.0%          |
|304/304    themint          themints       6-18      720   100.0%          |
|304/304    varmint          acts           8-19      660   100.0%          |
|448/448                     brokers        8-19      660   100.0%          |
|221/221    varuna           acts           8-19      660   100.0%          |
|233/340    viewmaster       viewmaster     24-hrs   1440   100.0%          |
|  2/270    viewmasterbs-bb  viewmaster     24-hrs   1440   100.0%          |
|308/308    viewmaster1      viewmaster     24-hrs   1440   100.0%          |
|269/375    viewmaster2      viewmaster     24-hrs   1440   100.0%          |
|462/462    viewmaster3      viewmaster     24-hrs   1440   100.0%          |
|743/743    vips             vips           8-19      660   100.0%          |
|211/339    wwfocascade      cascade        24-hrs   1440   100.0%          |
|                                                                          |
|Explanation of outages:                                                   |
 --------------------------------------------------------------------------
```

```
                    DATA CENTER MORNING REPORT


    ---------------------------------        ---------------------------------
    |         DCS Statistics        |        |        SOtool Statistics       |
    |-------------------------------|        |--------------------------------|
    | DCS Extracts created......03.08|        |  #Application Trans.....143,546|
    | DCS CCDs online...........03:38|        |  #System Transactions...348,557|
    | DCS CAS Q  (07:00)..........99|        |  Response Avg(seconds).....1.67|
    | DCS CAS1 Q (07:00)...........0|        |  #Users: High-water mark....550|
    |                               |        |  Avg # Thru-out day........502|
    ---------------------------------        ---------------------------------


    *******************************************************************************
    **                                                                         **
    **                  Sunglobe and Score information                         **
    *******************************************************************************
    **                                                                         **
    **   End User schedules finished at 01:35                                  **
    **                                                                         **
    **        BBB schedules finished at 00:48                                  **
    **                                                                         **
    *******************************************************************************
    **      Score Information         |        Sunglobe Information           **
    *******************************************************************************
    **                                                                         **
    **   Data Ready for download at 01:37  |   Data Ready for download at :    **
    **   The Load began at 02:21           |   The Load began at :             **
    **   The Load finished at  04:39       |   The Load finished at :          **
    **   The Application online at 04:44   |   The Application online at :     **
    **                                                                         **
    *******************************************************************************



    Notes:
```

```
    <---------------------Status of Production Reports----------------->

    ------------------------------------
    |          Abends/Exceptions        |
    ------------------------------------

     UNIX: vista


    ------------------------------------
    |     Unresolved Abends             |
    ------------------------------------

     UNIX: none

    ------------------------------------
    |     Jobs Not Yet Completed        |
    ------------------------------------

     UNIX: none
```

```
                    DATA CENTER MORNING REPORT

Wednesday                                            May 11, 1994

-----------------------------------------------------------------
          Availability in 24-hour Period (07:00 through 07:00)
-----------------------------------------------------------------

           *************  Mainframe Systems  ***********

  Day/Hi   System       Application   Uptime   Mins   Percent   Outages
  =======  ======       ===========   ======   ====   =======   =======
   87/196  MVS1                       24-hrs   1440   100.0%
   87/235               TPX           24-hrs   1440   100.0%
   57/71                IDMSPROD      2130-21  1410   100.0%
   87/157               IDMSSHAD      2130-21  1410   100.0%
   87/196               TSO1          24-hrs   1440   100.0%
   87/306  MVS2                       24-hrs   1440   100.0%
   84/193               IDMSPRD2      2130-21  1410   100.0%
   87/310               IDMSPREP      06-21    900    100.0%
   87/285               IDMSDEVL      06-01    1140   100.0%
   87/310               IDMSPILT      01-19    1140   100.0%
   87/169               IDMSICMS      01-19    1140   100.0%
   87/273               TSO2          24-hrs   1440   100.0%
  129/310  VM/XA                      24-hrs   1440   100.0%
  129/310  VM/SP        Control       24-hrs   1440   100.0%

           *************  HP Systems  ************

  Day/Hi   System       Application   Uptime   Mins   Percent   Outages
  =======  ======       ===========   ======   ====   =======   =======
  463/463  HERA         FMS           24-hrs   1440   100.0%
  407/407  ZEUS         FMS           24-hrs   1440   100.0%
  610/610  HARPO                      24-hrs   1440   100.0%

Outages:
-----------------------------------------------------------------
```

An Example Morning Report   219

```
                    DATA CENTER MORNING REPORT


-----------------------------------        ------------------------------------
|      Production JOB Status      |        |      Production REPORT Status     |
-----------------------------------        ------------------------------------
|Total Production Jobs     1,063|          |Scheduled Prod Reports        454|
|      (MVS=966     HP=97 )      |         |      (MVS=452     HP=2   )       |
|                               |          |On-time A history          5/124|
|                               |          |A's Due 08:00  (169/169)    100%|
|                               |          |B's Due 08:00  ( 54/54 )    100%|
|                               |          ------------------------------------
-----------------------------------


-----------------------------------        ------------------------------------
|      IDMSPROD STATISTICS       |         |      IDMSPRD2 STATISTICS        |
-----------------------------------        ------------------------------------
|CORPDB Online            21:05|           |DPLXDB Online            21:05|
|#Users: High-water mark    279|           |#Users: High-water mark     97|
|#Users: Thru-out day       978|           |#Users: Thru-out day       519|
|Systems transaction   345,853|            |Systems tranactions     50,470|
|Times at Max Tasks           0|           |Times at Max Tasks           0|
-----------------------------------        ------------------------------------


-----------------------------------        ------------------------------------
|    IDMSPROD APPLICATION STATS  |         |    IDMSPRD2 APPLICATION STATS   |
-----------------------------------        ------------------------------------
| Appl Transactions     276,850|           | Appl Transactions      27,884|
| <1 sec Response         95.71|           | <1 sec Response         96.47|
| >3 sec Response          0.61|           | >3 sec Response          0.71|
| Appl Abends                 1|           | Appl Abends                 0|
| Appl Deadlocks             51|           | Appl Deadlocks              0|
-----------------------------------        ------------------------------------


-----------------------------------        ------------------------------------
|     Application Statistics     |         |     Miscellaneous Statitics     |
-----------------------------------        ------------------------------------
| BBB Extracts            01:43|           | MVS1 Avg Cpu 8:00-5:00    31.7%|
| Inqcas to Mfgpro        19:54|           | MVS2 Avg Cpu 8:00-5:00    19.4%|
| VM_Control Availability   yes|           | MVS Tape Mounts           467|
|                               |          | Total Print Pages      44,534|
-----------------------------------        ------------------------------------


Notes:
```

```
                    DATA CENTER MORNING REPORT

  <--------------------Status of Production Reports------------------->

--------------------------------------
|        Abends/Exceptions          |
--------------------------------------
  MVS : jeic016d,jcic016d
  H/P : none


--------------------------------------
|      Unresolved Abends            |
--------------------------------------
  MVS : none
  H/P : none


--------------------------------------
|      Jobs Not Yet Completed       |
--------------------------------------
  MVS : none
  H/P : none


--------------------------------------
|    Reports not Printed By 08:00   |
--------------------------------------
          "A"          "B"
         none          none
```

E

Sun ConsoleServer

Note – This tool is available through SunIntegration Services.

One of the tools we implemented in our "lights-out" production environment was Sun ConsoleServer. Console servers give technical personnel console-port access to many servers from a workstation on the network. This access normally eliminates the need to address a server via a character terminal physically attached to the server. Console servers give system programmers/administrators remote access to servers for diagnostics and root access from any workstation across the network, including both internet and modem access.

The basic functions of the console server provide:

- Automatic sensing of hostname or host state of all systems connected to the desktop serial lines

- Ability to configure the console window environment with labeled icons and windows as well as a pull-down menu

- Utilities that interface to CU, giving useful feedback by checking to see if the requested resource is in use

- Utility that gives exact location of a specified host connected to the console server

Some of the benefits of Sun ConsoleServer are:

- The ability to keep an electronic log of all messages that go to the console in the system by tracking console error messages for future debugging

- Local and remote access to multiple servers even when they are down

Figure F-1 shows the concept of the Sun ConsoleServer.

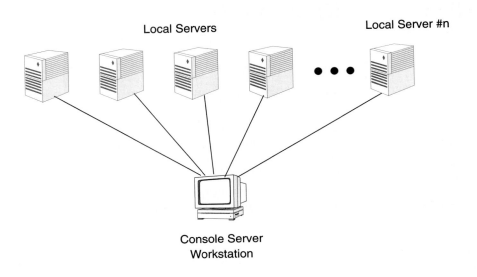

Figure F-1   Sun ConsoleServer

A system programmer can log in on to the system from home via the Xterminal to a console server and perform analysis related to network problems (if required), to system or hardware problems, and to reboot any server immediately. This access allows the technician to perform all analysis from home, eliminating the need to drive into work; it also eliminates the need for computer operator intervention. This is what 99.9% availability is all about.

Controls Multiple Hosts from a Single Desktop

Sun ConsoleServer replaces multiple ASCII terminals serving as system consoles with a single desktop SPARCstation. The use of Sun ConsoleServer reduces total hardware cost while saving on space and power consumption. Sun ConsoleServer also offers several additional benefits. It allows support staff to control multiple systems from a single location in the data center; it keeps a log history of console messages; and it permits support staff to access the console functions from remote locations.

When a system problem occurs, support staff often need to know what messages have gone to the console. An ordinary terminal can keep only a screenful or two and then the information is lost. The Sun ConsoleServer solution using OpenWindows allows one to keep a log of all messages that go to console with virtually no limit.

By placing the server console connections on a Sun system, the support staff gains network access to a server's console from a remote location, such as the office or home. This can eliminate unnecessary travel and save time. Combined, these abilities — resource savings, logging, and remote access — make Sun ConsoleServer a very attractive alternative to the one-terminal-per-server solution.

Sun ConsoleServer includes utilities for the following functions:

- Automatic sensing of hostname and host state

- Configuration of the console window environment with labeled icons and windows as well as a pull-down menu

- Establishment of serial line connection to a host's console

- Determining the physical wire on which a given host is attached

Table F-1 describes features and benefits of the Sun ConsoleServer.

Table F-1   Features and Benefits of Sun ConsoleServer

Features	Benefits
Replaces up to 24 or more ASCII terminals with a single SPARC desktop footprint.	• Saves space • Reduces power consumption and heat load • Provides a convenient single control location in the data center • Decreases hardware cost
OpenWindows front end	• Easy point-and-click interface
Automatic configuration	• Eases initial installation with large numbers of hosts
Console log history	• Enables support staff to diagnose problems more quickly • Reduces downtime
Ability to access any console over the network	• Saves support staff's time • Reduces travel costs • Reduces downtime

F

At Sun, Sun ConsoleServer has been deployed in server rooms around the world. Sun administrators perform remote administration on multiple servers, even when they are down or unreachable. This ability to perform remote system administration has allowed administrators to solve problems from home any time of the day or night.

Measuring Performance

Measuring performance on an on going basis is key to providing high RAS. The discipline of "managing what you measure" is the methodology used to track and report performance as it relates to the services provided. It is also a way to communicate service levels as negotiated between the customers of the service and the service providers.

This appendix contains examples of two service level reports:

- The Metrics Report
  This report is a measurement (metric) of key system indicators to both manage and assess the overall performance of all systems to the end-user.

- The Focus Report
  This report is provided to senior IT management of key metrics that measure against overall IT service goals. It also contains the 6-Sigma report used for quality improvement as it relates to the Malcolm Baldridge award for quality.

Both of these reports were developed and modified over a period of several years and were instrumental in the success of RAS at Sun. They became key communication tools for both the customer and the senior IT management team. (Similar metrics were used for tracking our mainframe environments.)

Even though a company may have different reporting and quality requirements, these examples are provided as a way to get started or to enhance existing reporting requirements.

Metrics Report

The Metrics Report is a monthly report depicting service performance to end-users. This report includes the following:

- IT System Administration — Customer Satisfaction Survey Feedback
- IT System Administration — Server Availability Area 1
- IT UNIX Data Center — System Availability
- IT System Administration — Telecommunications Work Requests
- IT System Administration — Work Requests
- IT System Administration — Telecommunications Trouble Tickets
- IT System Administration — Trouble Tickets

IT System Administration — Customer Satisfaction Survey Feedback

ServiceDesk is a problem management and reporting tool. One of its functions is to measure customer satisfaction. ServiceDesk includes a user-friendly GUI frontend that allows the end-user to double-click on one of three icon faces: a happy face, a straight (noncommital) face, and a frowning face. A happy face indicates a high level of customer satisfaction, while a frowning face indicates the customer has a problem with the service provided. When the Data Center receives a frowning face response from a customer, it is chartered to call the user back and discuss the problem. The goal is to receive no more than 2% frowning faces in any one fiscal year.

Figure G-1 shows a sample System Administration Customer Satisfaction Survey Feedback Report, which is a triple-bar chart with the x-axis depicting each month and the y-axis showing the percentage of icon face responses in each of the three categories: Smileys, Straight Faces, and Frowns.

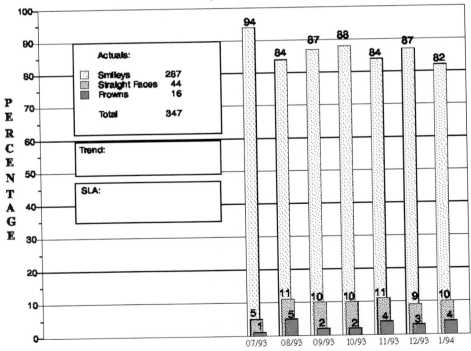

Figure G-1   Sample of an IT System Administration — Customer Satisfaction Survey Feedback Chart

IT System Administration — Server Availability Area 1

This report shows server availability for all non mission critical (but still production) servers in any one geographical territory. These servers are for the end-user environments supporting each LAN. Non-mission critical servers are *not* located in an environmentally controlled Data Center with UPS and other amenities that usually come with a Data Center. They are, however, located in secured rooms designed to hold servers. The goal is to keep the servers functioning at 100% availability with the average performance being 99.6% or better in any given month.

Figure G-2 shows a sample IT System Administration Server Availability Area 1 report, which is a single-bar chart with the x-axis depicting each month and the y-axis showing the percentage of uptime usage of these servers.

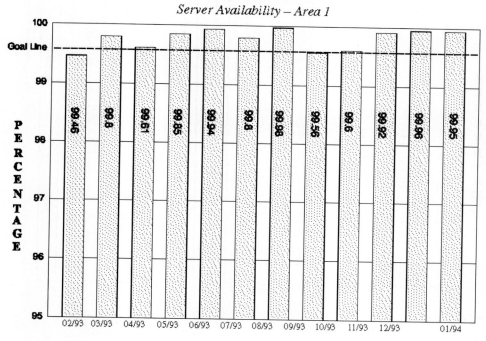

Figure G-2   Sample of an IT System Administration — Server Availability Area 1 Chart

IT UNIX Data Center — System Availability

This report shows server availability for all mission critical production servers, most of which reside in the Data Center. The goal is to keep the servers functioning at 100% availability with the average performance being 99.8% or better in any given month.

Figure G-3 shows a sample IT UNIX Data Center System Availability report, which is a single-bar chart with the x-axis depicting each month and the y-axis showing the percentage of uptime usage of these servers.

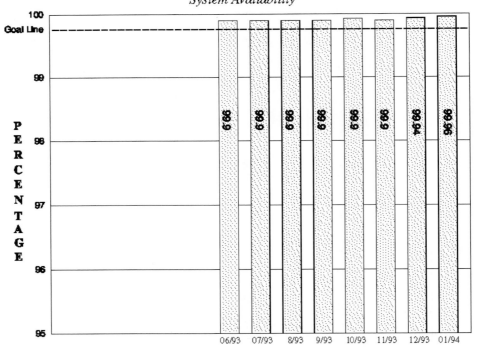

Figure G-3   Sample of IT UNIX Data Center — Server Downtime Chart

IT System Administration — Telecommunications Work Requests

This report shows the number of Work Requests (WRs) received, completed, and still outstanding by the Telecommunications group. Examples of Work Requests include a request for a new phone, an office move, or new voice mail. The goal is to complete all requests within five working days.

Figure G-4 shows a sample IT System Administration Telecommunications Work Requests report, which is a triple-bar chart with the x-axis depicting each month and the y-axis showing the number of scheduled jobs in each of three categories: Work Received, Work Completed, and Outstanding Work. (The y-axis is started at 0 scheduled jobs and goes up to 500 in increments of 50.)

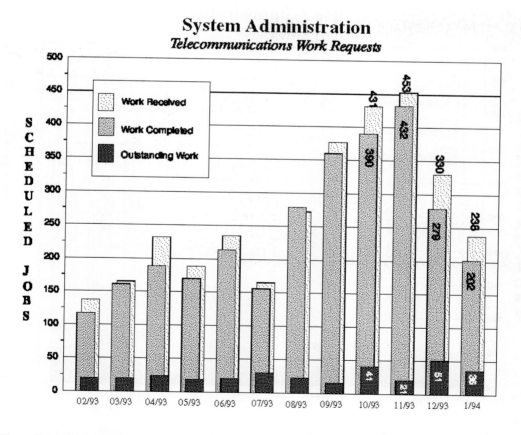

Figure G-4   Sample of an IT System Administration — Telecommunications Work Requests Chart

IT System Administration — Work Requests

This report shows the number of Work Requests (WRs) received, completed, and still outstanding by the System Administration group. Examples of these Work Requests include office moves and hardware installations or upgrades. The goal is to complete all requests within five working days.

The IT System Administration Work Requests report is a triple bar chart with the x-axis depicting each month and the y-axis showing the number of scheduled jobs in each of three categories: Work Received, Work Completed, and Outstanding Work. (The y-axis is started at 0 scheduled jobs and goes up to 600 in increments of 60.)

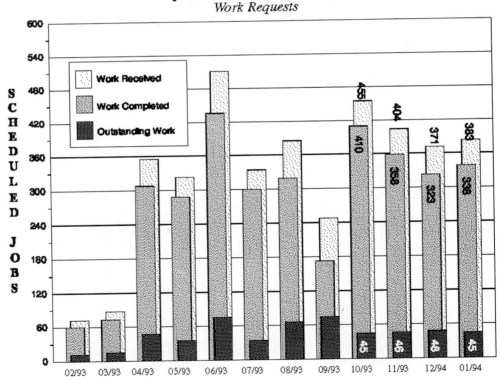

Figure G-5   Sample of an IT System Administration — Work Requests Chart

IT System Administration — Telecommunications Trouble Tickets

This report shows the number of trouble tickets (TTs) received by the Telecommunications group. Examples of these trouble tickets include LAN wiring, phone problems, and voice mail issues. The goal is respond to all trouble tickets within 2 hours and to resolve each ticket within 24 hours.

Figure G-6 shows the IT System Administration Telecommunications Trouble Tickets report, which is a single-bar chart with the x-axis depicting each month and the y-axis showing the number of scheduled jobs, that is, the number of trouble tickets received. (The y-axis is started at 0 scheduled jobs and goes up to 90 in increments of 10.)

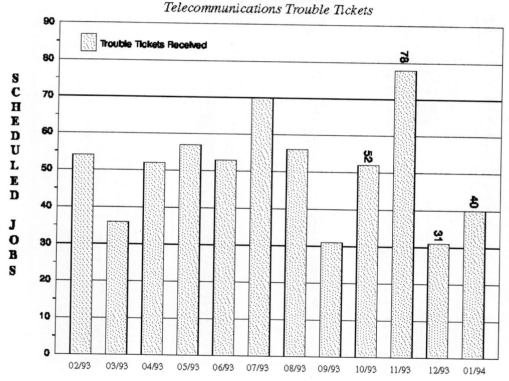

Figure G-6   Sample of an IT System Administration — Telecommunications Trouble Tickets Chart

IT System Administration — Trouble Tickets

This chart shows the number of trouble tickets (TTs) received by the System Administration staff. Examples of these trouble tickets include hardware, software, printer, or network problems. The goal is respond to all trouble tickets within 2 hours and to resolve each ticket within 24 hours.

The IT System Administration Trouble Tickets report is a double-bar chart with the x-axis depicting each month and the y-axis showing the number of scheduled jobs — both the number of trouble tickets received and the number of tickets cleared. (The y-axis is started at 0 scheduled jobs and goes up to 450 in increments of 50.)

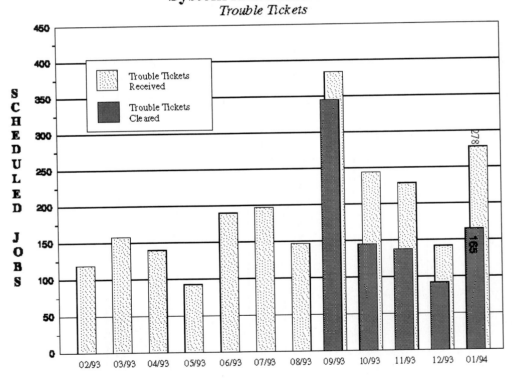

Figure G-7   Sample of an IT System Administration — Trouble Tickets Chart

Focus Report

The Focus Report is a monthly report that tracks Server Availability, Work Requests (WRs) and trouble tickets (TTs) as reported to senior IT management to assess performance against overall IT goals. This four-page report includes two pages of tabular data for each of the following categories and two pages of actual graphs for each category:

- LAN server availability
- Work requests
- Trouble tickets
- UNIX Data Center Server downtime minutes

The Focus Report produces what is known as the 6-Sigma report, which is the industry-standard reporting structure used for quality improvement for those companies who are looking to earn the Malcolm Baldrige award for quality.

LAN Server Availability

This report shows non-mission critical production server availability and is generated using data supplied by the monthly Metrics Server Report. It depicts total server availability in minutes as well as the actual downtime, also in minutes. The formula (with sample data) shown in Table G-1 is used to generate the LAN Server Availability report.

Table G-1   Formula for Generating LAN Server Availability Report

Minutes of downtime from Server Report (that is, Failures)	961
Days in the month (excluding weekends and holidays)	19
Hours in the day (= 12) x 60 minutes =	720
X the number of servers	114
= Opportunities for the month (in minutes)	82080
Opportunities minus the downtime minutes = Success	81119
Success divided by opportunities = Server % Availability	98%
(1,000,000 divided by opportunities) times Failures = DPM (defects per million)	11,708

Figure G-8 shows the graph that is generated using the data in Table G-1, which includes a single-bar chart with the x-axis depicting each month and the y-axis showing the percentage of server availability. (The y-axis begins at 95.0% and goes to 100.0% in increments of 0.5%.) On the face of each monthly bar are the number of minutes of downtime and the DPM (defects Per million).

Success is computed as follows:

- Outstanding 99.9%
- Satisfactory 99.5%
- Minimum 99.0%

In summary, this example data shows that LAN Server Availability (January) was at 98% success with 961 minutes of monthly downtime and a DPM (defects Per million) of 11,708.

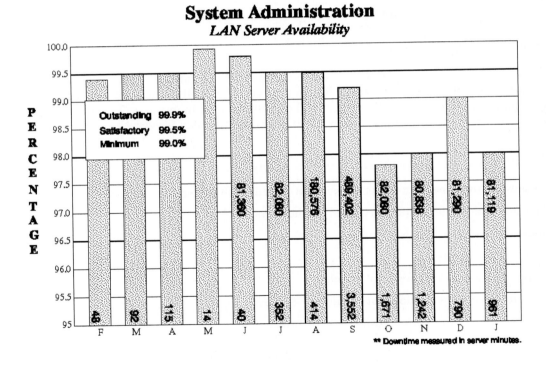

Figure G-8   Sample of a Focus Report LAN Server Availability Chart

Work Requests

This report is for tracking all system administration Work Requests (WRs) and Communication Work Requests (CWRs), such as new phones, workstation upgrades, or office moves. For each type of Work Request, two numbers are captured: the larger number is for the total number of requests that have been closed within the Service Level Agreement (SLA) time period; the smaller number is for the Work Requests that are still outstanding. The goal is to complete all requests within five working days.

Large office moves (the last two lines on the chart below) include office moves of more than five people. These are tracked separately and are coordinated with facilities, that is, they are not submitted via a Work Request.

Table G-2 shows a sample of the data needed to generate the report for Work Requests.

Table G-2   Sample Data for Work Requests Report

Number of Work Requests closed within SLA:	338
Number of Work Requests closed outside SLA (Failures):	45
Number of CWRs closed within SLA:	202
Number of CWRs closed outside SLA (Failures):	36
Number of large office Moves closed within SLA:	44
Number of large office Moves closed outside SLA (Failures):	0

Table G-3 shows the formula (with sample data) used to generate the report.

Table G-3   Formula for Generating Work Requests Report

Add (Work Requests and CWR's) that were closed within SLA	540
(WRs and CWRs) x 5 (steps) = Opportunities	2700
Moves closed within SLA =	44
Moves x 3 (steps) = Opportunities	132
Add Opportunities 2700 + 132 = Total Opportunities	2832
Add Work Requests, CWRs, and Moves closed outside SLA = Failures	81
Subtract Failures from Total Opportunities = Success	2751
Success divided by Opportunities = % Performance	97%
(1,000,000 divided by Opportunities) x Failures = DPM (defects per million)	28,601

Figure G-9 shows the graph generated using the above data and is a single-bar chart with the x-axis depicting each month and the y-axis showing the percentage of actions completed. (The y-axis begins at 75% and goes to 100% in increments of 2%.) On the face of each monthly bar are the number of failures and the DPM.

System Administration
Work Requests

	Outstanding	98%
	Satisfactory	97%
	Minimum	95%

Bars (F–J): 774, 749, 1,067, 1,012, 3,415, 18,615, 3,210, 3,199, 4,540, 4,145, 3,103, 2,692

Failures: 72, 39, 89, 91, 45, 46, 104, 81

NOTE: Total number of actions completed. Objective is to complete all requests in 5 days.

Figure G-9   Sample of a Work Requests Chart

Success is computed as follows:

- Outstanding 98%
- Satisfactory 97%
- Minimum 95%

In summary, the sample data indicates that the number of incomplete TTs/CWRs/Moves (i.e., Failures) was at 97% success with 81 actual failures and a DPM of 28,601 (January). The total opportunities equalled 2,832.

Trouble Tickets

This report is for tracking all trouble tickets (TTs) and Ten Minute Tickers (TMTs). TTs are logged in through ServiceDesk; TMTs are not. TMTs are not formally documented through any system; they are informal TTs where a System Administrator helps out an end-user without having submitted a TT report (e.g., the end-user stops the System Administrator in the hallway and asks for impromptu help). Both TTs closed within SLA time, and those still outstanding (that is, TTs that were not resolved within 24 hours) are listed.

Table G-4 shows a sample of the data needed to generate a Trouble Tickets report.

Table G-4   Sample Data for Trouble Tickets Report

Number of trouble tickets closed within SLA:	165
Number of trouble tickets closed outside SLA (failures):	113
Number of Ten Minute Tickers for the group:	800

Table G-5 shows the formula (with sample data) used to generate the Trouble Tickets report.

Table G-5   Formula to Generate Trouble Tickets Report

Trouble Tickets and TMTs closed within SLA = Opportunities	965
Trouble Ticket Failures:	113
Subtract Failures from Total Opportunities = Success	852
Success divided by Opportunities =% Performance	88%
1,000,000 divided by Opportunities x Failures = DPM (defects per million)	117,098

The graph shown in Figure G-10 was generated using the above dataand is a single-bar chart with the x-axis depicting each month and the y-axis showing the percentage of actions completed. (The y-axis begins at 75% and goes to 100% in increments of 2%.) On the face of each monthly bar are the number of failures and the DPM.

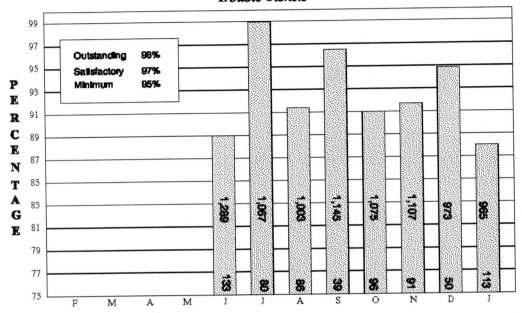

System Administration
Trouble Tickets

Figure G-10 Sample of a Trouble Tickets Chart

Success is computed as follows:

- Outstanding 98%
- Satisfactory 97%
- Minimum 95%

In summary, this report shows that the number of incomplete trouble tickets (that is, failures) was at 88% success with 113 actual failures and a DPM of 117,098 for January.

UNIX Data Center Server Downtime Minutes

This report covers mission critical production servers and is generated using data supplied by the monthly Metrics Server Report. It depicts server availability in total possible minutes available and the actual downtime in minutes.

Table G-6 shows the formula (with sample data) used to generate the UNIX Data Center Server Downtime Minutes report.

Table G-6   Formula to Generate UNIX Data Center Server Downtime Minutes Report

Minutes of downtime from Server Report (Failures):	1465
Days in the month (excluding weekends and holidays)	19
Hours in the day (= 12) x 60 minutes =	720
x the number of servers	103
= Opportunities for the month (in minutes)	74160
Subtract the downtime minutes from Opportunities = Success	72695
Success divided by Opportunities = Server % Availability	98%
(1,000,000 divided by Opportunities) x Failures = DPM (defects per million)	19,754

A graph generated using the data in Table G-6 includes a single-bar chart with the x-axis depicting each month and the y-axis showing the percentage of server availability. (The y-axis begins at 95.0% and goes to 100.0% in increments of 0.5%.) On the face of each monthly bar are the number of minutes of downtime and the DPM.

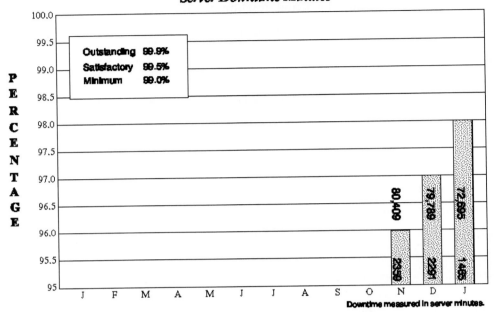

Figure G-11 *Sample of an IT UNIX Data Center Chart*

Success is computed as follows:

- Outstanding 99.9%
- Satisfactory 99.5%
- Minimum 99.0%

In summary, this sample data indicates the mission critical Server Availability was at 98% success with 1465 minutes of monthly downtime and a DPM of 19,754.

Service Level Agreement

The objective of the Service Level Agreement (SLA) is to define a framework for managing the quality and quantity of delivered services, in the face of changing business needs and user requirements, at a price the business is able to afford. Specifically, this document intends to:

- Synchronize IT services with the business needs of the customers

- Set the correct level of service expectations and responsibilities for both IT and the customer

- Enable IT to be an effective and flexible partner to the business unit, aiding rapid response to the changing business environment

- Enable IT to plan for the delivery of required services at the lowest cost to the customer

- Enable IT to maintain quality and visibility of the services that they can provide, and thus demonstrate value for money

System Administration is responsible for the design, delivery, configuration, management, and support of all the resources necessary to provide the infrastructure of office systems in line with our IT architecture and the business units that use the service(s).

System Administration is chartered to provide:

- Fast and effective reaction to user problems
- A stable and consistent systems environment
- A flexible and responsive partnership
- Value for money

Specific services will be:

- Configuration and maintenance of desktop, client and software servers, and printer resources
- Change management/addition and moves of office systems resources
- Configuration and maintenance of the office LAN resources
- User access control and security of office systems resources

H

Table H-1 describes the specific services provided by each group.

Table H-1   Services Provided

Group	Services Provided
System Administration	Hardware installation • Workstations • Printers • Peripherals • Options
	Hardware troubleshooting • Workstations • Printers • Peripherals • Options
	Third-party hardware installation • Color printers • Scanners • Modems • Fax modems
	Network connectivity and troubleshooting • Ethernet • Starlan • MUX boxes
	Third-party hardware troubleshooting • Color printers • Scanners • Modems • Fax modems
	Operating system installations • Solaris 2
	Operating system support • Troubleshooting • Kernel configuration • Patch distribution

Table H-1   Services Provided (Continued)

Group	Services Provided
Server Support	Hardware installation • Servers • Peripherals • Options
	Operating system installations • Solaris 2
	Special services for client/server • Exports • Automounting • Home directories • Mail • User accounts
	Network connectivity
	User home and mail backups and restores
	System resource management
Software Support	Software distribution management
	Application support
Network Support	NIS/NIS+ management
Customer Support	Single point of contact
	ServiceDesk
	5 x 24, 2 x 8 phone support
	5 x 24, 2 x 8, on-site availability
System Security	Routine security audits
	Securing privileged login access
	Controlling access to local networks
Moves	Intercampus moves
	Intracampus moves
	Single-user moves
	Multiple-user moves
System Architecture	Performance tuning
	Capacity planning
	System resources

General Services

Trouble Ticket Resolution

Trouble tickets (TTs) are defined as any problem a user may have with his or her workstation. This does not include an upgrade, a move, or a new installation. Trouble tickets can be submitted through our ServiceDesk tool. When a user submits a ServiceDesk trouble ticket, the first line of support is the Assistance Center. When the Assistance Center cannot provide the appropriate level of support, the ticket is transferred to either the System Administrator or the appropriate IT support group.

System Administration will respond within 2 hours of the time the trouble ticket was submitted. The trouble ticket will be resolved within 24 hours. On the average, trouble tickets are resolved within 4 hours of the time the ticket was submitted.

Work Requests

Work requests (WRs) are tasks that a user requests to have his or her workstation upgraded or installed. Moves are not considered work requests. An example of a work request would be to install a new workstation or to add more memory.

System Administration will complete Work Requests within 5 business days from the time the request was submitted.

Notes and Restrictions

1. Root access to systems supported by Client Services

   The general rule will be that no user/system that is supported by IT will be allowed root-level access to staff outside of IT. If a user requires root access to an IT-supported system, service will be provided on a best-effort basis. No user will have root privileges on any computer system other than those specifically agreed to in the SLA. Root access will be granted only when there is a specific application-related requirement that can only be met through use of root access. Normally, only primary customer support personnel will be granted root access. If personnel other than the primary customer request root access, it will be granted with the approval of the primary customer.

2. Informal services

   These are services provided by IT on a best-effort basis with no guarantees.
   - Nonstandard software installation
   - *Ad-hoc* technical assistance/training/consulting
   - User-specific backups/restores

3. Table H-2 lists the customer's responsibilities.

Table H-2   Customer Responsibilities

Responsibility	Description
Training	The customer should ensure that adequate resources are available to ensure user training on the desktop environment and applications in use in their environment. IT will specifically not deliver training sessions.
Passwords	The customer is expected to work closely with IT to ensure that all users carefully select, control, and regularly change user passwords in line with corporate security policy.
Feedback	The customer is responsible for giving feedback on service levels and business requirements at regular review meetings and user surveys.
Finance	The customer is responsible for obtaining the appropriate capital assets to ensure sufficient computing environment. The customer is responsible for obtaining funding and approval through his/her business unit for all related incremental capital and expense.
Communication and commitment	The customer is responsible for the communication and commitment of SLA within the business unit.
OS releases	Supported Sun operating systems will be limited to FCS (First Customer Shipping) versions only. The level of operating system on each workstation and server will be based on the business requirement.
Personal capacity management	Each individual user is expected to manage his or her own disk space usage.
Backups/restores	All IT client servers will be backed up on a daily basis. Requests for restores will be completed within 24 business hours following submission of the request.
Server room management	The server rooms will be managed to ensure adequate environment for systems within them at the lowest capital cost.

Table H-2   Customer Responsibilities (Continued)

Responsibility	Description
Printers	The quantity and location of printer resources will be provided by the customer. The customer will be responsible for providing all printer resources, including print engines, printers, and printer consumables (e.g., toner, paper, etc.). Additionally, the customer will be responsible for managing the replacement of printer consumables. Supported printer devices are limited to Sun printers only.
Nonproduction systems	Service Level Agreements will be established only for those systems that provide computing resources for direct production requirements or research and development support for production requirements.
Budget for special services	Senior management will allocate money and resources to meet customer needs. If the resources allocated are insufficient, IT and the customer will negotiate a reduced level of service. Services above the line are budgeted services that IT agrees to provide. Services below the line must be discarded or budgeted separately. The normal hourly rate for special services is $60 US per hour. Emergency services (unplanned/critical time frame) are charged at $120 US per hour. This is to absorb the cost of contracting services.

Outline of a Service Level Agreement Document

The following outline represents the topics to consider in writing a Service Level Agreement.

Scope and Purpose of the Agreement

- Purpose
- Scope
- Approval Process
- Review Team

Service Requirements

- Response Definition
- Technical Response Commitments
- Priority Definitions (As Defined by the End-user)

Trouble Call General Background

- Overview
- Call Flow During IT Assistance Center Business Hours
- Call Flow Outside of 6s AC Business Hour

Trouble Ticket Escalation Call Flow

- Priority 1 Business Hours Trouble Call
- Priority 1 After Hours Trouble Call
- Priority 1 Trouble Call From Babss
- Priority 2 Trouble Calls Call Flow
- Priority 3 Trouble Calls Call Flow

IT Organizational Information

- Responsibilities
- Service Hours (all times PST)
  - Backup and Restore
  - Network Support
  - Hardware Support
  - Printing Support

Priority-One Corrective Action

- Root Cause Reporting
- Corrective Action Report

Process Corrective Action

- Purpose
- Nonconformance Defined
- Metrics
- Process
- First Management Review
- Second Management Review

H

Rightsizing the New Enterprise

Internal Support Agreement for the Data Center

The Support Agreement described in this appendix is the agreement used between the different organizations within the Data Center. It defines how they interact with each other in supporting this new distributed environment. It also describes how the Data Center organization interacts with other IT organizations. This agreement establishes a commitment between these organizations as well as escalation procedures. The goal of this support agreement is to solidify and clarify each group's expectations and to build on efficient and timely service between groups.

Production Support (UNIX)

IT Production Support Services is made up of several groups.

- System Administration supports the Production Environment (non-mission critical) in various data centers. The support by this group is the minimum support provided.

- Support for the Mission Critical Business Systems involves the Production Control Group, the DBA Group, the Technical Support Group (System Programming), Data Center Operations, and, if applicable, the Network Services Group.

Production Escalation

Production escalation will be followed according to the support group information as defined in the UPA.

Special Requests

Special requests or systems maintenance on production or development machines are to be submitted to the appropriate support alias for that application. These requests are reviewed to determine whether the changes will affect other applications or dependencies.

Production Control

The Production Control Group has responsibility for coordinating the productionalization of new business applications and the implementation of new releases to existing applications.

Additionally the Production Control Group supports the following services:

- New/modified application implementation
  - Act as main contact between project members and IT
  - Assist movement through implementation process
  - Assist with UPA information and ensure that steps are followed, in order and in the proper time sequence
  - Interface to other groups
  - Consult with development of structures, crons, error messages, and so forth
  - Act as repository of source code (including scripts and tables)
  - Assist in development and execution of Assistance Center training
  - Reserve or coordinate process for necessary footprint for new servers

- Application support
  - Maintain scheduling, edit crontab, start, restart jobs
  - Start, restart, or kill applications
  - Disk file maintenance: add/delete files or parameters
  - Perform migrations

Migrations

All source code will be migrated to, and held in, repository by the Software Environment Support group (of Production Control). The movement of code to this repository will be required as part of the beta test release. This will signal the official "code freeze." Executables will either be picked up from the development environment or created as part of the migration.

Distribution will occur from this source repository, either through SunDANS (Sun's Distribution Administration of Network Services) or some other means.

Modifying Source

Source code can be checked out from this repository for later modification. It is suggested that this be the method used, as it will ensure that the production version is the basis for future changes.

Assistance Center Training

Production Control will assist the Development Group to create and conduct support training for the Assistance Center.

Technical Support

The Technical Support Group provides the following functions for all production servers:

- Installing software
  - Load OS on new machines
  - Load OS upgrades on existing machines
  - Load unbundled software and their upgrades
  - Installing a binary into the system directory structure
  - Format disk
  - Partition disk

- Configuring software
  - Kernel
  - Optional hardware
  - Modem ports
  - Terminals
  - Printers
  - Network
  - Manipulation/modification of any system daemon that is run as root
  - Manipulation/modification of any system file owned by root
  - Maintain the /etc/rc* files

- Maintaining/configuring system security
  - Add user account for rlogin and rsh capabilities
  - Establish groups of users
  - Secure privileged login access on a machine
  - Control access to machines on network

- Establishing communication
  - UUCP or tip communication
  - Electronic mail

- Establishing and maintaining network services
  - Network file system
  - Maintain any network-related configuration files

- Maintaining system
  - Maintain file system
  - Perform backup
  - Restore files and system

- Managing disk resources
  - Install and configure devices based on the configuration provided by UNIX DBA

- Maintaining hardware
  - Coordinate hardware maintenance/installation

- Supporting systems
  - Implement/maintain a standard hardware and software environment for production systems
  - Provide operating system environments with related vendor program products that are reliable, current, and secure

- Supporting applications
  - Monitor daily processing, capacity, performance, and usage
  - Manage and maintain the security and integrity of corporate data and production databases
  - Support remote production servers
  - Act as technical consultants to development and support groups for application design, maintenance, and debugging

Database Administration

The Database Administration (DBA) Group is responsible for supporting the database functions of applications. They take ownership of database servers and software.

DBMS Software Support

- Install and upgrade Database Management System software with new releases and maintenance releases

- Install DBMS patches as supplied by the vendor as needed, in coordination with UNIX Technical Support and the Application Support staff

- Provide consultation support to Technical Support regarding OS release implementation

- Make recommendations for software products and utilities used to enhance DBMS usage and throughput

- Provide 24 hour, 7-day/week, 365-days/year on-call support for production DBMS problem resolution

Database Support

- Responsible for physical integrity of the production databases, includes regularly scheduled verification procedures and correction of errors

- Responsible for verification and correction of errors on nonproduction status databases on an as-requested basis

- Responsible for architectural procedures for business continuation planning (that is, backup and recovery) as required by system availability agreements for each application

- Provide database support for disaster recovery in conjunction with Technical Support

- Perform database modification function against production applications (such as alter table)

- Maintain system runtime configuration information to define DBMS's execution

- Assist Application Support staff in providing device configuration data (hardware and software) for UNIX Technical Support UPA agreement (such as disk usage or memory)

- Monitor informational and error logs for messages specific to system operation

- Responsible for maintaining and providing DBA-level access as required for all production status applications on production and support/staging environments

- Responsible for database performance tuning

- Responsible for monitoring physical capacity

- Responsible for monitoring database user access

- Provide problem resolution support for DBMS-related errors

Vendor Interface

Coordinate with DBMS software vendors and other internal support groups (for example, Sybase contact).

Application Support

- Provide consultation support for logical database design for database applications in production and development environments

- Provide consultation and development support for the physical database design for database applications in production and development environments

- Enforce conformance to database and data center standards in application systems prior to production implementation and during UNIX Production Acceptance (UPA) cycle

- Provide consultation for selection of the DBMS

- Provide consultation for system configuration of new applications; such as use of raw partitions versus file system, client/server architecture

- Support impact analysis activity related to application design and modification

- Provide problem resolution support for DBMS application related errors

- Provide support and input to programming staff and UNIX Technical Support in the development of the application UPA document

Security/Access Support

Consult with Application Developers in architecting and designing security methodologies to establish end-user access to the database.

Request Response

Each request made to the DBA staff will be reviewed and planned on an as-requested basis. Efforts will be made to meet the application/project time requirements.

Other Groups

Network Support

Network Support will provide the following data communications support:

- Ethernet
- Communications outside of SWAN network
- Mainframe-to-UNIX communications
- Network planning and consultation
- Gateway support

Ancillary Server Rooms

Note – This section pertains to any server room other than the main Data Center.

Since these machines are located at sites that do not have full-time Data Center staff associated with them, there will be occasions when on-site, hands-on tasks need to be performed. The following tasks may need to be performed and will be coordinated by the Data Center and communicated to the Site Supervisor for System Administration when needed:

- Boot from console
- Check network and power connection
- Check status light on disk drive
- Power cycle a server
- Notify IT Production Support Services of machine room operations that affect the uptime of the machine (such as power outages, cooling, and network)

≡ I

Recommended Reading

This appendix is a listing of the recommended books for mainframers transitioning to UNIX as mentioned in Chapter 7, "Transitioning and Training Staff.

Title	Author	Publisher
General UNIX		
Design and Implementation of 4.3BSD UNIX Operating System	Leffler/McKusick/ Karels/ Quarterman	Addison-Wesley
Design of the UNIX Operating System	Bach	Prentice Hall
Guide to Solaris	Pew	SunSoft Press/ Ziff-Davis Press
Inside Solaris: SunOS & OpenWindows	Kitalong/Lee/Marzin	New Riders Press
Mastering Solaris	Heslop and Angell	Sybex
A Practical Guide to the UNIX System V Release 4.0, 2ed	Sobell	Addison-Wesley
UNIX in a Nutshell for System V & Solaris 2.0	Gilly and staff	O'Reilly & Associates
UNIX System V Release 4: An Introduction	Rosen/Rosinski/Farber	Osborne/ McGraw-Hill
The Waite Group's UNIX System V Primer, 2ed	Waite/Martin/Prata	Sams Publishing
UNIX System Administration		
All About Administering NIS+, 2ed	Ramsey	SunSoft Press/ Prentice Hall
Essential System Administration	Frisch	O'Reilly & Associates

Title	Author	Publisher
UNIX System Administration (continued)		
Learning the vi Editor	Lamb	O'Reilly & Associates
Solaris System Administrator's Guide	Winsor	SunSoft Press/ Ziff-Davis Press
Solaris Advanced System Administrator's Guide	Winsor	SunSoft Press/ Ziff-Davis Press
Solaris Implementation: A Guide for System Administrators	Becker/Morris/Slattery	SunSoft Press/ Prentice Hall
A System Administrator's Guide and Basic Networking on the Sun Workstation	Becker and Slattery	Springer-Verlag
Sun Performance and Tuning: SPARC and Solaris	Cockcroft	SunSoft Press/ Prentice Hall
System Performance Tuning	Loukides	O'Reilly & Associates
UNIX System Administration Handbook	Nemeth/Snyder/ Seebass	Prentice Hall
UNIX Programming		
Advanced Programming in the UNIX Environment	Stevens	Addison-Wesley
Advanced UNIX Programming	Rochkind	Prentice Hall
The AWK Programming Language	Aho/Kernighan/ Weinberger	Addison-Wesley
KornShell Programming Tutorial	Rosenberg	Addison-Wesley
Programming Perl	Wall and Schwartz	O'Reilly & Associates
sed & awk	Dougherty	O'Reilly & Associates
UNIX Applications Programming: Mastering the Shell	Swartz	Sams Publishing

Title	Author	Publisher
UNIX Programming (continued)		
The UNIX C Shell Field Guide	Anderson and Anderson	Prentice Hall
The UNIX Programming Environment	Kernighan and Pike	Prentice Hall
UNIX Shell Programming, rev. ed.	Kochan andWood	Hayden
UNIX System Programming: A Programmer's Guide to Software Development	Salama and Haviland	Addison-Wesley
UNIX Networking		
Analyzing Sun Networks	Malamud	Van Nostrand
Managing NFS and NIS	Stern	O'Reilly & Associates
TCP/IP and NFS: Internetworking in a UNIX Environment	Santifaller	Addison-Wesley
UNIX Network Programming	Stevens	Prentice Hall
The X Window System: Programming and Applications with Xt, OPEN LOOK edition	Young and Pew	Prentice Hall
UNIX Security		
Practical UNIX Security	Garfinkel and Spafford	O'Reilly & Associates
UNIX System Security: A Guide for Users and System Administrators	Curry	Addison-Wesley
C and C++ Programming		
A Book on C: Programming in C, 2ed	Kelley andPohl	Addison-Wesley
The C Programming Language, 2ed, ANSI C version	Kernighan and Ritchie	Prentice Hall
C++ Primer, 2ed	Lippman	Addison-Wesley
Expert C Programming: Deep C Secrets	van der Linden	SunSoft Press/ Prentice Hall

Title	Author	Publisher
C and C++ Programming (continued)		
Programming in ANSI C	Kochan	Hayden
Programming in C++	Dewhurst and Stark	Prentice Hall
Using C on the UNIX System	Curry	O'Reilly & Associates
Database		
The Guide to SQL Server	Nath	Addison-Wesley
A Guide to Sybase and SQL Server	McGoveran and Date	Addison-Wesley
Oracle: The Complete Reference	Koch	Osborne/ McGraw-Hill
The Practical SQL Handbook: Using Structured Query Language	Emerson/Darnovsky/ Bowman	Addison-Wesley

Most Frequently Asked Q & A

These are 104 of the most frequently asked customer questions *with answers* based upon over 1700 customer presentations done over the past two years. The answers are necessarily brief; please refer to the appropriate sections of the book for further detail.

1. What were some of your major obstacles in rightsizing Sun's operations?

Data Center philosophies versus UNIX methodologies: We found that UNIX people did not have a clear understanding of what it meant to support a mission critical production environment. What they were lacking were disciplines.

People issues: Transitioning mainframers to support UNIX was essential. They understand our business and, most importantly, they know how to implement and support mission critical environments.

Investing in tools for integrated environments: Acquiring the funding for the tools we developed internally was a painful process. Upper management, who came from what we call "UNIX university" (i.e., an academic environment, such as the University of California at Berkeley or Stanford University), did not understand the importance of this, but we knew that as long as the mainframes were around, these tools were essential in supporting a heterogenous environment.

Organizational issues: To decentralize, or to centralize? How do you organize to support this new mission critical production environment? We actually tested both organizations.

2. What was the size of your IT staff when you started 5 years ago and what is it today?

Five years ago we had 24 people in Computer Operations: 1 Data Center Manager, 5 supervisors, 15 operators, and 3 report distribution people. Today, we have 3 supervisors and 7 operators all reporting to a Technical Support Manager. We have cut our staff in half. The Technical Support Manager is responsible for Computer Operations, Production Control, and System Programming.

There is no longer a need for a separate Computer Operations Manager because we have automated most of the functions performed by the operators — which is key for high availability and reducing infrastructure costs. We recommend that the Technical Support Manager can now handle the System Programming and Computer Operations responsibilities. However, there is one function you will always need, even in a distributed environment, and that is a tape librarian.

3. Do you run a "Lights-Out" Data Center environment?

We are 90% there. The last piece of the puzzle is to implement a silo system or jukebox for automatic tape loading. Right now, that is the main reason for still having any type of Computer Operations staff at all. Once we have implemented an automated backup device, Computer Operator intervention will no longer be required.

4. What were the organizational issues?

Many, but to summarize it all in a few lines: Half of the business units had their own IT UNIX support organizations residing in the division, while we resided in the Data Center environment, that is, the "old mainframers" supporting the other half of the business units in a centralized paradigm. Well, these other organizations never had to deal with those controls and disciplines that we were accustomed to, such as change control, measuring performance, availability, disaster recovery, and so forth. Because these other organizations lacked these disciplines, their online availability numbers were 85% at best case (some could not even tell us because they never managed to high availability), while we were at 99.9%. Another problem was that each support organization had only enough personnel to handle their day-to-day activities.

A few years back our Data Center took over responsibility for one of these distributed support groups. Well they protested because they did not want to be part of this mainframe group; they believed that their support paradigm was the way of the 1990s. We did not know what to do, maybe they were right, so we let both groups go as they were for about a year to see which group would work better. One other important note was the fact that there were only six people in the distributed support group, including the manager. Whentwo people were out for whatever reason, they were in trouble. Well, guess which organizational structure won?

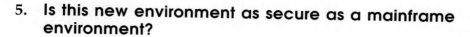

5. **Is this new environment as secure as a mainframe environment?**

Yes. The tools are there today. We used CA TopSecret on the mainframe; we looked for the tools with the same features based on mainframe functionality.

6. **Describe your computer center strategy related to client/server.**

Our strategy was to implement fully centralized control with decentralized operations. Centralized control means that production servers are as if they were in the computer center itself, even if they were not. This strategy allows us to implement a fully distributed environment with the same high availability and fewer resources to manage it. Our obstacle was to implement all processes and tools based on mainframe functionality because we knew that paradigm worked. We just customized and automated those processes based on the requirements of our business units.

7. **What are the business drivers for your strategy?**

- Provide high (RAS) Reliability, Availability, and Serviceability for our customers
- Lower the costs to support our infrastructure. We need to stay competitive with the industry.

8. **Rank these value drivers in order of importance in your computer center strategy.**

Both are equally important.

9. **Is it improving service delivery to the end-user?**

Yes. We are empowering people to do their jobs at their desks. Also, we are getting the right information to the right people to do their jobs, which improves productivity and business processes. (Please refer to Chapter 12, "Some Things to Consider When Rightsizing.")

10. **Does it optimize end-user access and use of IT?**

Yes. It has actually given Sun a competitive advantage in the industry. (Please refer to Chapter 12, "Some Things to Consider When Rightsizing.")

11. Does it shorten time to market (i.e., corporate products, IT enablers)?

Yes. We have supported processes to increase inventory cycle turns to 12 per year; this is unheard of in the computer industry. (Please refer to Chapter 12, "Some Things to Consider When Rightsizing.")

12. How did you go about implementing your strategy?

We started with an architecture statement, had it approved by senior management, and then developed an implementation plan based on the approved architecture.

13. How were your clients involved in getting your strategy?

Business units drive all business system issues. IT application developers are located within each business unit; they define system needs based on business requirements. We support the implementation of the solution through the UPA process.

14. How do you measure IT effectiveness and efficiency?

IT provides metrics and a scorecard to senior management based on agreed Service Levels. (Please refer to Appendix G, "Measuring Performance.")

15. Do you have formal service agreements with clients? How are they negotiated?

Yes. We negotiate with all clients about the level of service they are looking for prior to bringing an application within the Data Center. Each business unit has its own special requirements; this is all negotiated within the UPA process.

16. Have you built an infrastructure that is cohesive and yet durable enough to support heterogenous support needs? If so, what was the key to developing this infrastructure?

We believe that the key to a successful rightsizing endeavor is to establish an infrastructure that can support a heterogenous environment — both in the Data Center and on the Network. As an example, we were able to achieve 99.9% system on-line availability with 222 servers, *without* any specialized high-availability tools. It all starts with the infrastructure.

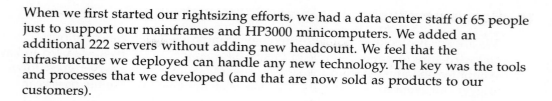

When we first started our rightsizing efforts, we had a data center staff of 65 people just to support our mainframes and HP3000 minicomputers. We added an additional 222 servers without adding new headcount. We feel that the infrastructure we deployed can handle any new technology. The key was the tools and processes that we developed (and that are now sold as products to our customers).

17. What specific computing center processes have you employed that you believe have dramatically impacted systems performance and reliability (e.g., platform standardization, operation tools, quality process)?

We have taken all the processes that we have developed within the mainframe environment and have put that same thinking into the tools we developed for our new distributed environment, that is, preventive maintenance. On the mainframe, we have a tool called `erep` that monitors the hardware for potential problems. We then schedule downtime to fix the problem — a *novel* idea. We developed the same type of tool in our distributed environment that polls every server for potential hardware problems and reports back to us so we can schedule downtime as well.

The most important process that we developed and our number one priority was the UPA process. This process was our methodology for supporting distributed mission critical production applications. It is explained in great detail in the book. Without it, we would not be here today talking about rightsizing (and our replacements would be here talking about something else!).

18. How do you select the system and utility software that you run? Is it best characterized as requiring the use on an "SOE" (standard operating environment) or do the clients predicate the software that is used?

We treat each application as a unique program. We talk with each user to evaluate their needs and then base our decision on those needs. This is part of the UPA culture/methodology. We have one overall guiding factor: the Solaris operating environment. Clients can pick whatever software they want as long as it runs within Solaris.

19. How is new technology used in your strategy?

We are always looking at new technology to improve the efficiency of our infrastructure. A good example of this is auto-paging. In the past, we used to have computer operators monitoring server outages. Today when a server goes down, it triggers an event to our beepers. This has been deployed within the past year.

This tool was pulled from an Internet bulletin boards and customized to work in our shop. Automation is the key in supporting a distributed environment from a centralized location. In the past, we used to have a computer operator sitting there, waiting for a problem to happen — and then call someone else to fix the problem when one did occur. Why? Now it is fully automated for high availability by passing over one unnecessary step. When that server goes down, a System Programmer is paged automatically.

20. What functions does your System Administrator perform?

- Workstation support
- Disaster recovery
- Security
- Telecommunications
- Moves
- User training
- Desktop database administration
- Performance and tuning
- Software distribution support
- Hardware maintenance
- Hardware installation
- Software configuration
- Software installation

21. What are your System Administrator User Support ratios?

One System Administrator for every 125 users.

22. What training do you provide for System Administrators?

Basic training includes:
- SPARC maintenance
- Peripherals maintenance
- Installation and networking
- System administration for Solaris
- Shell programming
- Desktop applications
  - Interleaf, FrameMaker, WordPerfect
  - Lotus
  - Sybase
- Customer skills
  - Quality awareness
  - Quality customer service
  - Managing interpersonal relationships
  - Negotiating skills

23. How did you train Application Programmers?

Once again, the key was to provide the opportunity to everyone. Curriculums were established through one of our divisions called SunServices. At one time, they were all COBOL programmers. Today, they use C and C++.

24. How are backups performed for non-mission critical environments?

All backups to our non-mission critical, yet production, environments are done disk to disk (i.e., automated scripts) on a nightly basis. They are then dumped to tape every two weeks and sent off-site. It is easier and more responsive to restore from disk than it is to restore from tape — you know how those users lose their files.

25. Do you support standard sets of software?

Yes, and multiples of each. As an example, for desktop publishing we use WordPerfect, InterLeaf, FrameMaker, and IslandPresents™. These are the desktop publishing tools supported by IT. The users can purchase their own software but, if they do, they must get their support elsewhere.

26. How do you collaborate with your clients to understand their needs?

Everything is communicated via the UPA process. It is our "bible" for implementing and supporting business systems. Remember the old data center paradigm? We used to be isolated from our user community, but, with the UPA process, we put a team up front during the system design and development to understand the issues and requirements. We call it "Personalized Communications." (Please read Chapter 6, "Implementing and Supporting Distributed Applications," for more information about the UPA process.)

27. How do you fund the infrastructure and/or strategic work that is planned?

We provide input to our VP during our budget cycle as to how much money is needed for tools, development costs, and hardware.

28. Do you charge back the cost of your Data Center processing to client organizations?

Yes, we charge back the cost of Data Center processing to our clients. We keep our chargeback process as simple as possible. We are *not* a profit center; we just charge back the cost of our services. As an example, we charge clients a standard price for each server that we support; we keep it simple, regardless of the size of each system — whether you have one user or one hundred users, you are charged the same rate. (Please refer to Chapter 12, "Some Things to Consider When Rightsizing.")

29. If you do charge back the cost, please describe briefly your products and services.

The services for which we charg back are:
• Desktop support
• Telephone
• Voicemail
• Network services
• Assistance Center
• Software distribution
• Data Center support
• Workstation moves
• Telephone moves/adds/changes

(Please refer to Chapter 12, "Some Things to Consider When Rightsizing.")

30. **Do you have different classes of service for your clients (e.g., 7x24 vs. 8-5, disaster recovery grades of service)? Please describe your classes of service.**

Currently we provide two classes of service:

7x24 - Applications/Hardware are monitored and supported 24 hours a day. This includes UPS, disaster recovery, technical support, DBA support, and computer operations.

5x12 - Applications/Hardware are supported 12 hours a day and 5 days a week. This includes backups, technical support, and DBA support.

31. **How did the estimated savings of your strategy compare to the real savings after implementation?**

The real cost reduction in infrastructure (20-30%) is based on our implementation of centralized control. (Please refer to Chapter 12, "Some Things to Consider When Rightsizing.")

32. **Do the demands on your organization outweigh the resources that you have? If so, how do you balance this?**

Yes. This will always be the case in Data Processing. But the new processes that we have implemented have made us much more efficient. As an example, the UPA process we talk about with regularity was originally 200 pages thick and very cumbersome. This process added to our backlog. Today, it is an asset because the actual process is only 7 pages thick; we have streamlined our entire methodology to support over 100 applications.

The other key factor was implementing a "lights-out" data center environment to handle additional servers without adding resources.

33. What are the main cost factors in your cost reduction strategy (e.g., force reduction, platform downsizing, Data Center elimination)?

The way to reduce overall costs is based on reducing infrastructure costs. As examples:

a. "Lights-out" operations

b. Improving System Administration-to-user ratios. Currently, we support 125 users with each System Administrator. We would like to improve those ratios.

c. Lower hardware and software costs by moving to the client/server model

34. How large is your network (e.g., number of LUs, FEPs, routers, terminals, PCs)?

23,000 nodes and 200 routers, all using Sun equipment.

35. Do you have a documented network architecture and/or engineering guidelines?

Yes. (Please refer to Chapter 4, "The Network," for specifics.)

36. What logical subnetwork types do you have (SNA, DECNet, TCP/IP, Datakit, bridged, etc.)?

TCP/IP, EX100, and EX400.

37. Do you use any mainframe channel-to-channel or channel-to peripheral extension equipment?

Yes. We use a channel-to-channel adapter to transfer data from the mainframe over to a UNIX platform. This also allows the user to emulate a 3270 IBM terminal.

38. How do you measure availability?

We have a system monitor script that we created that will denote any outage to a mission critical server. This report calculates any outage and delivers a server availability report to the management staff once a day. (Please refer to Chapter 8, "System Management Tools," for further details on the Morning Report.)

39. How do you manage system changes in a distributed environment?

Change control is used to handle any planned outage that we may encounter. Change control is emailed to our users once a week denoting any outages that may occur for the next 2 weeks. It is the same change control system that we used on the mainframe, but we also added some additional features. (See Chapter 8, "System Management Tools," for more information.)

40. How do you manage disk space?

We have another homegrown shell script called DiskPatrol. DiskPatrol will poll all production servers once a day to see if we are reaching a critical point in our disk partitions.

41. How do you manage and track hardware problems?

We use another shell script called prevent_maint, which has the same functionality as the mainframe product called erep. It manages and tracks hardware problems for us, and, just like the mainframe, it will warn us if there is a potential hardware problem, which we will then schedule downtime to fix.

42. Is your network engineered for disaster recovery and/or continuous operations?

Yes, it is. We have a tool called SunNet Manager that can manage our network from any one of our major hubs. As an example, in October 1989 we experienced a 7.1 earthquake in the San Francisco Bay Area where we work. Things got pretty bad; the Data Center functioned all right, but we started losing circuits. Dallas, Texas, which is one of the locations at which we have this product running, saw that we were having problems, so they took complete ownership of the network for the interim.

43. How do you fund the network infrastructure (e.g., by user, with corporate funding, by computer center funding)?

By user. Each employee is charged for network connectivity. Everyone at Sun has a workstation on their desktop to perform many different functions. One thing that is common to all is that everyone communicates via email, which means network connectivity.

44. Is network operations part of computer operations or is it a standalone organization?

Standalone. It reports into the network group. Although it is not a part of the Computer Operations staff, it is still under our overall IT group, which is basically a utilities organization. Our organization supports Data Centers, networking, and System Administration functions all around the world.

45. How many people support your network infrastructure (engineering, implementation, and operations)?

We have 10 people to monitor the United States and 10 additional people worldwide.

46. In regard to workload management and performance analysis, what performance monitoring tools and data are available?

There are many tools available for monitoring performance, among them are sar, proctool, iostat, statit, and SunNet Manager. Sun publishes the Solaris 2.x performance handbook, which is updated with new data for each release of the OS (typically twice a year).

47. What type and frequency of performance tracking and reporting run on Sun's production systems?

We use SunNet Manager to track performance issues, that is, CPU utilization, disk I/O, memory, and so forth on a daily basis.

48. Are Service Level Agreements (SLAs) defined for application performance?

Currently, the majority of our SLAs revolve around availability. SOTool is the only current application that we have an SLA for application performance. SOTool is one of our largest UNIX applications with anywhere from half a million to three fourths of a million transactions a day. The SLA for availability is monitored via the Morning Report.

49. What are SLAs reported against?

For the most part, we use the Morning Report to show system availability. The Morning Report tracks availability for all servers and tracks performance issues with certain mission critical applications like the SOTool mentioned above.

50. How are tape management and file backup functions handled by Sun?

Today, all of the day-to-day backups and tape management are handled by the Computer Operations staff. As mentioned earlier, we still have seven computer operators performing backups. Now, this is not their only job responsibility; we still have three HP3000 minicomputers that need manual intervention. The way it currently works is that our swingshift computer operators load each server with 8mm cartridges, then our automated Tape Management scripts kick in based on each server's availability hours. We perform incrementals nightly and do full dumps on the weekend. Our graveyard shift will then removes the cartridges.

51. What is Sun's volume of tape processing disk MB backup nightly, per system and overall?

It changes every night, but a ballpark figure would be approximately 270GB for incrementals and approximately 400GB for full volume backups.

52. What is Sun's frequency of file backup, retention periods, and total tapes supported? What type of tape is used?

a. We do incremental backups Sunday through Thursday with our full volume backups done on Friday night.

b. The retention period varies with each backup:

Daily	= 1 Week
Weekly	= 4 Weeks
Monthly	= 13 Months
Quarterly	= 2 Years
Yearly	= 7 Years

We perform 135 backups per night. Each backup requires 1 tape.

c. We are currently using 8M tapes.

53. What tape management and catalogs are used?

Since we could not find a tape management system four years ago, we took a Sun Tape Backup product (called Backup Copilot™) and incorporated some additional functionality. We are currently using an enhanced version of Sun's original product (now called Online: Backup). This version includes a UNIX TMS (Tape Management System) patch that enables us to read the label of the tape and ensures that we have the right tape mounted. In this way, we never write over a production tape.

54. What components for tape management and file backups meet Sun's needs in the current environment?

Much of the tape management functionality that was lacking early on, for example, standard labeling, offsite retention criteria, and so forth, has been built into the product. We invested heavily (1 person year) to provide for this functionality. The products were not very robust in 1989.

55. What areas of tape management and file backups can or should be improved?

The product in which we have invested heavily still does not perform database backups. We have to dump raw partition to a UNIX file system and then back it up to tape, wasting both disk space and time. It also did not support jukeboxes or silos. These two areas are probably the two that are worth mentioning.

The product we use is called Online Backup. We started enhancing and redeveloping this tool in 1989 to give it the same tape management functionality as we had on the mainframe. We did not add everything, as we knew the tools would eventually be available in the marketplace — and they are here today!

56. How much concurrent tape backup is done per system?

One.

57. Are backups automated, or are they still performed manually?

The backups are automated, but the mounting and unmounting of the tapes are currently manual processes.

58. What is the best tape backup/restore product that supports a heterogenous environment?

The product called Networker™ from Legato is probably the best one to support a heterogeneous environment.

59. How do you back up remote systems? Over the network or locally?

Very few systems are backed up over the net; only extremely mission critical systems are handled this way. Nine out of 10 times, we will contract with our local System Administrators to perform these backups. We use the same tape backup product for the ones we back up over the net.

60. Do you use a jukebox, cylo, or stacker device? If yes, what type?

No. We are currently doing a product analysis of tape storage devices.

61. How do you back up databases?

We have database utilities that dump the database to flat files on a disk. Then we back up the flat files. This is still one of the limitations that we have in our product. When we installed our tape backup product, we knew it was going to be a short-term solution.

62. What is the best tape media product to use?

After a lengthy analysis, we decided to use 3M® tapes.

63. What tools does Sun use for system management?

a. Job scheduling — cron (will be transitioning to AutoSys)

b. Console management — Console servers

c. Disk and data management (i.e., aging unused datasets) — We use an internally developed product called DiskPatrol which monitors disk space at all locations. We do not yet have a product that manages aging unused data sets.

d. Auto-paging — internally developed scripts

e. Output distribution — Sun Paperless Reporter

    f.   Software distribution — SunDANS

    g.   Problem/change management — internally developed scripts

    h.   Security — ASET (BoKS is also used)

    i.   Network management — SunNet Manager

    j.   Managing availability — The Morning Report

    k.   Tape management — Online Backup

64. Do any of the tools used run from a central location, or do they run individually on each production system?

They run on one centralized production server. We have agents that run on every server; we view the results from one centralized location.

65. What products were reviewed for each of the functions, and why was the chosen package selected?

A detailed description of each tool is provided in the book.

66. What shortcomings and/or problems have been encountered in installing and running the selected packages?

Please see Chapter 8, "System Management Tools," for this information.

67. Do the Operations staff feel that the current packages support their needs?

They feel that the tools we have in place today support all of their needs. These are the same people who were using the mainframe tools, and we know that mainframe tools were the best tools around. No complaints from our staff at all. But this was because if the tools did not have the same functionality as our legacy environment; we had no choice but to develop them from scratch or enhance the available tools.

68. How do you support mission critical distributed applications? Is there a methodology?

The UPA process is our methodology and our guideline. (Please refer to Chapter 6, "Implementing and Supporting Distributed Applications," for a detailed explanation.)

69. How is the UPA document kept up to date?

We have a constant communication process with the users. Whenever there is a new release of an application, a review of the associated UPA is required. Enhancements will be applied if necessary.

70. Is the network key to distributed computing?

Yes. Having the network topology in place allows a distributed solution to be a business rather than a network issue.

71. How long have standards been in place?

Five years.

72. How are the standards working?

They are working fine. Conforming to standards was a necessity for us because of the different types of hardware and OS versions we were supporting. The more standards in the environment, the fewer resources it takes to support that environment

73. What is the staff's gut feeling about the extra overhead that the standards introduced?

At first, the UNIX people did not want to bother with standards because they felt like standards would slow them down. However, in the long run, they realized it was easier to provide maintenance/upgrades for a standard configuration than for a nonstandard configuration.

74. Are tools available to administer the standards? Were these purchased or developed?

We developed our own tools in 1989, 1990, and 1991 because tools were not readily available on the marketplace.

75. What is the staff's reaction to the tools developed or purchased to administer the standards?

The same group that developed the standards also developed the tools to administer them.

76. What kind of disaster backup plans are in place?

We have a disaster recovery plan that took us 1.5 years to develop. (Please refer to Chapter 11, "Data Center Disaster Recovery Plan.")

77. What is the location of the alternate server system?

For performing our disaster recovery drills, we use one of our existing server rooms which is in another building but on the same campus. These servers are dedicated to disaster recovery.

78. What are the SLAs for recovery to a backup system?

We have an SLA with our archive vendor that states that any tape can be returned from the vault within 90 minutes. We guarantee a 24-hour turnaround to bring up a mission critical system

79. What type of training is provided to the Operations staff, operations support staff, and development staff for UNIX, C, and Sun standard practices and procedures?

We sent the Operations staff to the following classes:

a. System administration essentials for Solaris (a 3-day introductory class)

b. Shell programming (a 1-week class)

c. System administration (a 1-week in-depth class)

(Please see Chapter 7, "Transitioning and Training Staff," for more information.)

80. Is training updated periodically?

Yes. When we see a new class that we feel is pertinent to the Operations staff, we ask that they attend it.

81. What was the fallout rate on staff for the mainframes?

Twenty percent wanted to stay with the mainframes; it was their choice. (Please refer to Chapter 7, "Transitioning and Training Staff.")

82. How long did it take to train a mainframe MVS person?

This depends on the person. They can be trained as quickly as three months or as long as ten months.

83. Were there any morale issues?

None at all. The key was to provide the *opportunity* to everyone. (Please refer to Chapter 7, "Transitioning and Training Staff.")

84. Did you train everyone?

Yes. We gave every person the opportunity to attend classes. Not everyone went to all of the classes; we didn't have a huge training budget. We sent people to a minimum set of classes so that they would be involved with our projects to develop the tools we needed. It is very important that once people attend class, they need to get involved in projects. (Please refer to Chapter 7, "Transitioning and Training Staff," for further details.)

85. What is Sun's experience regarding hardware failure rates?

There have been very few hardware failures. We currently use MTBF-Tool (Mean Time Between Failure) to evaluate our hardware failures. This is similar to RPLUS on the mainframe.

86. Are certain types of hardware more prone to failure than others?

Yes. Tape drives and disk drives tend to have the highest failure rates, which are relatively low considering their rate of failure.

87. What are Sun's SLAs for recovering an application from a hardware failure?

This depends on the application. A mission critical application will be fixed as soon as possible. A non-mission critical application will be fixed at the earliest convenient time.

88. Does Sun have any mission critical 24x7 applications running on UNIX systems?

Yes. We are currently running approximately 90+ mission critical applications. The user defines the application as being "mission critical" during the UPA process.

89. What steps are taken to ensure higher or 100% availability of these applications and files?

We use disk mirroring on servers to ensure high availability. We are also looking at other third-party applications for high availability. But, as stated throughout the book, we were able to attain 99.9% availability without any special high availability tools, such as RAID™. The infrastructure is the key. Purchasing high availability tools is the "icing on the cake" — perhaps attaining 99.999...% availability.

90. How will Sun address support for mission critical 24x7 applications as more of these applications are moved to the UNIX environment?

Support will be provided in the same way that we support other applications today. Our operations center is situated in such a way that adding more applications will not cause a problem. As stated in the book, the key is to build a strong, solid infrastructure that can handle new technologies.

91. What type of automatic OS installation mechanism is used by Sun's Operations staff?

During our internal transition from SunOS 4.x to Solaris 2.x, we used a product that is part of the Solaris operating environment to upgrade overnight over 100 workstations at a time without operator intervention. We set up the configuration files the day before, and, when we came in the next morning, they were running Solaris. This saved enormous amounts of time and afforded the desktop users an uninterrupted workflow.

92. On the SPARCcenter 2000, how does the system recover when a CPU failure, memory failure, or I/O failure occurs?

The operating system will configure out the defective part, and, depending on the severity of the problem, it may reboot itself.

93. **What impact does the recovery mechanism have on applications running on the system at the time the failure occurred?**

Once again, this depends on the error. We will reboot if needed.

94. **They say that it is costlier to implement a distributed environment. What are your experiences?**

We did not see it that way. (Please refer to Chapter 12, "Some Things to Consider When Rightsizing.")

95. **How do you perform extracts from the mainframe?**

Batch jobs run on the mainframe to extract the data. Then the data is transferred to a UNIX platform via MVSNFS.

96. **How do you handle software distribution?**

Please refer to Appendix A, "SunDANS."

97. **How do you play transactions in a heterogeneous environment, mainframe, and UNIX RDBMS?**

With a product we developed internally called SunRAI. (Please refer to Appendix B, "SunRAI," for a detailed explanation.)

98. **How do you keep databases in sync?**

With SunRAI.

99. **How do you distribute batch reports in a distributed environment?**

With a product we developed called Sun Paperless Reporter.

100. **How do you escalate problems in a distributed environment?**

It is part of our auto-paging process. We developed a tool that will automatically escalate to the next level as required.

101. What were some of your greatest challenges?

The obstacles were very painful. The most difficult challenge was selling the whole concept of mainframe disciplines to a UNIX company. (Please refer to Chapter 12, "Some Things to Consider When Rightsizing.")

102. Are System Management Tools available today that do not require additional development?

Yes. Please refer to Chapter 8, "System Management Tools," for a list of the tools that we believe will work in a heterogenous environment.

103. Do you still have a centralized Help Desk function (i.e., an Assistance Center)?

Yes, but our plan is to eliminate the Help Desk within the next year. We have already bypassed Help Desk when it comes to our mission critical applications.

When a problem occurred with a server in the past, the operator monitoring the master console would notice that a portion of the screen would turn red and an alarm would sound. The operator would then phone a Technical Support person. The other scenario was that if the user detected a problem, the user would call the Help Desk and then the Help Desk would call the appropriate support person. To us, both methods introduced too many wasted cycles. All of these little issues are what we are referring to when we talk about the infrastructure, and they represent 99.9% on-line availability in a fully distributed environment supporting over 200 servers.

What we did to expedite solutions to server problems was to implement an automated paging mechanism that would automatically beep an on-call Technical Support person. We now use this 'auto-paging' whenever a server goes down. A Technical Support person is automatically paged not by an operator nor by the Help Desk, but by a tool. Precious minutes are thereby saved, and, by the time a problem was detected prior to auto-paging, the new auto-paging method already has someone working on a problem resolution.

We have also developed an on-line problem management and reporting tool called ServiceDesk that gives users the ability to report system administration-related calls on-line, thereby bypassing the Help Desk. If a user has a problem with the workstation, telephone, network connection, or anything to do with the desktop environment, it is reported directly to their System Administrator who is responsible for closure and coordination of that "ticket." ServiceDesk also has a very user-friendly GUI interface with a Customer Satisfaction section. (See Appendix D, "ServiceDesk," for further details on ServiceDesk.)

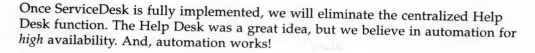

Once ServiceDesk is fully implemented, we will eliminate the centralized Help Desk function. The Help Desk was a great idea, but we believe in automation for *high* availability. And, automation works!

104. With all the network connectivity, your network costs must be outrageous. How do you justify such a cost?

Surprisingly, our network costs are very low. We deliver network connectivity to all Sun employees (with bandwidth to support performance) at a very low cost. With centralized control, a more homogeneous environment, network management standards, and effective negotiations with our vendors, we have been able to supply the network at a very competitive rate.

Rightsizing the New Enterprise

Glossary

10BaseT hub

Industry standard for twisted-pair ethernet connectivity.

abort

To terminate, in a controlled manner, a processing activity in a computer system because it is impossible or undesirable for the activity to proceed.

access

To obtain entry to or to locate, read into memory, and make ready for some operation. Access is usually used with regard to disks, files, records, and network entry procedures.

account

See *user account*.

address

(1) A number used by the system software to identify a storage location.
(2) In networking, a unique code that identifies a node to the *network*.

administration

See *system administration* and *network administration*.

alias

(1) In electronic mail, an easy-to-remember name used in place of a full name and address. Also, a name used to identify a distribution list — several user names grouped under a single name.

(2) An alternate label. For example, a label and one or more aliases may be used to refer to the same data element or point in a computer program.

(3) A distortion or artifact in the digital reproduction of an audio waveform that results when the signal frequency is too high compared to the sampling frequency.

aliasing

The jagged artifact in a line or in the silhouette of a curve that results from drawing on a raster grid. Aliasing occurs in all graphical images drawn on raster displays, but it is especially noticeable in low-resolution monitors. The sampling frequency is a major factor in aliasing. Synonymous with *jaggies*.

American National Standards Institute (ANSI)

An organization that reviews and approves product standards in the United States. In the electronics industry, its work enables designers and manufacturers to create and support products that are compatible with other hardware *platforms* in the industry. Examples are *PHIGS* and *GKS*. See also *International Organization for Standardization (ISO)*.

American Standard Code for Information Interchange (ASCII)

The standard binary encoding of alphabetical characters, numbers, and other keyboard symbols.

ANSI

See *American National Standards Institute (ANSI)*.

API

See *application programming interface (API)*.

application

A software program specially designed for a particular task or the specific use of a software program. Graphics applications are usually designed to enable the user to manipulate data or images, or to create images from data or from a library of shapes.

application programming interface (API)

(1) The interface to a library of language-specific subroutines (called a *graphics library*) that implement higher-level graphics functions. See also *binding*.

(2) A set of calling conventions defining how a service is invoked through a software package.

architecture

The specific components of a computer system and the way they interact with one another.

architecture statement

A definite plan for an enterprise of the changes, requirements, and developments to take place over the next three to five years. For example, a network architecture statement would be a 3-to-5 year plan that defines the networking infrastructure required to support business requirements.

archive

A collection of several files bundled into one file by a program (such as ar, tar, bar, or cpio) for shipment or *archiving*.

archiving

The storage of backup files and associated journals, usually for a given period of time.

ASCII

(Pronounced "as-kee.") See *American Standard Code for Information Interchange (ASCII)*.

Asynchronous Transfer Mode(ATM)

One of the new protocols being utilized to support different network packet structures and higher network bandwidth requirements.

ATM

See *Asynchronous Transfer Mode*.

auto-dial

The feature of a modem that opens a telephone line and initiates a call by transmitting a stored telephone number as a series of pulses or tones.

auto-recognition

When a network gateway or router is connected to the network, the network management system, that is, SunNet Manager, automatically recognizes that it is on the network and starts to manage it.

backbone

The primary connectivity mechanism of a hierarchical distributed system. All systems that have connectivity to an intermediate system on the backbone are assured of connectivity to each other. This mechanism does not prevent systems from setting up private arrangements with each other to bypass the backbone for reasons of cost, performance, or security.

backup

A copy on a diskette, tape, or disk of some or all of the files from a hard disk. There are two types of backups: a full backup and an incremental backup. Synonymous with "dump." See *full dump* and *incremental dump*.

backup device

The device that receives a backup copy of files — a floppy drive, tape drive, or disk.

baud rate

The rate at which information is transmitted between devices; for example, between a terminal and the computer. Often incorrectly assumed to indicate the number of bits per second (bps) transmitted, baud rate actually measures the number of events, or signal changes, that occur in 1 second. Because one event can actually encode more than one bit in high-speed digital communications, baud rate and bits per second are not always synonymous, and the latter is the more accurate term to apply to modems. For example, a so-called 9600-baud modem that encodes four bits per event actually operates at 2400 baud but transmits 9600 bits per second (2400 events times 4 bits per event) and thus should be called a 9600-bps modem.

binary

From bi-, meaning two; generally, a term describing a system, statement, or condition that has two components, alternatives, or outcomes. In mathematics, binary is the base-2 number system, in which values are expressed as combinations of two digits, 0 and 1.

binding

(1) Language-dependent code that allows a software library to be called from that computer language.

(2) The process during which a client finds out where a server is so that the client can receive services. *NFS* binding is explicitly set up by the user and remains in effect until the user terminates the bind, for example, by modifying the /etc/fstab file. NIS binding occurs when a client's request is answered by a server and is terminated when the server no longer responds.

(3) A logical relationship between any two elements, such as a file type, an application, a print script, a color, a filter, or another element that can be used for displaying or operating on a file. Thus, an application can be bound to a print script so that files the user generates with that application always print in a particular way.

bit

Short for "binary digit." Indicates the smallest unit of information stored in a digital memory. Binary digits indicate two possible values: on and off. A single bit is represented in memory as 0 (off) and 1 (on).

boot

A method that loads the system software into memory for execution.

bridge

A device that connects two or more physical networks and forwards packets between them. Bridges can usually be made to filter packets, that is, to forward only certain traffic. Related devices are: repeaters which simply forward electrical signals from one cable to another; and full-fledged *routers* which make routing decisions based on several criteria. In International Organization for Standardization's open systems interconnection (OSI) terminology, a bridge is a data link layer intermediate system.

campus

A group of buildings utilized by a company to share common resources, for example, manufacturing or engineering.

CDDI

High-speed 100Mb Ethernet using twisted-pair wire technology.

central control

A specification that only one central support group serves the following functions:

- Testing for quality on a timely basis
- Decreasing labor costs through the use of one location
- Simplifying problem determination
- Implementation and support

central processing unit (CPU)

The part of the computer in which calculations and manipulations take place.

client

(1) In the *client-server model* for file systems, the client is a machine that remotely accesses resources of a compute server, such as compute power and large memory capacity.

(2) In the client-server model for window systems, the client is an *application* that accesses windowing services from a "server process." In this model, the client and the server can run on the same machine or on separate machines. See also *dataless client*, *diskless client*, and *diskfull client*.

client-server model

A common way to describe network services and the model user processes (programs) of those services. Examples include the name-server/name-resolver paradigm of the *domain name system (DNS)* and file-server/file-client relationships such as *NFS* and diskless hosts. See also *client*.

client system

A system on a network that relies on another system, called a *server system*, for resources such as disk space.

closed architecture

Any computer design with specifications not freely available. Such proprietary specifications make it difficult or impossible for third-party vendors to create ancillary devices that work correctly with a closed-architecture machine; usually, only its original master can build peripherals for such a machine. Contrast with *open architecture*.

compressed export

A dump that has been compressed to save size.

concurrent manager

Oracle process that does a data synchronization to make sure that application transactions are in sync.

console

A terminal, or a dedicated window on the screen, where system messages are displayed.

console server

Replaces multiple ASCII terminals serving as system consoles with a single desktop SPARCstation.

CPU

See *central processing unit (CPU)*.

crontab

A file that lists commands to be executed at specified times on specified dates.

cu

The actual command to connect a console server to a host device. It calls up another UNIX system, a terminal, or possibly a non-UNIX system, then manages an interactive conversation. It is convenient to think of cu

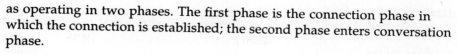

as operating in two phases. The first phase is the connection phase in which the connection is established; the second phase enters conversation phase.

data compression

Application of an algorithm to reduce the bit rate of a digital signal, or the bandwidth of an analog signal, while preserving as much as possible of the information—usually with the objective of meeting the constraints in subsequent portions of the system.

data dictionary

The roadmap of how data objects relate to one another. It defines ownership and where the data can be found.

data encrypting key

A key used to encipher and decipher data intended for programs that perform encryption.

data encryption standard (DES)

A commonly used, highly sophisticated algorithm developed by the U. S. National Bureau of Standards for encrypting and decrypting data.

data segment

The portion of the disk where the actual data is stored.

data server

Relational Database Management System, or a distributed system that stores or houses data.

database consistency checkers

Locations where the database goes through and checks for page allocations and possible index corruption.

database dump

A full dump of the database. It is the same as doing a full dump on UNIX file systems.

database lock

The method used by the database server to eliminate the possibility of database corruption

database management system (DBMS)

A software system facilitating the creation and maintenance of a data base and the execution of programs using the database.

database objects
Tables, triggers, and stores procedures that make up a database.

dataless client
A *client system* that relies on a *server system* for its home directory and data storage, and on a local disk for its root directory and swap space. See also *diskless client* and *diskfull client*.

DBA
Data Base Administrator — responsible for data base integrity for all production server locations, including problem control, new database releases, security, and contact for third-party vendors in handling problems and bug patches.

DBCC errors
Any error messages that come out of database consistency checkers.

DBMS
See *database management system (DBMS)*.

decentralizing network operations
Utilizing other hub locations or third-party vendors to assist in managing the network.

device
A hardware component, such as a printer or disk drive, acting as a unit to perform a specific function.

device-independent
Software that has been written expressly for portability across dissimilar computer systems. An *industry-standard* graphics library, such as *PHIGS*, is a device-independent interface.

device name
The name that the system uses to identify a device. For example, /dev/rst0 (or just rst0) is the device name for a 1/4-inch tape drive.

directory
A type of file that can contain common files and other directories.

directory path name
The complete name by which the directory is known. The *path name* gives the sequence of directories by which the directory is linked to the *root directory*

Rightsizing the New Enterprise

disk

A round platter, or set of platters, of a magnetized medium organized into concentric tracks and sectors for storing data such as files.

diskette

A 3.5-inch removable storage medium.

diskfull client

A *client* on a network that relies on a *server* for resources, such as files, but has its own local disk for data storage. Some of its files are local while others can be remote. The remote files can be obtained from any machine running as a network fileserver. Contrast with *diskless client* and *standalone*.

diskless client

A *client* on a network that relies on a *server* for all of its disk storage and has no local disk drive. Contrast with *diskfull client* and *standalone*.

disk partition

A portion of the *disk* reserved for a specific file system and function.

distributed file system

A file system that exists on more than one server, enabling each user to access files on it or on other servers.

domain

(1) In the Internet, a part of a naming hierarchy. Syntactically, an Internet domain name consists of a sequence of names (labels) separated by periods (dots). For example, "tundra.mpk.ca.us."

(2) In International Organization for Standardization's open systems interconnection (OSI), "domain" is generally used as an administrative partition of a complex distributed system, as in MHS private management domain (PRMD) and directory management domain (DMD).

(3) At Sun, a campus environment or geographic area (such as east, west, or central).

domain name

The name assigned to a group of systems on a local network that share administrative files. The domain name is required for the network information service database to work properly. Se also *domain*.

domain name system (DNS)

The distributed name/address mechanism used in the Internet.

download

Extracting data from a central source (e.g., a mainframe) and delivering it to a client/server RDBMS for local use.

dumb terminal

A terminal that lacks any local "intelligence." Sometimes referred to as a *TTY* terminal.

electronic label

Machine-readable internal label for Tape Management Software.

email

Electronic mail. See also *mail*.

emulate

To imitate one system with another, primarily by hardware, so that the imitating system accepts the same data, executes the same computer programs, and achieves the same results as the imitated system.

enterprise-wide database

A central database that contains all data required to run the enterprise and its business systems.

environment

The conditions under which a user works while using the UNIX system. A user's environment includes those things that personalize the user's login and how the user is allowed to interact in specific ways with UNIX and the computer. For example, the shell environment includes such things as the shell prompt string, specifics for backspace and erase characters, and commands for sending output from the terminal to the computer.

error log

Log to which the database server writes error messages or conditions.

Ethernet

A type of local area network that enables real-time communication between machines connected directly together through cables. Ethernet was developed by Xerox in 1976, originally for linking minicomputers at the Palo Alto Research Center. A widely implemented network from which the IEEE 802.3 standard for contention networks was developed, Ethernet uses a bus topology (configuration) and relies on the form of access known as *CSMA/CD* to regulate traffic on the main communication line. Network nodes are connected by coaxial cable (in either of two

Rightsizing the New Enterprise

varieties known as thin and thick) or by twisted-pair wiring. Thin Ethernet cabling is 5 millimeters (about 0.2 inch) in diameter and can connect network stations over a distance of 300 meters (about 1000 feet). Thick Ethernet cabling is 1 centimeter (about 0.4 inch) in diameter and can connect stations up to 1000 meters (about 3300 feet) apart.

event processing

A program feature belonging to more advanced operating-system architectures such as UNIX. Programs used to be required to interrogate, and effectively anticipate, every device that was expected to interact with the program, such as the keyboard, mouse, and printer. Unless sophisticated programming techniques were used, one or two events happening at the same instant would be lost. Event processing solves this problem through the creation and maintenance of an event queue.

execute

(1) To run a file as a program.

(2) To perform one or more instructions. In programming, execution implies loading the machine language code of the program into memory and then performing the instructions.

export

The process by which a server advertises the file systems that it allows hosts on a network to access.

extract

Usually a batch job that selects specific data from one database to another.

FDDI

An emerging high-speed networking standard. The underlying medium is fiber optics, and the topology is a dual-attached, counter-rotating token ring. FDDI networks can often be spotted by the orange fiber cable.

file

A sequence of bytes constituting a unit of text, data, or program. A file can be stored in the system memory or on an external medium such as tape or disk.

file name

The name of a file as it is stored in a directory on a disk. See also *path name*.

file permissions
> A set of permissions assigned to each file and directory that determines which users have access to read, write, and execute its contents.

filtering
> In computer graphics, an image-processing technique that reduces unwanted features or colors in an image.

firewall
> Security processes installed on a router or a gateway that allow each network packet to be monitored and that detect any unauthorized access or virus.

floppy drive
> An electromechanical device that reads data from and writes data to floppy disks.

footprint
> A term used in data center environments for standard hardware configuration, size, and dimensions.

full dump
> A copy of the contents of a file system backed up for archival purposes. Contrast with *incremental dump*.

gateway
> (1) The original Internet term for what is now called a *router* or more precisely, IP router. In modern usage, the terms "gateway" and "application gateway" refer to systems that do translation from some native format to another. Examples include X.400 to/from RFC 822 electronic mail gateways.
>
> (2) Technology that connects Ethernet connections without using long distance link; for example, building to building or LAN to LAN. It will also provide security to block packets from a LAN or building.

global
> Having extended or general scope. For example, a global substitution of one word for another in a file affects all occurrences of the word. In networking, global refers to worldwide connectivity.

global file
> A file containing information such as user, host, and network names, network-wide in scope.

global mainframe database

A company or enterprise-wide database that is attached to the mainframe at a centralized location. See also *enterprise-wide database*.

global variable

A variable whose value can be accessed and modified by any statement in a program. That is, the variable is visible to the entire program, including statements and functions.

graphical user interface (GUI)

The graphical user interface, or GUI, provides the user with a method of interacting with the computer and its special applications, usually via a mouse or other selection device. The GUI usually includes such things as windows, an intuitive method of manipulating directories and files, and icons.

group

A collection of users who are referred to by a common name. There are two types of groups: default user group and standard user group.

GUI

See *graphical user interface (GUI)*.

hard link

A directory entry that references a file on disk. More than one such directory entry may reference the same physical file.

hardware

(1) The mechanical and electrical components of a computer system.

(2) The components of a computer system responsible for user input, display, and mathematical processing. Often the term hardware is used in specific reference to the computing power of the CPU or the graphics accelerator, or both. Another term for the collection of compute hardware is *platform*.

help

An OPEN LOOK® GUI implementation that usually provides on-screen help for each element in a window. The application provides help for application functions and elements.

heterogenous network

A network composed of systems of more than one architecture. Contrast with *homogeneous network*.

hit ratio

In memory caching systems, the ratio by which the required data is found in memory rather than retrievable from disk.

homogeneous network

A network composed of systems of only one architecture. Contrast with *heterogenous network*.

hostid

See *system ID*.

ICMP

Errors occur from time to time in all networks and nodes. These must be notified to those responsible or to those concerned. The notification is the responsibility of the Internet Control Message Protocol (ICMP).

image

A picture or graphic representation of an object.

incremental dump

A duplicate copy of only those database files that have changed since a certain date. An incremental dump is used for archival purposes. Contrast with *full dump*.

industry standard

Elements of a computer system hardware or software subsystem that have been standardized and adopted by the industry at large. Standardization occurs in two ways: through a rigorous procedure followed by the *ANSI* and *ISO* organizations or through wide acceptance by the industry.

infrastructure

The functions that perform utility services, such as networking, data center, and system administration. Each organization should have an *architecture statement* defining the organizational structure and operational procedures.

input

Information fed to a command, a program, a terminal, a person, and so on.

intelligent hub

A network hub that has the intelligence to allow software execution that monitors the desktop.

International Organization for Standardization (ISO)

An international agency that reviews and approves independently designed products for use within specific industries. ISO is also responsible for developing standards for information exchange. Its function is similar to that of *ANSI* in the United States. Also known as "International Standards Organization."

internet

A collection of networks interconnected by a set of routers that enable them to function as a single, large virtual network.

Internet

(Note the capital "I.") The largest internet in the world consisting of large national backbone nets (such as *MILNET, NSFNET,* and *CREN*) and a myriad of regional and local campus networks all over the world. The Internet uses the Internet Protocol suite. To be on the Internet the user must have IP connectivity, that is, be able to *Telnet* to—or *ping*—other systems. Networks with only email connectivity are not actually classified as being on the Internet.

Internet Control Message Protocol (ICMP)

See *ICMP*.

Internet protocol (IP)

See *IP*.

IP

The cornerstone of the TCP/IP architecture. All computers in the Internet understand IP. The main tasks of IP are the addressing of the computers and the fragmentation of packets; it contains no functions for end-to-end message reliability or for flow control. IP makes the best effort to forward packets to the next destination, although the forwarding is not guaranteed. The main attributes of IP are: connections protocol, fragments (divides) packets if necessary, addressing via 32-bit Internet addresses, 8-bit transport protocol addresses, maximum packet size of 65535 bytes, contains only a header checksum, no data checksum, protocol fields which are not always required are optional, finite packet lifetime, best-effort delivery.

ISO

See *International Organization for Standardization (ISO)*

job number

A number that the system assigns to each process running on that machine.

LAN

See *local area network (LAN)*.

"Lights-Out" Data Center

Terminology used for a data center that uses no human Computer Operator intervention. All tools and processes have been automated so that no human intervention is required to run computer room functions.

load sharing

A protocol that can switch network packets between connections.

loading

Putting the machine-language instructions of a program into memory.

local

Having limited scope. Contrast with *global*.

local area network (LAN)

A group of computer systems in close proximity that can communicate with one another via some connecting hardware and software.

local bisync 3270

IBM or compatible character-based bisynchronous dumb terminal.

localized database

A database that takes the current time, date, and language that would be installed for local use at a local site.

log in

To gain access to the system, usually by typing a user name and a password, so that the user can begin a work session.

login directory

The directory the user is placed in after logging in. Usually, the home directory.

login name

The name by which the computer system knows the user.

login prompt

The string of characters that the system displays to let the user know that it is ready to accept the user name.

Rightsizing the New Enterprise

log out

To end a session on the system, usually when the user finishes work. Further access requires a user ID and password.

machine language

The basic set of instructions understood by a given computer. These instructions are represented internally by means of a binary code.

mail

A computer system facility that enables the sending and holding of mail messages via the computer.

mailbox

A disk storage area assigned to a particular network user for receipt of electronic messages.

mail gateway

A machine that connects two or more electronic mail systems (especially dissimilar mail systems on two different networks) and transfers messages between them. Sometimes the mapping and translation can be quite complex, and generally it requires a store-and-forward scheme whereby the message is received from one system completely before it is transmitted to the next system after suitable translations.

man pages

UNIX on-line command reference. Abbreviation for manual pages.

master server

The server that maintains the master copy of the network information service database. It has a disk and a complete copy of the operating system and network information.

message

Information generated by a process that informs users about the status of that process.

modem

Short for modulator/demodulator. A device that enables a machine or terminal to establish a connection and transfer data through telephone lines. Because a computer is digital and a telephone line is analog, modems are needed to convert digital into analog and vice versa. When transmitting, modems impose (modulate) a computer's digital signals onto a continuous carrier frequency on the telephone line. When receiving, modems sift out (demodulate) the information from the carrier and transfer it in digital form to the computer. Modems operating over telephone lines typically transmit at speeds ranging from 300 to 9600 baud. Higher rates of operation are also possible but are generally constrained by the limitations of the telephone lines themselves. See also *baud rate*.

modem pool

One central server with modems attached (up to 32) and a rotary of telephone access numbers.

monitor

The video display that is part of a workstation. The term monitor usually refers to a video display and its housing. The monitor is attached to the workstation by a cable.

mount

The process of accessing a directory on a disk attached to a machine making the mount request or remote disk on a network.

mounting

The process of making a file system accessible over the network by executing the `mount` command.

mount point

A directory on a workstation to which you *mount* a file system that exists on a remote machine.

multiuser system

Any computer system that can be used concurrently by more than one person. Although a microcomputer shared by several people can be considered a multiuser system, the term is generally reserved for machines that are accessed by several or many people through communications facilities or via network terminals.

network

Technically, the hardware connecting various distributed and/or remote systems enabling them to communicate.

network administration

Tasks of the person who maintains a network, such as adding systems to a network or enabling sharing between systems.

network administrator

The person who maintains a network.

network bandwidth

Capacity available between two networked locations, for example, 56Kb, T1, or 10Mb.

Network Design and Development Group

Essential to implementation of central control in the network. Responsible for designing the architecture, implementing the appropriate wide-area, metropolitan-area, campus-area, and local-area networking topologies, and defining the Network Management Strategy.

network file system (NFS)

NFS is a network file sharing system specifically developed by Sun for UNIX.

network hub

The location that contains network routers and provides network management to other hubs or locations.

network information service (NIS)

A distributed network database containing key information about the systems and the users on the network. The NIS database is stored on the *master server* and all the *slave servers*.

network management station (NMS)

The system responsible for managing a (portion of a) network. The NMS talks to network management agents, which reside in the managed nodes, via a network management protocol.

Network Management Strategy

Defines guidelines for making the transition through the various stages of development in the implementation of the tools, structure, and protocol that directly relate to the management of the network.

network management tool

Software responsible for managing the network and has the capacity to decentralize operations; for example, SunNet Manager.

network router

(1) An Ethernet connection that connects different locations over a leased circuit or satellite.

(2) The hub connectivity between cities, campuses, and/or buildings.

NFS

See *network file system.*

object

(1) In the OPEN LOOK GUI, an item that a user sees.

(2) A graphics entity. A single image or model defined in 2-D or 3-D space.

object code

Output from a compiler or assembler that is itself executable machine code or is suitable for processing to produce executable machine code.

object file

A file containing *machine language* code. An executable file.

on-line

Connected to a system or network and in operation.

open architecture

A term used to describe any computer or peripheral design that has published specifications. A published specification enables third parties to develop add-on hardware for an open-architecture computer or device. Contrast with *closed architecture*.

open system

In communications, especially with regard to the ISO open interconnection model, a computer network designed to incorporate all devices—regardless of manufacturer or model—that can use the same communications facilities and protocols. See also *open architecture*.

operating system

A collection of programs that monitor the use of the system and supervise the other programs executed by it.

Oracle system-level statistics

The accounting mechanism that the Oracle database server uses to keep track of changes made to the database.

orasrv process

Automated ways to verify that the Oracle Server process is functioning properly and that local users can connect.

ordinary file

In UNIX, a file containing text data that is not executable.

output

Information produced by a command, program, or such, and sent elsewhere; for example, to the terminal, to a file, or to a line printer.

owner

(1) The person who created a file or directory.

(2) The attribute of a file or directory that specifies who has owner permissions.

package

(1) A collection of software grouped for modular installation.

(2) A computer application consisting of one or more programs created to perform a particular type of work — for example, an accounting package or a spreadsheet package.

packet

A group of information in a fixed format that is transmitted as a unit over communications lines.

packet switching

A concept wherein a network transmits packets over connections that last only for the duration of the transmission. A packet switching network handles information in small units, breaking long messages into multiple packets before routing. Although each packet may travel along a different path and the packets composing a message may arrive at different times or out of sequence, the receiving computer reassembles the original message. This repackaging is called packet assembly and disassembly. Standards for packet switching on networks are documented in the CCITT recommendation X.25.

partition

The unit into which disk space is divided by software.

password

A security measure used to restrict access to computer systems and sensitive files. A password is a unique string of characters that a user types in as an identification code. The system compares the code against a stored list of authorized passwords and users. If the code is legitimate, the system allows the user access, at whatever security level has been approved for the owner of the password.

password protection

The use of passwords as the method of allowing only authorized users access to a computer system or its files.

path name

The location of a file or directory in the UNIX file system.

performance monitor

A process or program that appraises and records status information about various network or system devices and other processes.

permissions

The attribute of a file or directory that specifies who has read, write, or execution access.

platform

The foundation technology of a computer system. Because computers are layered devices composed of a chip-level hardware layer, a firmware and operating-system layer, and an applications program layer, the bottom layer of a machine is often called a platform, as in "a *SPARC* platform." However, designers and users of applications software view both the hardware and systems software as the platform because both provide support for an application.

plug-compatible

An adjective describing hardware equipped with connectors that are equivalent both in structure and in usage. For example, most modems having DB-25 connectors on their rear panels are plug-compatible; that is, one can be replaced by another without the cable having to be rewired.

port

(1) In computer hardware, a location for passing data in and out of a computing device. Microprocessors have ports for sending and receiving data bits; these ports are usually dedicated locations in memory. Full computer systems have ports for connecting peripheral devices such as printers and modems.

(2) In computer programming, to change a program in order to run it on a different computer.

(3) To move documents, graphics, and other files from one computer to another.

(4) The abstraction used by Internet transport protocols to distinguish among multiple simultaneous connections to a single destination host. See also *selector*.

proactive approach (to network management)

The processes where the network management tool automatically recognizes events that are occurring in the network and takes action to rectify the situation.

processor

A hardware device that executes the commands in a stored program in the computer system. In addition to the *central processing unit (CPU)*, many sophisticated graphics systems contain a dedicated processor for use in the graphics accelerator.

process status

The current state of a process, that is, running, stopped, waiting, error, and so on.

program

A sequence of instructions telling a computer how to perform a task. A program can be in *machine language* or it can be in a higher-level language that is then translated into machine language.

protocol

A formal description of messages to be exchanged and rules to be followed for two or more systems to exchange information.

prototyping

Analyzing multiple vendors to determine the best implementation to meet an architecturally defined solution.

query

(1) The process by which a master station asks a slave station to identify itself and give its status.

(2) The process of extracting data from a database and presenting it for use.

(3) A specific set of instructions for extracting particular data repetitively. For example, a query might be created to present sales figures for a particular region of the country. This query could be run periodically to obtain current reports.

queue

(1) A line or list formed by items in a system waiting for service.

(2) To arrange in, or form, a queue.

(3) A multielement data structure from which (by strict definition) elements can be removed only in the same order in which they were inserted; that is, it follows a first-in-first-out (FIFO) constraint.

quit

To stop in an orderly manner; to execute the normal shutdown of a program and return control to the operating system.

RAS

Reliability, Availability, and Serviceability.

raw partition

Disk space utilized by the database engine that is not partitioned within the UNIX file structure.

real time

(1) An event or system that must receive a response to some stimulus within a narrow, predictable time frame. Usually, this requires that the response is not strongly dependent on system performance parameters that are highly variable, such as a processor load or interface latency.

(2) The accelerated graphics processing that makes objects appear to move naturally and at a speed that appears realistic. Also, the visual result of some combination of effective transformation algorithms, fine-tuning of the graphics software to the graphics hardware, double buffering, and graphics accelerators.

record

(1) As a verb, to retain information, usually in a file.

(2) As a noun, a data structure that is a collection of fields (elements) each with its own name and type.

record locking

A strategy employed in distributed processing and other multi-user situations to prevent more than one user at a time from writing data to a record.

recover

To return to a stable condition after some error has occurred. When a program recovers from an error, it stabilizes itself and continues carrying out instructions without user intervention. When a computer user recovers lost or damaged data, a recovery program searches for and salvages whatever information remains in storage. When a database is recovered, it is returned to a previous stable condition after some problem, such as abnormal termination of the database program, has caused the data to lose its integrity.

recoverable error

A nonfatal error—one that can be successfully managed by software, as when the user enters a number when a letter is required.

redirect output

To send results of an operation to a different medium than is otherwise anticipated; for example, to redirect output from the screen to the printer. Also known as *redirection*.

rightsizing

The process of determining the most effective platform on which a business system should execute; for example, central versus distributed, mainframe versus client-server.

rlogin

A service offered by UNIX that enables users of one machine to log in to other UNIX systems (for which they are authorized) and interact as if their terminals were connected directly. Similar to *Telnet*.

ROM

Read-only memory.

root directory

The base directory from which all other directories stem, directly or indirectly.

router

A system responsible for making decisions about which of several paths network (or Internet) traffic will follow. To do this, it uses a routing protocol to gain information about the network, and algorithms to choose the best route based on several criteria known as "routing metrics." In International Organization for Standardization's open systems interconnection (OSI) terminology, a router is a network layer intermediate system. See *gateway*, *bridge*, and *network router*.

routing

The process of determining a pathway for data to get from one machine in a network to another machine through a *gateway* or a *router*.

Sbus machine

A single board system that resides in custom enclosures with no room for additional boards of the same size to be added. Any additions to the system are via the small Sbus cards that plug into the SBus connectors provided on the CPU card itself. All SBus systems use a Single Inline Memory Module (SIMM) parity memory system.

scope

The range over which an action or definition applies.

script

A type of program that consists of a set of instructions to an application or utility program. A script usually consists of instructions expressed using the application's or utility's rules and syntax, combined with simple control structures such as loops and if/then expressions.

selector

The identifier used by an International Organization for Standardization's open systems interconnection (OSI) entity to distinguish among multiple service access points at which it provides services to the layer above.

serial port

An external computer port or a connection that is used for *serial transmission*.

serial transmission

A method in which bits that compose a character are transmitted sequentially as contrasted with parallel or simultaneous transfer.

server

(1) In the *client-server model* for file systems, the server is a machine with compute resources (and is sometimes called the compute server), and large memory capacity. Client machines can remotely access and make use of these resources. In the client-server model for window systems, the server is a process that provides windowing services to an application, or "client process." In this model, the client and the server can run on the same machine or on separate machines.

(2) A daemon that actually handles the providing of files.

server system

A system that is on a *network* and provides resources, such as disk space, software services, and file transfers, to other systems.

shell

A programmable command interpreter. The shell provides direct communication between the user and the operating system.

Simple Network Management Protocol (SNMP)

The open network protocol of choice for TCP/IP-based network management systems.

simple path name

A file or directory name, without mention of any associated directories, that you use to access a file or directory in the working directory.

slave server

A server system that maintains a copy of the *network information service (NIS)* database. It has a disk and a complete copy of the operating system.

SNMP

See *Simple Network Management Protocol*.

SunDANS

Tool through which software updates are distributed across the network. It provides the ability to distribute from a central location.

source code

The uncompiled version of a program written in a language such as C, C++, or Pascal. The source code must be translated to machine language by a program known as the *compiler* before the computer can execute the program.

SPARC

The 32-bit Scalable Processor ARChitecture from Sun. SPARC is based on a reduced instruction set computer (RISC) concept. The architecture was designed by Sun and its suppliers in an effort to significantly improve price and performance. SPARC is a registered trademark of SPARC International, Inc.

specific address

(1) An address that identifies a storage location or a device without the use of any intermediate reference.

(2) An address permanently assigned by the designer to a storage location.

(3) Synonymous with explicit address, machine address, specific address.

standalone

(1) A computer that does not require support from any other machine. It must have its own disk and may or may not be attached to an Ethernet network. It must have some type of medium, such as CD-ROM or tape drive, for software installation. Synonymous with *single system*.

(2) A standalone diagnostic means the program can load from either local disk or Ethernet and runs in a non-UNIX environment.

standard tape labeling

Standardized internal and external alphanumeric labeling on tape recorded media.

subdirectory

A directory that resides within another directory.

subnet

See *subnetwork*.

SunNet Manager

A network management tool developed at Sun Microsystems that proactively monitors network events over the wide-area, campus-area, and local area networks. It is essential to providing centralized control.

subnetwork

A collection of International Organization for Standardization's open systems interconnection (OSI) end systems and intermediate systems under the control of a single administrative domain and using a single network access protocol. Examples: private X.25 networks, collection of bridged LANs.

Sun Paperless Reporter

A rightsizing on-line report distribution and viewing tool. Formerly called *ViewMaster*.

SunRAI

The Remote Application Interface developed at Sun Microsystems. Promotes interaction between any third-party RDBMS, as well as any mainframe DBMS. It is a key tool for supporting multiple integrated environments.

swap

To write the active pages of a job to external storage (*swap space*) and to read pages of another job from external page storage into real storage.

swapping area

See *swap space*.

swap space

The memory used for the transfer of a currently operating program from system memory to an external storage device. Also known as *swapping area*.

Sybase devices

Physical resources available to the Sybase RDBMS system.

system

A computer that enables a user to run computer programs.

system administration

The tasks of a person who performs maintenance to systems, servers, or desktop machines attached to a network. Also manages and supports the LAN with control of the building-level gateway down to the desktop.

system administrator

The person who performs system administration functions.

system daemon

A process that performs a particular system task. Daemons are separate programs rather than parts of the kernel.

system ID

A sequence of numbers, and sometimes letters, that is unique to each system and is used to identify that system.

system name

The unique name assigned to a system on a network.

tape librarian

A person who manages a physical tape library. Tapes are a means of storing critical data or information. The media can be kept at any location and reused as defined by the tape librarian.

TCP

See *Transmission Control Protocol (TCP)*.

terminal

A process running on a machine that originates with the physical device called a terminal, or as the software representation of such a physical device, like a window.

tip communication

A software product used by console servers to establish communication between the console server monitor and its client remote hosts.

token ring network

A local area network formed in a ring (closed loop) topology that uses token passing as a means of regulating traffic on the line.

tool

A package of compact, well-designed programs designed to do a specific task well. Several tools can be linked together to perform more complex tasks.

toolkit

A set of programs and predefined routines that a programmer can use in writing a program for a particular machine, environment, or application.

transaction dump

An incremental accounting of transactions played against the database.

Transmission Control Protocol (TCP)

(1) Transmission Control Protocol (TCP) is a protocol of the transport layer, and thus lies above the IP. Its main task is the reliable transportation of data through the network.

(2) The major transport protocol in the Internet suite of protocols providing reliable, connection-oriented, full-duplex streams.

transparent

(1) In computer use, an adjective describing a device, function, or part of a program that works so smoothly and easily that it is invisible to the user.

(2) In communications, an adjective describing a mode of transmission in which data can include any characters, including device-control characters, without the possibility of misinterpretation by the receiving station — for example, early termination because the data contains a character that the receiving device interprets as "end of transmission."

transparent access

Use of files, data, and programs that are part of another file system on a network.

trend analysis

History of data (such as capacity or performance) over time, for example, day, month, or year.

UDP

See *User Datagram Protocol.*

UNIX Production Acceptance (UPA)

Guideline/process developed to support and implement distributed mission critical business systems with mainframe disciplines and central control.

user account

A record of essential user information that is stored on the system. Each user who accesses a system has a user account.

User Datagram Protocol (UDP)

A connectionless transport protocol. Its attributes are connectionless, addressing via port numbers, data checksums, very simple, best-effort forwarding.

user-defined

Something determined by the user.

user interface

See *graphical user interface (GUI)*.

user name

A combination of letters, and possibly numbers, that identifies a user to the system.

utility

A standard program, usually furnished at no charge with the purchase of a computer, that performs specific housekeeping functions.

utility services

Network, data center, and system administration are defined as centralized utility functions. These are also defined as the *infrastructure*.

uucp

UNIX-to-UNIX copy program. A protocol (UUCP) used for communication between consenting UNIX systems.

ViewMaster

An internal Sun acronym used to define a rightsizing on-line report distribution and viewing tool. Renamed to *Sun Paperless Reporter*.

VMEbus

An interfacing system that connects data processing, data storage, and peripheral control devices in a closely coupled configuration. The VMEbus structure can be described in two ways: mechanically and functionally. The mechanical specification includes physical dimensions of su-tracks, backplanes, and plug-in boards. The functional specification describes how the bus works, what functional modules are involved in each transaction, and the rules that define behavior.

WAN

See *wide-area network (WAN)*.

wide-area network (WAN)

A network consisting of many systems that provide file transfer services over a large physical area, sometimes spanning the globe. A WAN can span between different locations, regions (for example, cities or states), and countries.

window

In applications and graphical interfaces, a portion of the screen that can contain its own document or message. In window-based programs, the screen can be divided into several windows, each of which has its own boundaries and can contain a different document (or another view into the same document). Each window might also contain its own menu or other controls, and the user might be able to enlarge and shrink individual windows at will. See also *window system*.

window system

A system that provides the user with a multiuse environment on the display device. Separate windows are like separate displays on the monitor screen. Each window can run its own application. The user brings up some number of windows for various applications, and the window system handles the communications between each of the applications and the hardware.

wrappers

"Expert systems" that embody product-access information necessary to maintain those systems and products in thousands of separate locations. They can automate installation steps, present product-specific messages, and perform usage tracking (for example, for licensing).

Index

console servers, basic functions, 223
console-port access, 223
controlled user access, 9
COPS, 148
Corporate Information Security (CIS), 148
Corporate Systems, 13
cost analysis, 174
cost reduction
    hardware, 176
    labor, 177
    software, 176
Crack, 148
curriculum
    costs, 174
    education, 80
    training, 80
customer responsibilities, 247
customer satisfaction, 205, 228
customer satisfaction tool, 204

D

data, 36, 37
data center, 14
    architecture statement, 52
    change control, 105
    current state of infrastructure, 53
    development of, 51
    functional support, 52
    implementation of, 56
    infrastructure, 52
    operational standards and procedures, 55
    organizational chart, 53
    organizational structure, 53
    problem management, 107
    roles and responsibilities, 52
    services of, 55
    staffing requirements, 84
    support, 58
    target state of infrastructure, 54
Data Center Availability report, 241
data depository, 4
data dictionary, 4
data distribution mechanism, 197

data warehouse, 4
database
    support, 255
    utilities, 114, 139
Database Administration services, 254
database administration staff, 85
Database Administrator (DBA), 58, 67
Database Administrators, responsibilities of, 58
dataless client, 133
dataless_backup, 139
DBMS software support, 254
decentralized network control, 43
decentralized network operations, benefits
    of, 43
decentralized operations, 5
decentralizing network operations, 42
deploying functions, across networks, 41
desktop security, 147
DeskTop Tool, 204, 207
desktop tools support, 133
desktop, definition of, 205
dial-in modem pools, security for, 147
disaster recovery
    plan, 152
    process, 155
    restore script, 158
disaster recovery team, rsponsibilities of, 157
diskpatrol, 139
distmgr, 185
Distributed Administration of Network Services
    (SunDANS), 21, 185
distributed computing environments, types
    of, 131
distribution-management mechanism
    (distmgr), 185
Domain Name Service (DNS), 155
downloading data, 23
dux, 139

E

education curriculum, 80
employee to SA ratio, 132

Rightsizing the New Enterprise

senior technical personnel, 175
server availability, 236, 241
Server Availability report, 229, 235
server room standards, 180
server rooms, 57, 257
server type, 57
Service Level Agreement (SLA), 131, 243
service level expected from System
    Administration, 131
service level reports, 227
serviceability (RAS), 56
ServiceDesk, 228
    authorization process, 207
    customer satisfaction, 205
    graphical tools, 204
    information flow, 213
    overview, 206
ServiceDesk Rating Report, 228
ServiceDesk tools, 207
session login management, 47
session termination, 48
shell scripts, 82, 99
SNM, 43, 112
software
    controlling, 9, 10
    initial costs, 174
    standards, 31
    standards, required, 55
software server, 133
software, reducing costs, 176
staffing requirements, 84
stages of developing an enterprise-wide
    network, 28
standard services, provided by System
    Administration, 138
standards, production, 73
strategic hub locations, 41
strategies to view the network
    inside-out, 32
    outside-in, 32
Sun ConsoleServer, 223
    features and benefits, 225
    utilities, 225

Sun Paperless Reporter, 22, 65, 197
    benefits of, 201
    distribution of reports, 199
    features of, 199
    overview of, 197
    report distribution, 201
    report flow diagram, 200
    viewing reports, 200
Sun Remote Application Interface (SunRAI), 21,
    22, 191
Sun servers, 57
Sun Wide Area Network (SWAN), 27, 138
Sun workstations, 57
SunDANS, 21, 185, 252
    benefits of, 188
    features of, 185
    how it works, 187
SunIntegration Services, 185, 191, 197, 215, 223
SunIRS, 107
SunNet Manager (SNM), 29, 33, 112
SunRAI, 22, 35, 179, 191
    application components, 193
    architecture, 193
    client components, 194
    features and benefits, 191
    remote components, 194
SunServices, 81
Support Agreement, 251
SWAN, 27, 138, 154
SWAN sites, 27
SWAN topology map
    Europe, 38
    Pacific Rim, 39
    United States, 37
SYBASE, 197, 200, 201
Sybase, 23, 114
    scripts, 114
    Utilities Release 1.0, 115
    Utilities Release 2.0, 116
System Administration
    charter, 243
    improving ratios, 132
System Administration report, 229, 232, 234
System Administrator (SA), 205